T0238772

SQL Server 2019 AlwaysOn

Supporting 24x7 Applications with Continuous Uptime

Third Edition

Peter A. Carter

Apress®

SQL Server 2019 AlwaysOn: Supporting 24x7 Applications with Continuous Uptime

Peter A. Carter
Botley, UK

ISBN-13 (pbk): 978-1-4842-6478-2
ISBN-13 (electronic): 978-1-4842-6479-9
https://doi.org/10.1007/978-1-4842-6479-9

Copyright © 2020 by Peter A. Carter

This work is subject to copyright. All rights are reserved by the Publisher, whether the whole or part of the material is concerned, specifically the rights of translation, reprinting, reuse of illustrations, recitation, broadcasting, reproduction on microfilms or in any other physical way, and transmission or information storage and retrieval, electronic adaptation, computer software, or by similar or dissimilar methodology now known or hereafter developed.

Trademarked names, logos, and images may appear in this book. Rather than use a trademark symbol with every occurrence of a trademarked name, logo, or image we use the names, logos, and images only in an editorial fashion and to the benefit of the trademark owner, with no intention of infringement of the trademark.

The use in this publication of trade names, trademarks, service marks, and similar terms, even if they are not identified as such, is not to be taken as an expression of opinion as to whether or not they are subject to proprietary rights.

While the advice and information in this book are believed to be true and accurate at the date of publication, neither the authors nor the editors nor the publisher can accept any legal responsibility for any errors or omissions that may be made. The publisher makes no warranty, express or implied, with respect to the material contained herein.

Managing Director, Apress Media LLC: Welmoed Spahr
Acquisitions Editor: Jonathan Gennick
Development Editor: Laura Berendson
Coordinating Editor: Jill Balzano

Cover image designed by Freepik (www.freepik.com)

Distributed to the book trade worldwide by Springer Science+Business Media LLC, 1 New York Plaza, Suite 4600, New York, NY 10004. Phone 1-800-SPRINGER, fax (201) 348-4505, e-mail orders-ny@springer-sbm.com, or visit www.springeronline.com. Apress Media, LLC is a California LLC and the sole member (owner) is Springer Science + Business Media Finance Inc (SSBM Finance Inc). SSBM Finance Inc is a **Delaware** corporation.

For information on translations, please e-mail booktranslations@springernature.com; for reprint, paperback, or audio rights, please e-mail bookpermissions@springernature.com.

Apress titles may be purchased in bulk for academic, corporate, or promotional use. eBook versions and licenses are also available for most titles. For more information, reference our Print and eBook Bulk Sales web page at http://www.apress.com/bulk-sales.

Any source code or other supplementary material referenced by the author in this book is available to readers on GitHub via the book's product page, located at www.apress.com/9781484264782. For more detailed information, please visit http://www.apress.com/source-code.

Printed on acid-free paper

*This book is dedicated to my inspirational children,
Reuben, Iris, and Finola.*

Table of Contents

About the Author

Peter A. Carter is a SQL Server expert with over 15 years of experience in developing, administering, and architecting SQL Server platforms and data-tier applications. Peter was awarded an MCC by Microsoft in 2011, and it sits alongside his array of MCTS, MCITP, MCSA, and MCSE certifications in SQL Server from version 2005 onward. His passion for SQL Server shows through in everything he does, and his goal is that his passion for the technology will inspire others.

About the Technical Reviewer

Ian Stirk is a freelance SQL Server consultant based in London. In addition to his day job, he is an author, creator of software utilities, and technical reviewer who regularly writes book reviews for www.i-programmer.info.

He covers every aspect of SQL Server and has a specialist interest in performance and scalability. If you require help with your SQL Server systems, feel free to contact him at ian_stirk@yahoo.com or www.linkedin.com/in/ian-stirk-bb9a31/.

Ian would like to thank Peter Carter, Jonathan Gennick, and Jill Balzano for making this book experience easier for him.

None of us stands alone, and with this in mind, Ian would like to thank these special people: Mr. Courts, Graham Howes, Dave Starkey, Florence Dedeng, Meaza Yohannes, Feven Yohannes, and Adhanet Mehretab.

Ian's fee for his work on this book has been donated to World Child Cancer (www.worldchildcancer.org/).

Acknowledgments

I want to offer my thanks to the amazing Chris Dent, who once again helped me with my network configuration for this book.

I would also like to thank Ian Stirk, whose tech reviews always increase the quality of my books, with this book being no exception.

Introduction

SQL Server 2019 AlwaysOn is intended to be a quick start guide for DBAs who need to implement high availability and disaster recovery for their SQL Server workloads.

The book begins with a discussion of high availability concepts and methodologies, before a high-level overview of HA/DR technologies. Then, it's into the detail. We will discuss how to create Windows clusters, before looking at how to create SQL Server AlwaysOn Failover Clustered Instances.

The focus of the book then turns to AlwaysOn Availability Groups. Here, the book discusses how to create and configure Availability Groups for high availability and disaster recovery, both on Windows and Linux operating systems.

We then look at atypical use cases for AlwaysOn Availability Groups, such as clusterless and domain-independent availability groups, as well as configuring Availability Groups on Azure IaaS and Basic Availability Groups, for SQL Server Standard Edition.

Finally, the book looks at the operational side of AlwaysOn, with chapters covering the administration, monitoring, and troubleshooting of the technology.

CHAPTER 1

High Availability and Disaster Recovery Concepts

In today's 24×7 environments that are running mission-critical applications, businesses rely heavily on the availability of their data. Although servers and their software are generally reliable, there is always the risk of a hardware failure or a software bug, each of which could bring a server down. To mitigate these risks, business-critical applications often rely on redundant hardware to provide fault tolerance. If the primary system fails, then the application can automatically fail over to the redundant system. This is the underlying principle of high availability (HA).

Even with the implementation of HA technologies, there is always a small risk of an event that causes the application to become unavailable. This could be due to a major incident, such as the loss of a data center, due to a natural disaster, or due to an act of terrorism. It could also be caused by data corruption or human error, resulting in the application's data becoming lost or damaged beyond repair.

In these situations, some applications may rely on restoring the latest backup to recover as much data as possible. However, more critical applications may require a redundant server to hold a synchronized copy of the data in a secondary location. This is the underpinning concept of disaster recovery (DR). This chapter discusses the concepts behind HA and DR.

Level of Availability

The amount of time that a solution is available to end users is known as the *level of availability*, or *uptime*. To provide a true picture of uptime, a company should measure

1

© Peter A. Carter 2020
P. A. Carter, *SQL Server 2019 AlwaysOn*, https://doi.org/10.1007/978-1-4842-6479-9_1

the availability of a solution from a user's desktop. In other words, even if your SQL Server has been running uninterrupted for over a month, users may still experience outages to their solution caused by other factors. These factors can include network outages or an application server failure.

In some instances, however, you have no choice but to measure the level of availability at the SQL Server level. This may be because you lack holistic monitoring tools within the enterprise. Most often, however, the requirement to measure the level of availability at the instance level is political, as opposed to technical. In the IT industry, it has become a trend to outsource the management of data centers to third-party providers. In such cases, the provider responsible for managing the SQL servers may not necessarily be the provider responsible for the network or application servers. In this scenario, you need to monitor uptime at the SQL Server level to accurately judge the performance of the service provider.

The level of availability is measured as a percentage of the time that the application or server is available. Companies often strive to achieve 99%, 99.9%, 99.99%, or 99.999% availability. As a result, the level of availability is often referred to in 9s. For example, five 9s of availability means 99.999% uptime and three 9s means 99.9% uptime.

Table 1-1 details the amount of acceptable downtime per week, per month, and per year for each level of availability.

Table 1-1. *Levels of Availability*

Level of Availability	Downtime per Week	Downtime per Month	Downtime per Year
99%	1 hour, 40 minutes, 48 seconds	7 hours, 18 minutes, 17 seconds	3 days, 15 hours, 39 minutes, 28 seconds
99.9%	10 minutes, 4 seconds	43 minutes, 49 seconds	8 hours, 45 minutes, 56 seconds
99.99%	1 minute	4 minutes, 23 seconds	52 minutes, 35 seconds
99.999%	6 seconds	26 seconds	5 minutes, 15 seconds

All values are rounded down to the nearest second.

To calculate other levels of availability, you can use the script in Listing 1-1. Before running this script, replace the value of @Uptime to represent the level of uptime that you wish to calculate. You should also replace the value of @UptimeInterval to reflect uptime per week, month, or year.

Listing 1-1. Calculating the Level of Availability

```
DECLARE @Uptime      DECIMAL(5,3) ;

--Specify the uptime level to calculate

SET @Uptime = 99.9 ;

DECLARE @UptimeInterval VARCHAR(5) ;

--Specify WEEK, MONTH, or YEAR

SET @UptimeInterval = 'YEAR' ;

DECLARE @SecondsPerInterval FLOAT ;

--Calculate seconds per interval

SET @SecondsPerInterval =
(
SELECT CASE
        WHEN @UptimeInterval = 'YEAR'
                THEN 60*60*24*365.243
        WHEN @UptimeInterval = 'MONTH'
                THEN 60*60*24*30.437
        WHEN @UptimeInterval = 'WEEK'
                THEN 60*60*24*7
        END
) ;

DECLARE @UptimeSeconds DECIMAL(12,4) ;

--Calculate uptime

SET @UptimeSeconds = @SecondsPerInterval * (100-@Uptime) / 100 ;

--Format results
SELECT
    CONVERT(VARCHAR(12), FLOOR(@UptimeSeconds /60/60/24))   + ' Day(s), '
  + CONVERT(VARCHAR(12), FLOOR(@UptimeSeconds /60/60 % 24)) + ' Hour(s), '
  + CONVERT(VARCHAR(12),  FLOOR(@UptimeSeconds /60 % 60))    + ' Minute(s), '
  + CONVERT(VARCHAR(12),   FLOOR(@UptimeSeconds % 60))       + ' Second(s).' ;
```

Actual Availability

Now that we understand how to calculate the level of availability required by an application, we should also understand how to calculate the actual availability of an application. We can do this by discovering the MTBF (Mean Time Between Failures) and MTTR (Mean Time to Recover) metrics.

The MTBF metric describes the average length of time between failures. For example, imagine that we were reviewing the service logs for the past week and discovered that the Foo application has suffered three outages. There are 168 hours in a week and there have been three failures. We simply need to divide the number of hours within our time period by the number of failures. This will produce our MTBF. In this case, we have an MTBF of 56 hours.

MTTR can actually have two different meanings: Mean Time to Recover or Mean Time to Repair. When there is no HA or DR in place, then the MTTR metric describes the average length of time it takes for something that is broken to be repaired. This could potentially be an extended period of time, as we may need to wait for a service engineer to replace faulty hardware. When thinking about HA and DR, however, we use MTTR metric to mean Mean Time to Recover to record the duration of the outage. For example, if we have a three-node cluster and one of the nodes experiences a hardware failure, of course we need to fix this server, but from an application downtime perspective, we will only have an outage of a matter of seconds or minutes, while the service fails over and we still have resilience, meaning that the application's nonfunctional requirements are not impacted. Therefore, in this example, I will assume that MTTR is referring to "Mean Time to Recover."

We can calculate the MTTR by taking a sum of the total downtime duration within our period and dividing it by the number of failures. In this case, during our 168-hour period, we have had three failures and the total duration of downtime has been 12 minutes. Therefore, the MTTR for our Foo application is 4 minutes.

Now that we know our application's MTBF and MTTR, we can use these metrics to calculate the actual availability of our application. The formula for this is `(MTBF/(MTBF+MTTR))*100`. So in this case, we first need to convert our MTTR value to hours, so we have hours as our consistent unit. Four minutes is 0.06667 hours. Therefore, our calculation would be `(56/(56+0.6667))*100`. This makes our actual application availability 99.8811%.

Service-Level Agreements and Service-Level Objectives

When a third-party provider is responsible for managing servers, the contract usually includes service-level agreements (SLAs). These SLAs define many parameters, including how much downtime is acceptable, the maximum length of time a server can be down in the event of failure, and how much data loss is acceptable if failure occurs. Normally, there are financial penalties for the provider if these SLAs are not met.

In the event that servers are managed in-house, DBAs still have the concept of customers. These are usually the end users of the application, with the primary contact being the business owner. An application's business owner is the stakeholder within the business who commissioned the application and who is responsible for signing off on funding enhancements, among other things.

In an in-house scenario, it is still possible to define SLAs, and in such a case, the IT Infrastructure or Platform departments may be liable for charge-back to the business teams if these SLAs are not being met. However, in internal scenarios, it is much more common for IT departments to negotiate service-level objectives (SLOs) with the business teams, as opposed to SLAs. SLOs are very similar in nature to SLAs, but their use implies that the business do not impose financial penalties on the IT department in the event that they are not met.

Proactive Maintenance

It is important to remember that downtime is not only caused by failure but also by proactive maintenance. For example, if you need to patch the operating system, or SQL Server itself, with the latest service pack, then you must have some downtime during installation.

Depending on the upgrade you are applying, the downtime in such a scenario could be substantial – several hours for a stand-alone server. In this situation, high availability is essential for many business-critical applications – not to protect against unplanned downtime, but to avoid prolonged outages during planned maintenance.

Recovery Point Objective and Recovery Time Objective

The recovery point objective (RPO) of an application indicates how much data loss is acceptable in the event of a failure. For a data warehouse that supports a reporting application, for example, this may be an extended period, such as 24 hours, given that it may only be updated once per day by an ETL process and all other activity is read-only reporting. For highly transactional systems, however, such as an OLTP database supporting trading platforms or web applications, the RPO will be zero. An RPO of zero means that no data loss is acceptable.

Applications may have different RPOs for high availability and for disaster recovery. For example, for reasons of cost or application performance, an RPO of zero may be required for a failover within the site. If the same application fails over to a DR data center, however, five or ten minutes of data loss may be acceptable. This is because of technology differences used to implement intra-site availability and inter-site recovery.

The recovery time objective (RTO) for an application specifies the maximum amount of time an application can be down before recovery is complete and users can reconnect. When calculating the achievable RTO for an application, you need to consider many aspects. For example, it may take less than a minute for a cluster to fail over from one node to another and for the SQL Server service to come back up; however, it may take far longer for the databases to recover. The time it takes for databases to recover depends on many factors, including the size of the databases, the quantity of databases within an instance, and how many transactions were in-flight when the failover occurred. This is because all noncommitted transactions need to be rolled back.

Just like RPO, it is common for there to be different RTOs depending on whether you have an intra-site or inter-site failover. Again, this is primarily due to differences in technologies, but it also factors in the amount of time you need to bring up the entire estate in the DR data center if the primary data center is lost.

The RPO and RTO of an application may also vary in the event of data corruption. Depending on the nature of the corruption and the HA/DR technologies that have been implemented, data corruption may result in you needing to restore a database from a backup.

If you must restore a database, the worst-case scenario is that the achievable point of recovery may be the time of the last backup. This means that you must factor a hard business requirement for a specific RPO into your backup strategy. If only part of the database is corrupt, however, you may be able to salvage some data from the live database and restore only the corrupt data from the restored database.

Data corruption is also likely to have an impact on the RTO. One of the biggest influencing factors is if backups are stored locally on the server, or if you need to retrieve them from tape. Retrieving backup files from tape, or even from off-site locations, is likely to add significant time to the recovery process.

Note Backups directly to tape from SQL Server are deprecated. When this section refers to retrieving backups from tape, it is assuming a tape drive as the target for an enterprise backup solution that your database backups have been offloaded too.

Another influencing factor is what caused the corruption. If it is caused by a faulty IO subsystem, then you may need to factor in time for the Windows administrators to run the check disk command (CHKDSK) against the volume and potentially more time for disks to be replaced. If the corruption is caused by a user accidently truncating a table or deleting a data file, however, then this is not of concern.

Cost of Downtime

If you ask any business owners how much downtime is acceptable for their applications and how much data loss is acceptable, the answers invariably come back as zero and zero, respectively. Of course, it is never possible to guarantee zero downtime, and once you begin to explain the costs associated with the different levels of availability, it starts to get easier to negotiate a mutually acceptable level of service.

The key factor in deciding how many 9s you should try to achieve is the cost of downtime. Two categories of cost are associated with downtime: tangible costs and intangible costs. Tangible costs are usually fairly straightforward to calculate. Let's use a sales application as an example. In this case, the most obvious tangible cost is lost revenue because the sales staff cannot take orders. Intangible costs are more difficult to quantify but can be far more expensive. For example, if a customer is unable to place an order with your company, they may place their order with a rival company and never return. Other intangible costs can include loss of staff morale, which leads to higher staff turnover, or even loss of company reputation. Because intangible costs, by their very nature, can only be estimated, the industry rule of thumb is to multiply the tangible costs by three and use this figure to represent your intangible costs.

Once you have an hourly figure for the total cost of downtime for your application, you can scale this figure out, across the predicted life cycle of your application, and compare the costs of implementing different availability levels. For example, imagine that you calculate that your total cost of downtime is $2,000/hour and the predicted life cycle of your application is three years. Table 1-2 illustrates the cost of downtime for your application, comparing the costs that you have calculated for implementing each level of availability, after you have factored in hardware, licenses, power, cabling, additional storage, and additional supporting equipment, such as new racks, administrative costs, and so on. This is known as the total cost of ownership (TCO) of a solution.

Table 1-2. *Cost of Downtime*

Level of Availability	Cost of Downtime (Three Years)	Cost of Availability Solution
99%	$525,600	$108,000
99.9%	$52,560	$224,000
99.99%	$5,256	$462,000
99.999%	$526	$910,000

In this table, you can see that implementing five 9s of availability saves $525,074 over a two-9s solution, but the cost of implementing the solution is an additional $802,000, meaning that it is not economical to implement. Four 9s of availability saves $520,344 over a two-9s solution and only costs an additional $354,000 to implement. Therefore, for this particular application, a four-9s solution is the most appropriate level of service to design for.

Classification of Standby Servers

There are three classes of standby solution. You can implement each using different technologies, although you can use some technologies to implement multiple classes of standby server. Table 1-3 outlines the different classes of standby that you can implement.

Table 1-3. *Standby Classifications*

Class	Description	Example Technologies
Hot	A synchronized solution where failover can occur automatically or manually. Often used for high availability.	Clustering, AlwaysOn Availability Groups (Synchronous)
Warm	A synchronized solution where failover can only occur manually. Often used for disaster recovery.	Log Shipping, AlwaysOn Availability Groups (Asynchronous)
Cold	An unsynchronized solution where failover can only occur manually. This is only suitable for read-only data, which is never modified.	–

Note   Cold standby does not show an example technology because no synchronization is required and, thus, no technology implementation is required.

Summary

Your application's level of availability is measured as a percentage of time that the application is available to users. The level of availability is often referred in nines. For example, 99.9% uptime requirement is known as three 9s of availability. The higher the uptime requirement, the higher the cost of implementing the solution. Therefore, the level of uptime that you strive to achieve should be driven by SLAs and the cost of downtime.

Recovery point objective is a measure of how much data it is acceptable to lose in the event of a disaster. For example, if your only DR solution is backups and backups are scheduled to be taken every hour, you can achieve a recovery point objective of one hour. Recovery time objective is a measure of how long it will take to recover a solution after a failure. For example, if you have a recovery time objective of 30 minutes, then you must be able to restore service within half an hour.

It is important to determine the cost of downtime for your application, as this is one of the main drivers to determine your level of availability. The cost of downtime consists of both tangible and intangible costs. Tangible costs can be calculated, whereas intangible costs need to be estimated.

Redundant infrastructure helps you to maintain availability of your applications and services. A redundant server will be classified as hot, warm, or cold. A hot standby server is one which is kept synchronized with the live server and configured to allow automatic failover. This is suitable for HA scenarios. A warm standby server is one which is kept synchronized with the live server, but is not configured to failover automatically. Instead, an engineer must perform the failover manually. This is suitable for DR scenarios. A cold standby server is not kept synchronized with the live server and therefore cannot be failed over automatically. A cold standby server is suitable for DR scenarios where all data is read-only and never modified.

CHAPTER 2

Understanding High Availability and Disaster Recovery Technologies

SQL Server provides a full suite of technologies for implementing high availability and disaster recovery. The following sections provide an overview of these technologies and discuss their most appropriate uses.

AlwaysOn Failover Clustering

A Windows cluster is a technology for providing high availability in which a group of up to 64 servers works together to provide redundancy. An AlwaysOn Failover Clustered Instance (FCI) is an instance of SQL Server that spans the servers within this group. If one of the servers within this group fails, another server takes ownership of the instance. Its most appropriate usage is for high availability scenarios where the databases are large or have high write profiles. This is because clustering relies on shared storage, meaning the data is only written to disk once. With SQL Server–level HA technologies, write operations occur on the primary database and then again on all secondary databases, before the commit on the primary completes. This can cause performance issues. Even though it is possible to stretch a cluster across multiple sites, this involves SAN replication, which means that a cluster is normally configured within a single site.

Each server within a cluster is called a *node*. Therefore, if a cluster consists of three servers, it is known as a three-node cluster. Each node within a cluster has the SQL Server binaries installed, but the SQL Server service is only started on one of the nodes,

© Peter A. Carter 2020
P. A. Carter, *SQL Server 2019 AlwaysOn*, https://doi.org/10.1007/978-1-4842-6479-9_2

which is known as the *active node*. Each node within the cluster also shares the same storage for the SQL Server data and log files. The storage, however, is only attached to the active node.

Tip   In geographically dispersed clusters (known as geoclusters or stretch clusters), each server is attached to different storage. The volumes are updated by SAN replication or Windows Storage Replica (a Windows Server technology, introduced in Windows Server 2016, which performs storage replication). The cluster regards the two volumes as a single, shared volume, which can only be attached to one node at a time.

If the active node fails, then the SQL Server service is stopped and the storage is detached. The storage is then reattached to one of the other nodes in the cluster, and the SQL Server service is started on this node, which is now the active node. The instance is also assigned its own network name and IP address, which are also bound to the active node. This means that applications can connect seamlessly to the instance, regardless of which node has ownership.

The diagram in Figure 2-1 illustrates a two-node cluster. It shows that although the databases are stored on a shared storage array, each node still has a dedicated system volume. This volume contains the SQL Server binaries. It also illustrates how the shared storage, IP address, and network name are rebound to the passive node in the event of failover.

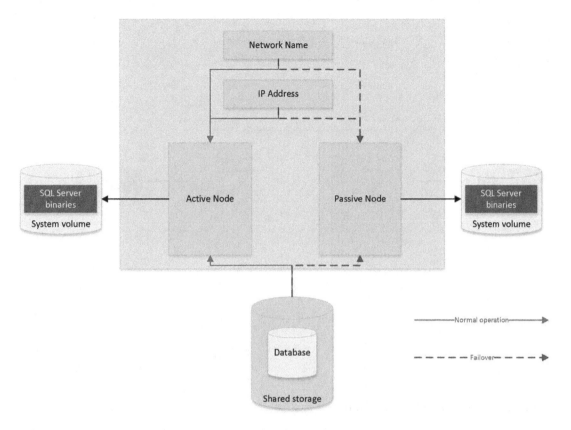

Figure 2-1. *Two-Node Cluster*

Active/Active Configuration

Although the diagram in Figure 2-1 illustrates an active/passive configuration, it is also possible to have an active/active configuration. Although it is not possible for more than one node at a time to own a single instance, and therefore it is not possible to implement load balancing, it is, however, possible to install multiple instances on a cluster, and a different node may own each instance. In this scenario, each node has its own unique network name and IP address. Each instance's shared storage also consists of a unique set of volumes.

Therefore, in an active/active configuration, during normal operations, Node1 may host Instance1 and Node2 may host Instance2. If Node1 fails, both instances are then hosted by Node2, and vice versa. The diagram in Figure 2-2 illustrates a two-node active/active cluster.

13

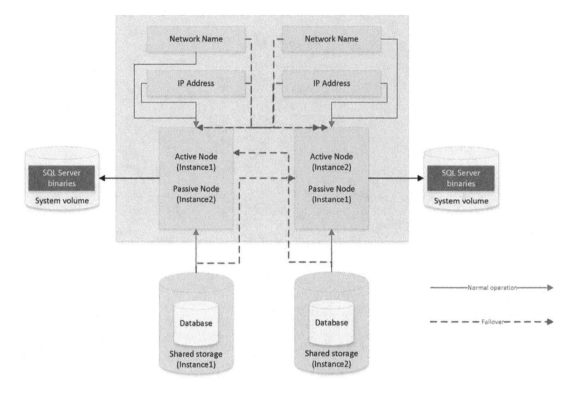

Figure 2-2. *Active/Active Cluster*

Caution   In an active/active cluster, it is important to consider resources in the event of failover. For example, if each node has 128GB of RAM and the instance hosted on each node is using 96GB of RAM and locking pages in memory, then when one node fails over to the other node, this node fails as well, because it does not have enough memory to allocate to both instances. Make sure you plan both memory and processor requirements as if the two nodes are a single server. For this reason, active/active clusters are not generally recommended for SQL Server.

Three-Plus Node Configurations

As previously mentioned, it is possible to have up to 64 nodes in a cluster. When you have three or more nodes, it is unlikely that you will want to have a single active node and two redundant nodes, due to the associated costs. Instead, you can choose to implement an N+1 or N+M configuration.

In an N+1 configuration, you have multiple active nodes and a single passive node. If a failure occurs on any of the active nodes, they fail over to the passive node. The diagram in Figure 2-3 depicts a three-node N+1 cluster.

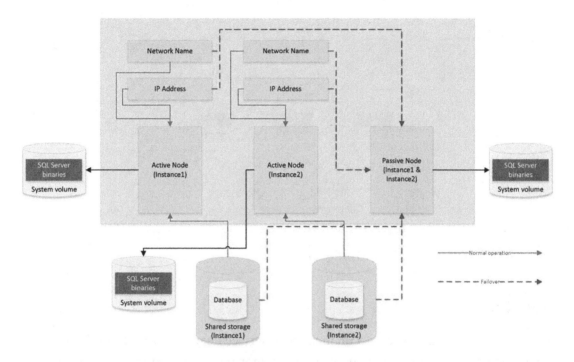

Figure 2-3. *Three-Node N+1 Configuration*

In an N+1 configuration, in a multifailure scenario, multiple nodes may fail over to the passive node. For this reason, you must be very careful when you plan resources to ensure that the passive node is able to support multiple instances. However, you can mitigate this issue by using an N+M configuration.

Whereas an N+1 configuration has multiple active nodes and a single passive node, an N+M cluster has multiple active nodes and multiple passive nodes, although there are usually fewer passive nodes than there are active nodes. The diagram in Figure 2-4 shows a five-node N+M configuration. The diagram shows that Instance3 is configured to always fail over to one of the passive nodes, whereas Instance1 and Instance2 are configured to always fail over to the other passive node. This gives you the flexibility to control resources on the passive nodes, but you can also configure the cluster to allow any of the active nodes to fail over to either of the passive nodes, if this is a more appropriate design for your environment.

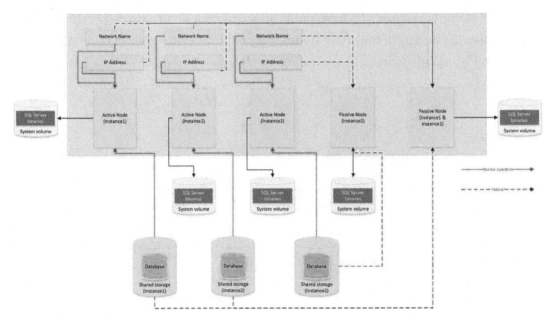

Figure 2-4. *Five-Node N+M Configuration*

Quorum

So that automatic failover can occur, the cluster service needs to know if a node goes down. In order to achieve this, you must form a quorum. The definition of a quorum is "The minimum number of members required in order for business to be carried out." In terms of high availability, this means that each node within a cluster, and optionally a witness device (which may be a cluster disk, a file share that is external to the cluster or Azure BLOB storage), receives a vote. If more than half of the voting members are unable to communicate with a node, then the cluster service knows that it has gone down and any cluster-aware applications on the server fail over to another node. The reason that more than half of the voting members need to be unable to communicate with the node is to avoid a situation known as a *split brain*.

To explain a split-brain scenario, imagine that you have three nodes in Data Center 1 and three nodes in Data Center 2. Now imagine that you lose network connectivity between the two data centers, yet all six nodes remain online. The three nodes in Data Center 1 believe that all of the nodes in Data Center 2 are unavailable. Conversely, the nodes in Data Center 2 believe that the nodes in Data Center 1 are unavailable. This leaves both sides (known as partitions) of the cluster thinking that they should take control. This can have unpredictable and undesirable consequences for any application that successfully connects to one or the other partition. The *Quorum = (Voting Members / 2) + 1* formula protects against this scenario.

Tip If your cluster loses quorum, then you can force one partition online, by starting the cluster service using the /fq switch. If you are using Windows Server 2012 R2 or higher, then the partition that you force online is considered the *authoritative partition*. This means that other partitions can automatically rejoin the cluster when connectivity is reestablished.

Various quorum models are available and the most appropriate model depends on your environment. Table 2-1 lists the models that you can utilize and details the most appropriate way to use them.

Table 2-1. *Quorum Models*

Quorum Model	Appropriate Usage
Node Majority	When you have an odd number of nodes in the cluster
Node + Disk Witness Majority	When you have an even number of nodes in the cluster
Node + File Share Witness Majority	When you have nodes split across multiple sites or when you have an even number of nodes and are required to avoid shared disks*

Reasons for needing to avoid shared disks due to virtualization are discussed later in this chapter.

Although the default option is one node, one vote, it is possible to manually remove a node's vote by changing the NodeWeight property to zero. This is useful if you have a *multi-subnet cluster* (a cluster in which the nodes are split across multiple sites). In this scenario, it is recommended that you use a file share witness in a third site. This helps you avoid a cluster outage as a result of network failure between data centers. If you have an odd number of nodes in the quorum, however, then adding a file share witness leaves you with an even number of votes, which is dangerous. Removing the vote from one of the nodes in the secondary data center eliminates this issue. From Windows Server 2019 onward, a file share witness can be any file share that supports SMB (Server Message Block) 2.0 or above. This includes USB keys attached to a network router, NAS (network-attached storage devices), and workgroup-joined computers running Windows.

Caution   A file share witness does not store a full copy of the quorum database. This means that a two-node cluster with a file share witness is vulnerable to a scenario known as *partition in time*. In this scenario, if one node fails while you are in the process of patching or altering the cluster service on the second node, then there is no up-to-date copy of the quorum database. This leaves you in a position in which you need to destroy and rebuild the cluster.

Modern versions of Windows Server also support the concepts of Dynamic Quorum and Tie Breaker for 50% Node Split. When Dynamic Quorum is enabled, the cluster service automatically decides whether or not to give the quorum witness a vote, depending on the number of nodes in the cluster. If you have an even number of nodes, then it is assigned a vote. If you have an odd number of nodes, it is not assigned a vote. Tie Breaker for 50% Node Split expands on this concept. If you have an even number of nodes and a witness and the witness fails, then the cluster service automatically removes a vote from one random node within the cluster. This maintains an odd number of votes in the quorum and reduces the risk of a cluster going offline, due to a witness failure.

Tip   If your cluster is running in Windows Server 2016 or higher, with Datacenter Edition, then Storage Spaces Direct is supported. This allows high availability to be realized, using locally attached physical storage, with a software-defined storage layer on top. A full conversation around Storage Spaces Direct is beyond the scope of this book, but further details can be found at docs.microsoft.com/en-us/ windows-server/storage/storage-spaces/storage-spaces-direct-overview.

AlwaysOn Availability Groups

AlwaysOn Availability Groups (AOAG) replaces database mirroring and is essentially a merger of database mirroring and clustering technologies. SQL Server is installed as a stand-alone instance (as opposed to an AlwaysOn Failover Clustered Instance) on each node of a cluster. A cluster-aware application, called an Availability Group Listener, is then installed on the cluster; it is used to direct traffic to the correct node. Instead of relying on shared disks, however, AOAG compresses the log stream and sends it to the other nodes, in a similar fashion to database mirroring.

AOAG is the most appropriate technology for high availability in scenarios where you have small databases with low write profiles. This is because, when used synchronously, it requires that the data is committed on all synchronous replicas before it is committed on the primary database. You can have up to eight replicas, including three synchronous replicas. AOAG may also be the most appropriate technology for implementing high availability in a virtualized environment. This is because the shared disk required by clustering may not be compatible with some features of the virtual estate. As an example, VMware does not support the use of vMotion, which is used to manually move virtual machines (VMs) between physical servers, and the Distributed Resource Scheduler (DRS), which is used to automatically move VMs between physical servers, based on resource utilization, when the VMs use shared disks, presented over Fiber Channel.

Tip   The limitations surrounding shared disks with VMware features can be worked around by presenting the storage directly to the guest OS over an iSCSI connection at the expense of performance degradation.

AOAG is the most appropriate technology for DR when you have a proactive failover requirement but when you do not need to implement a load delay. AOAG may also be suitable for disaster recovery in scenarios where you wish to utilize your DR server for offloading reporting. This allows the redundant servers to be utilized. When used for disaster recovery, AOAG works in an asynchronous mode. This means that it is possible to lose data in the event of a failover. The RPO is nondeterministic and is based on the time of the last uncommitted transaction.

In the old days, of database mirroring, the secondary database was always offline. This means that you cannot use the secondary database to offload any reporting or other read-only activity. It is possible to work around this by creating a database snapshot against the secondary database and pointing read-only activity to the snapshot. This can still be complicated, however, because you must configure your application to issue read-only statements against a different network name and IP address. Availability Groups, on the other hand, allow you to configure one or more replicas as readable. The only limitation is that readable replicas and automatic failover cannot be configured on the same secondaries. The norm, however, would be to configure readable secondary replicas in asynchronous commit mode so that they do not impair performance.

To further simplify this, the Availability Group Replica checks for the read-only or read-intent properties in an applications connection string and points the application to the appropriate node. This means that you can easily scale reporting and database maintenance routines horizontally with very little development effort and with the applications being able to use a single connection string.

Because AOAG allows you to combine synchronous replicas (with or without automatic failover), asynchronous replicas, and replicas for read-only access, it allows you to satisfy high availability, disaster recovery, and reporting scale-out requirements using a single technology. If you're sole requirement is read-scaling, as opposed to HA or DR, then it is actually possible to configure Availability Groups with no cluster, from SQL Server 2017 onward. In this case, there is no cluster service and hence no automatic redirection. Replicas within the Availability Groups use certificate when communicating with each other. This is also true if you configure Availability Groups without AD, in a workgroup, or cross-domain.

When you are using AOAG, failover does not occur at the database level, nor at the instance level. Instead, failover occurs at the level of the availability group. The availability group is a concept that allows you to group related databases together so that they can fail over as an atomic unit. This is particularly useful in consolidated environments, because it allows you to group together the databases that map to a single application. You can then fail over this application to another replica for the purposes of DR testing, among other reasons, without having an impact on the other data-tier applications that are hosted on the instance.

No hard limits are imposed for the number of availability groups you can configure on an instance, nor are there any hard limits for the number of databases on an instance that can take part in AOAG. Microsoft, however, has tested up to, and officially recommends, a maximum of 100 databases and 10 availability groups per instance. The main limiting factor in scaling the number of databases is that AOAG uses a database mirroring endpoint and there can only be one per instance. This means that the log stream for all data modifications is sent over the same endpoint.

Figure 2-5 depicts how you can map data-tier applications to availability groups for independent failover. In this example, a single instance hosts two data-tier applications. Each application has been added to a separate availability group. The first availability group has failed over to Node2. Therefore, the availability group listeners point traffic for Application1 to Node2 and traffic for Application2 to Node1. Because each availability group has its own network name and IP address, and because these resources fail over with the AOAG, the application is able to seamlessly reconnect to the databases after failover.

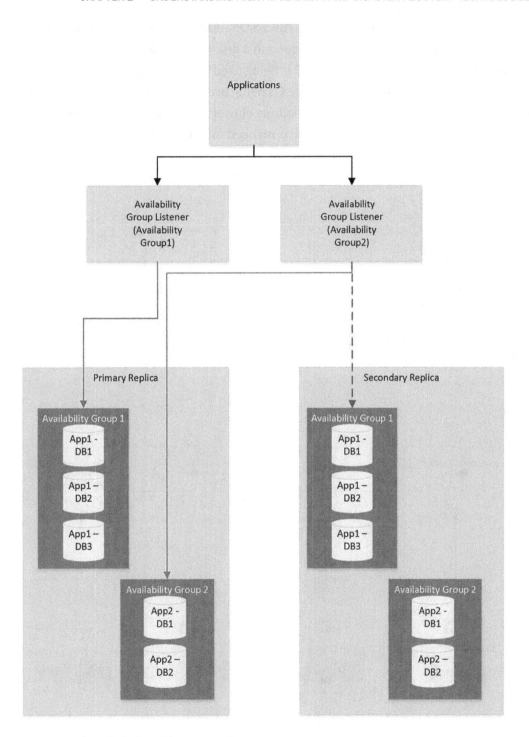

Figure 2-5. *Availability Groups Failover*

The diagram in Figure 2-6 depicts an AlwaysOn Availability Group topology. In this example, there are four nodes in the cluster and a disk witness. Node1 is hosting the primary replicas of the databases, Node2 is being used for automatic failover, Node3 is being used to offload reporting, and Node4 is being used for DR. Because the cluster is stretched across two data centers, multi-subnet clustering has been implemented. Because there is no shared storage, however, there is no need for SAN replication between the sites.

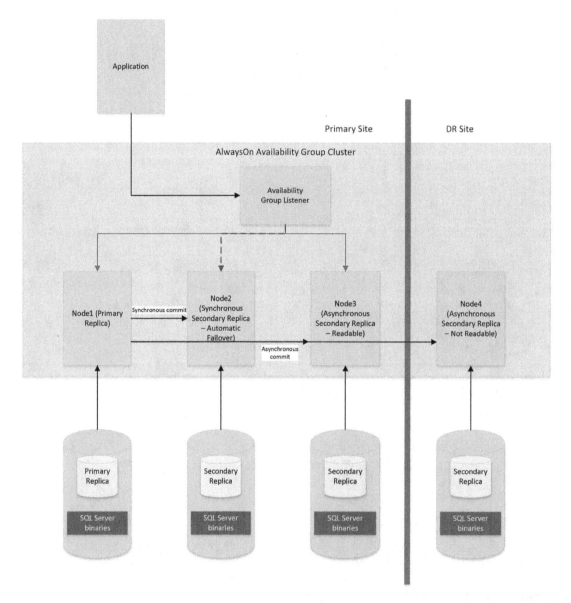

Figure 2-6. *AlwaysOn Availability Group Topology*

Automatic Page Repair

If a page becomes corrupt in a database configured as a replica in an AlwaysOn Availability Group topology, then SQL Server attempts to fix the corruption by obtaining a copy of the pages from one of the secondary replicas. This means that a logical corruption can be resolved without you needing to perform a restore or for you to run DBCC CHECKDB with a repair option. However, automatic page repair does not work for the following page types:

- File Header page

- Database Boot page

- Allocation pages

    - GAM (Global Allocation Map)

    - SGAM (Shared Global Allocation Map)

    - PFS (Page Free Space)

If the primary replica fails to read a page because it is corrupt, it first logs the page in the MSDB.dbo.suspect_pages table. It then checks that at least one replica is in the SYNCHRONIZED state and that transactions are still being sent to the replica. If these conditions are met, then the primary sends a broadcast to all replicas, specifying the PageID and LSN (log sequence number) at the end of the flushed log. The page is then marked as restore pending, meaning that any attempts to access it will fail, with error code 829.

After receiving the broadcast, the secondary replicas wait, until they have redone transactions up to the LSN specified in the broadcast message. At this point, they try to access the page. If they cannot access it, they return an error. If they *can* access the page, they send the page back to the primary replica. The primary replica accepts the page from the first secondary to respond.

The primary replica will then replace the corrupt copy of the page with the version that it received from the secondary replica. When this process completes, it updates the page in the MSDB.dbo.suspect_pages table to reflect that it has been repaired by setting the event_type column to a value of 5 (Repaired).

If the secondary replica fails to read a page while redoing the log because it is corrupt, it places the secondary into the SUSPENDED state. It then logs the page in the `MSDB.dbo.suspect_pages` table and requests a copy of the page from the primary replica. The primary replica attempts to access the page. If it is inaccessible, then it returns an error and the secondary replica remains in the SUSPENDED state.

If it can access the page, then it sends it to the secondary replica that requested it. The secondary replica replaces the corrupt page with the version that it obtained from the primary replica. It then updates the `MSDB.dbo.suspect_pages` table with an `event_id` of 5. Finally, it attempts to resume the AOAG session.

Note   It is possible to manually resume the session, but if you do, the corrupt page is hit again during the synchronization. Make sure you repair or restore the page on the primary replica first.

Log Shipping

Log shipping is a technology that you can use to implement disaster recovery. It works by backing up the transaction log on the principle server, copying it to the secondary server, and then restoring it. It is most appropriate to use log shipping in DR scenarios in which you require a load delay, because this is not possible with AOAG. As an example of where a load delay may be useful, consider a scenario in which a user accidently deletes all of the data from a table. If there is a delay before the database on the DR server is updated, then it is possible to recover the data for this table, from the DR server, and then repopulate the production server. This means that you do not need to restore a backup to recover the data. Log shipping is not appropriate for high availability, since there is no automatic failover functionality. The diagram in Figure 2-7 illustrates a log shipping topology.

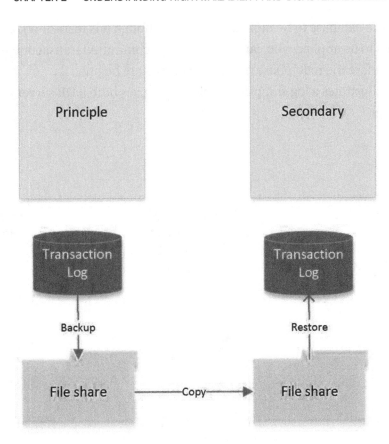

Figure 2-7. Log Shipping Topology

Recovery Modes

In a log shipping topology, there is always exactly one principle server, which is the production server. It is possible to have multiple secondary servers, however, and these servers can be a mix of DR servers and servers used to offload reporting.

When you restore a transaction log, you can specify three recovery modes: Recovery, NoRecovery, and Standby. The Recovery mode brings the database online, which is not supported with log shipping. The NoRecovery mode keeps the database offline so that more backups can be restored. This is the normal configuration for log shipping and is the appropriate choice for DR scenarios.

The Standby option brings the database online, but in a read-only state so that you can restore further backups. This functionality works by maintaining a TUF (Transaction Undo File). The TUF file records any uncommitted transactions in the transaction log. This means that you can roll back these uncommitted transactions in the transaction log, which allows the database to be more accessible (although it is read-only). The next time a restore needs to be applied, you can reapply the uncommitted transaction in the TUF file to the log before the redo phase of the next log restore begins.

Figure 2-8 illustrates a log shipping topology that uses both a DR server and a reporting server.

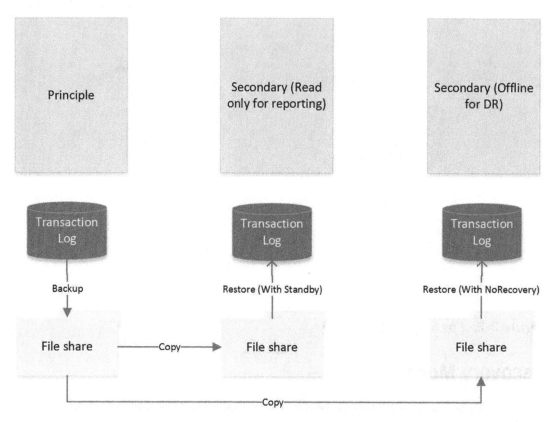

Figure 2-8. *Log Shipping with DR and Reporting Servers*

Remote Monitor Server

Optionally, you can configure a monitor server in your log shipping topology. This helps you centralize monitoring and alerting. When you implement a monitor server, the history and status of all backup, copy, and restore operations are stored on the monitor server. A monitor server also allows you to have a single alert job, which is configured to monitor the backup, copy, and restore operations on all servers, as opposed to it needing separate alerts on each server in the topology.

Caution   If you wish to use a monitor server, it is important to configure it when you set up log shipping. After log shipping has been configured, the only way to add a monitor server is to tear down and reconfigure log shipping.

Failover

Unlike other high availability and disaster recovery technologies, an amount of administrative effort is associated with failing over log shipping. To fail over log shipping, you must back up the tail end of the transaction log and copy it, along with any other uncopied backup files, to the secondary server.

You now need to apply the remaining transaction log backups to the secondary server in sequence, finishing with the tail-log backup. All of the restores are applied with the WITH NORECOVERY, expect for the final restore, which you apply using the WITH RECOVERY option to bring the database back online in a consistent state. If you are not planning to fail back, you can reconfigure log shipping with the secondary server as the new primary server.

Combining Technologies

To meet your business objectives and nonfunctional requirements (NFRs), you need to combine multiple high availability and disaster recovery technologies together to create a reliable, scalable platform. A classic example of this is the requirement to combine an AlwaysOn Failover Cluster with AlwaysOn Availability Groups.

The reason you may need to combine these technologies is that when you use AlwaysOn Availability Groups in synchronous mode, which you must do for automatic failover, it can cause a performance impediment. As discussed earlier in this chapter, the performance issue is caused by the transaction being committed on the secondary server before being committed on the primary server. Clustering does not suffer from this issue, however, because it relies on a shared disk resource, and therefore the transaction is only committed once.

Therefore, it is common practice to first use a cluster to achieve high availability and then use AlwaysOn Availability Groups to perform DR and/or offload reporting. The diagram in Figure 2-9 illustrates a HA/DR topology that combines clustering and AOAG to achieve high availability and disaster recovery, respectively.

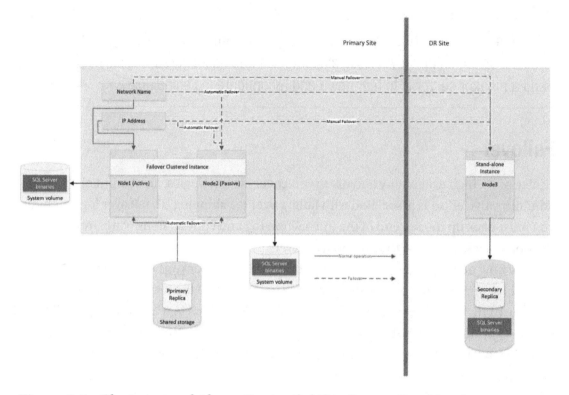

Figure 2-9. *Clustering and AlwaysOn Availability Groups Combined*

The diagram in Figure 2-9 shows that the primary replica of the database is hosted on a two-node active/passive cluster. If the active node fails, the rules of clustering apply, and the shared storage, network name, and IP address are reattached to the passive node, which then becomes the active node. If both nodes are inaccessible, however, the availability group listener points the traffic to the third node of the cluster, which is situated in the DR site and is synchronized using log stream replication. Of course, when asynchronous mode is used, the database must be failed over manually by a DBA.

Another common scenario is the combination of a cluster and log shipping to achieve high availability and disaster recovery, respectively. This combination works in much the same way as clustering combined with AlwaysOn Availability Groups and is illustrated in Figure 2-10.

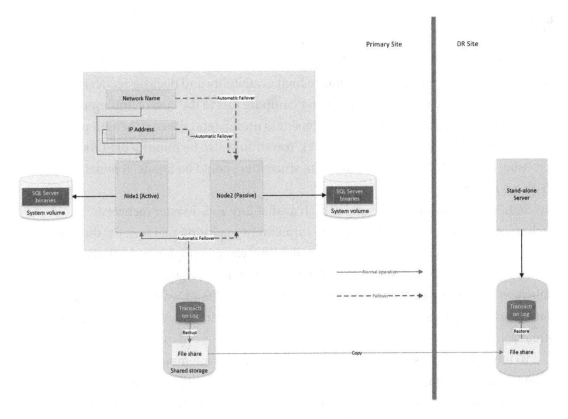

Figure 2-10. *Clustering Combined with Log Shipping*

The diagram shows that a two-node active/passive cluster has been configured in the primary data center. The transaction log(s) of the database(s) hosted on this instance are then shipped to a stand-alone server in the DR data center. Because the cluster uses shared storage, you should also use shared storage for the backup volume and add the backup volume as a resource in the role. This means that when the instance fails over to the other node, the backup share also fails over, and log shipping continues to synchronize, uninterrupted.

Caution   If failover occurs while the log shipping backup or copy jobs are in progress, then log shipping may become unsynchronized and require manual intervention. This means that after a failover, you should check the health of your log shipping jobs.

Summary

Understanding the concepts of availability is key to making the correct implementation choices for your applications that require high availability and disaster recovery. You should calculate the cost of downtime and compare this to the cost of implementing choices of HA/DR solutions to help the business understand the cost/benefit profile of each option (as discussed in Chapter 1). You should also be mindful of SLAs when choosing the technology implementation, since there could be financial penalties if SLAs are not met.

SQL Server provides a full suite of high availability and disaster recovery technologies, giving you the flexibility to implement a solution that best fits the needs of your data-tier applications. For high availability, you can implement either clustering or AlwaysOn Availability Groups (AOAG). Clustering uses a shared disk resource and failover occurs at the instance level. AOAG, on the other hand, synchronizes data at the database level by maintaining a redundant copy of the database with a synchronous log stream.

To implement disaster recovery, you can choose to implement AOAG or log shipping. Log shipping works by backing up, copying, and restoring the transaction logs of the databases, whereas AOAG synchronizes the data using an asynchronous log stream.

It is also possible to combine multiple HA and DR technologies together in order to implement the most appropriate availability strategy. Common examples of this are combining clustering for high availability with AOAG or log shipping to provide DR.

CHAPTER 3

Implementing a Cluster

Engineers may find the process of building and configuring a cluster to be complex and that they can implement many variations of the pattern. Although DBAs may not always need to build a cluster themselves, they do need to be comfortable with the technology and often need to provide their input into the process. They may also take part in troubleshooting issues discovered with the cluster.

For these reasons, this chapter discusses how to build a cluster at the Windows level and discusses some of the possible configurations. The demonstrations in this chapter use a prebuilt environment, consisting of two servers; ClusterNode1 and ClusterNode2. Both servers reside in a domain, named AlwaysOn.com. Five volumes have been presented to the nodes from a SAN and have been brought online and formatted on ClusterNode1, with the configuration detailed in Table 3-1.

Table 3-1. *Disk Configuration*

Drive Letter	Volume Label	Size	Comments
F	Data	10GB	Host SQL Server data files
L	Logs	3GB	Host SQL Server log files
T	TempDB	3GB	Host the TempDB data and log files
M	MSDTC	1GB	Host files associated with the MSDTC role
H	Quorum	1GB	Host a disk-based quorum witness

© Peter A. Carter 2020
P. A. Carter, *SQL Server 2019 AlwaysOn*, https://doi.org/10.1007/978-1-4842-6479-9_3

Tip   You may be surprised that there is a single volume allocated for data and log files, as a DBA's natural instinct is to separate these files onto separate drives. The important thing to remember here is that we are working with a SAN, and there is a very strong chance that even if we used separate volumes, those volumes would reside on the same physical spindles, meaning that separation is logical only. Also, if SAN snapshots are to be used, some SANs may require the data and log files to be stored on the same volume to ensure data consistency.

The scenario in this chapter requires us to build a two-node failover cluster, with a disk witness. Before we can do this, we will need to configure the Windows Cluster Service (WCS). We also need to configure an MSDTC (Microsoft Distributed Transaction Coordinator) Cluster Role, which will provide distributed transaction coordination for SSIS (SQL Server Integration Services). Additionally, we need to configure:

- The MSDTC role to failover with High priority (compared to other roles on the same cluster).

- Three failovers are allowed within any 24-hour period.

- Immediate failback is permitted.

Therefore, the complete list of tasks that we will perform is as follows:

- Install the failover cluster feature.

- Build a Windows Cluster, called ALWAYSON-C.

- Correctly configure the Quorum.

- Create a cluster role for MSDTC, called ALWAYSON-MSDTC-C.

- Configure the properties of the MSDTC role.

- Configure the Failover properties of the MSDTC role.

Tip   If you wish to build a cluster for learning purposes, but you do not have access to a domain, or a SAN, then the newer features of clustering allow you to simulate a very similar topology. Two virtual machines can be used as the cluster nodes. A third virtual machine, running the iSCSI Target feature of windows, can be used to present shared storage to each of these nodes. Even better – Windows Server 2016 and above allow for a cluster to be created on a workgroup, meaning that there is no need to create an additional VM to use as a domain controller. Be warned, however, that creating a cluster within a workgroup is only supported in PowerShell and not through Failover Cluster Manager. It is also important to be aware that from a SQL Server perspective, Availability Groups are supported on a workgroup cluster, but failover clustered instances are not.

Building the Cluster

Before you install a SQL Server AlwaysOn failover cluster instance, you must prepare the servers that form the cluster (known as nodes) and build a Windows cluster across them. The following sections demonstrate how to perform these activities.

Installing the Failover Cluster Feature

In order to build the cluster, the first thing we need to do is install the failover cluster feature on each of the nodes. To do this, we need to select the Add Roles and Features option in Server Manager. This causes the Add Roles and Features Wizard to display. The first page of this wizard offers guidance on prerequisites, as shown in Figure 3-1.

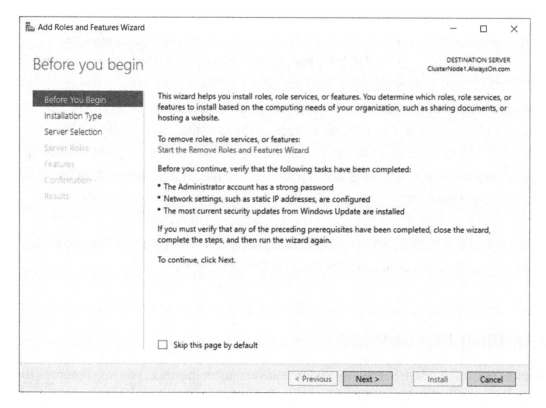

Figure 3-1. *The Before You Begin Page*

On the Installation Type page, ensure that Role-based or feature-based installation is selected, as illustrated in Figure 3-2.

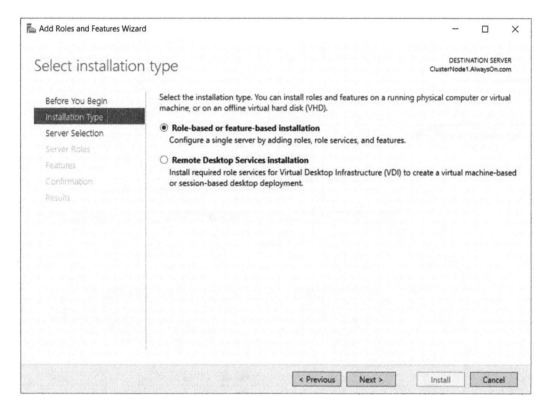

Figure 3-2. *The Installation Type Page*

On the Server Selection page, ensure that the cluster node that you are currently configuring is selected. This is illustrated in Figure 3-3.

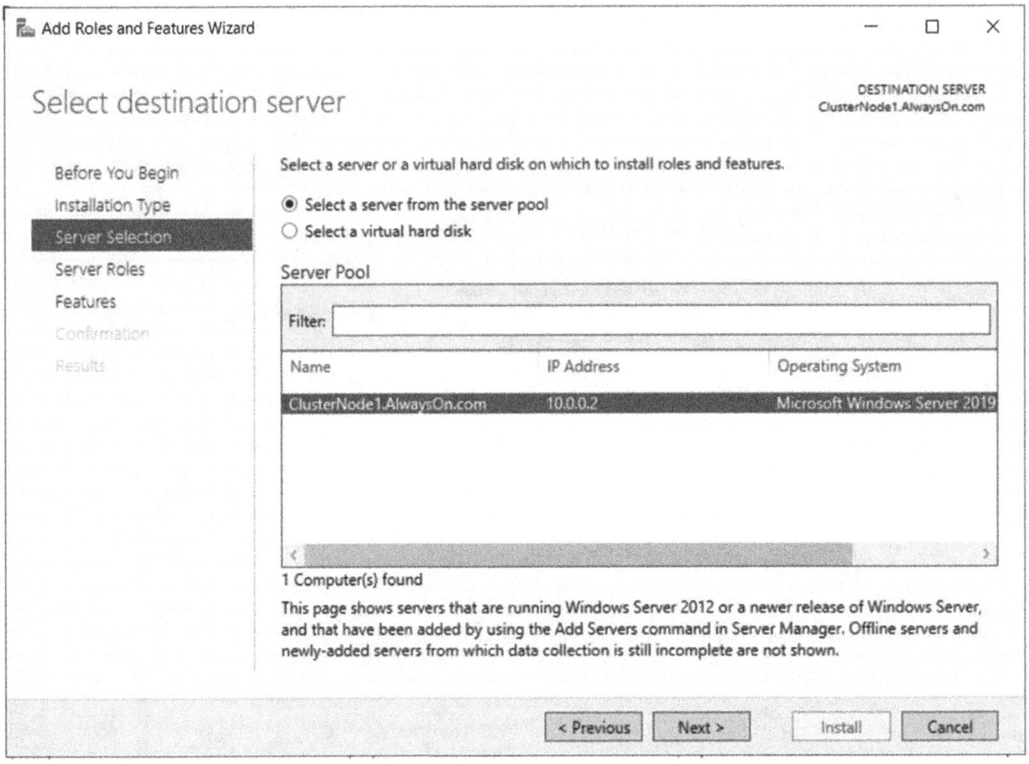

Figure 3-3. *The Server Selection Page*

The Server Roles page of the wizard allows you to select any server roles that you wish to configure. As shown in Figure 3-4, this can include roles such as Application Server or DNS Server, but in our case, this is not appropriate, so we simply move to the next screen.

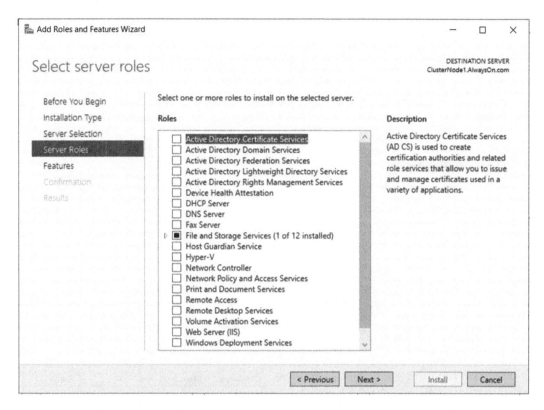

Figure 3-4. *The Server Roles Page*

On the Features page of the wizard, we need to select Failover Clustering, as shown in Figure 3-5. This satisfies the prerequisites for building the Windows cluster.

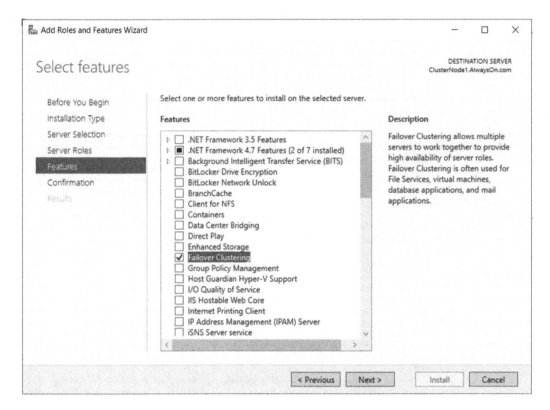

Figure 3-5. *The Features Page*

When you select Failover Clustering, the wizard presents you with a screen
(Figure 3-6) that asks if you want to install the management tools in the form of a check
box. If you are planning to manage the cluster directly from the nodes, check this option.

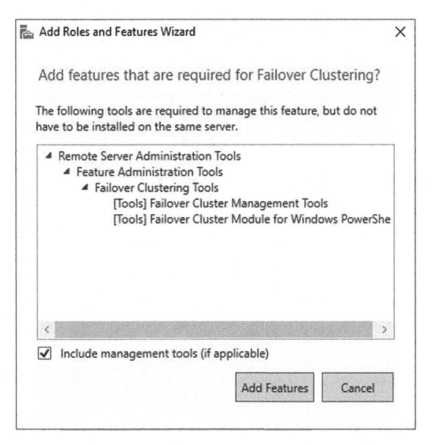

Figure 3-6. *Selecting Management Tools*

On the final page of the wizard, you see a summary of the features that are to be installed, as shown in Figure 3-7. Here, you can specify the location of the Windows media if you need to. You can also choose whether the server should automatically restart, if required. If you are building out a new server, it makes sense to check this box. However, if the server is already in production when you add the feature, make sure you consider what is currently running on the box, and whether you should wait for a maintenance window to perform a restart if one is needed.

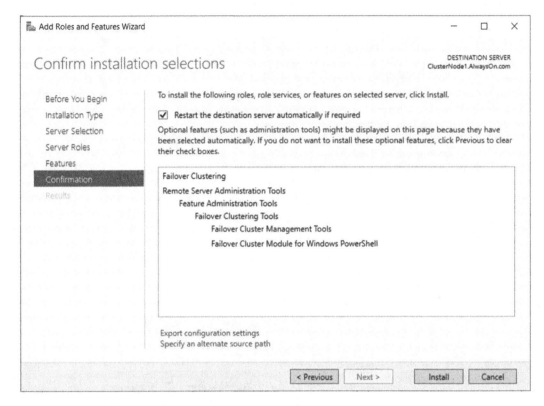

Figure 3-7. *The Confirmation Page*

As well as installation through Server Manager, cluster services can also be installed from PowerShell. The PowerShell command in Listing 3-1 achieves the same result as the preceding steps.

Listing 3-1. Installing Cluster Services

```
Install-WindowsFeature -Name Failover-Clustering –IncludeManagement
Tools -Verbose
```

Creating the Cluster

Once clustering has been installed on both nodes, you can begin building the cluster. To do this, connect to the server that you intended to be the active node, and run Failover Cluster Manager from Administrative Tools.

The Before You Begin page of the Create Cluster Wizard warns that Microsoft only supports clusters that pass all verification tests, as shown in Figure 3-8. The message also warns that you must be a local administrator on each node of the cluster. In previous versions of Windows Server, this meant that you must use a domain account that has local administrator rights on each server that will participate in the cluster. From Windows Server 2016 onward, however, the reliance on domain authentication has been removed, and the only requirement is that an account with local administrator rights exists on each node that has a consistent name and password. This allows for the creation of a cluster on a workgroup, or across multiple domains. Neither of these options were available in previous versions of Windows Server.

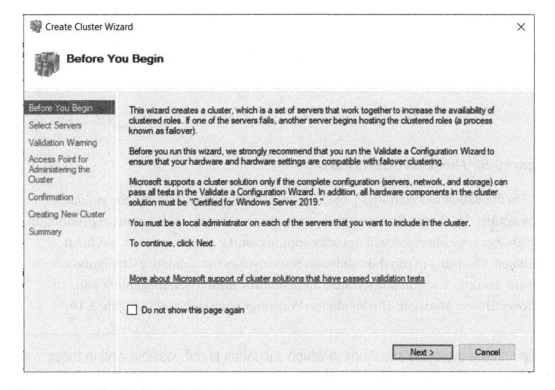

Figure 3-8. *The Before You Begin Page*

On the Select Servers screen of the wizard, you need to enter the names of the cluster nodes. This is illustrated in Figure 3-9. In our case, our cluster nodes are named ClusterNode1 and ClusterNode2, respectively. If they were part of a domain, however, then the domain name and suffix would be appended to the server name.

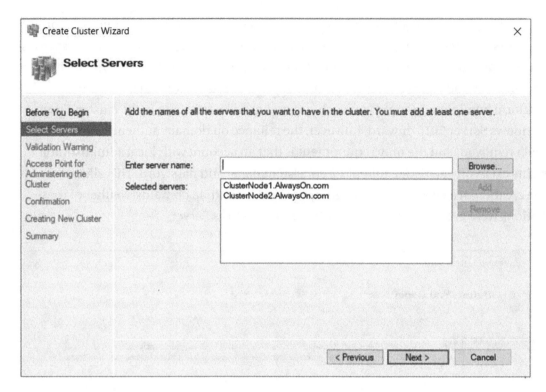

Figure 3-9. *The Select Servers Page*

On the Validation Warnings page, you are asked if you wish to run the validation tests against the cluster. You should always choose to run this validation for production servers, because Microsoft will not offer support for the cluster unless it has been validated. Choosing to run the validation tests invokes the Validate a Configuration Wizard. You can also run this wizard independently from the Management pane of Failover Cluster Manager. The Validation Warnings page is shown in Figure 3-10.

Tip   There are some situations in which validation is not possible, and in these instances, you need to select the No, I Do Not Require Support… option. For example, some DBAs choose to install one-node clusters instead of stand-alone instances so that they can be scaled up to full clusters in the future, if need be. This approach can cause operational challenges for Windows administrators, however, so use it with extreme caution.

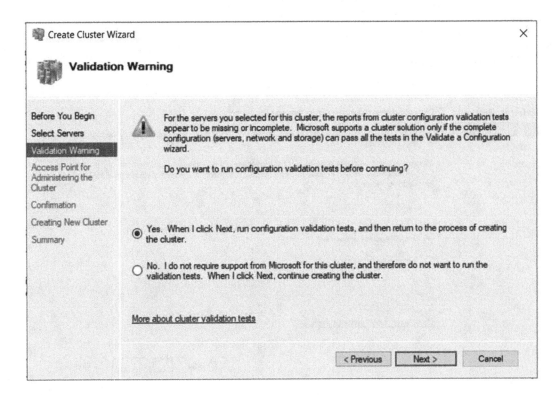

Figure 3-10. *The Validation Warning Page*

After you pass through the Before You Begin page of the Validate a Configuration Wizard, you see the Testing Options page. Here, you are given the option of either running all validation tests or selecting a subset of tests to run, as illustrated in Figure 3-11. Normally when you are installing a new cluster, you want to run all validation tests, but it is useful to be able to select a subset of tests if you invoke the Validate a Configuration Wizard independently after you make a configuration change to the cluster.

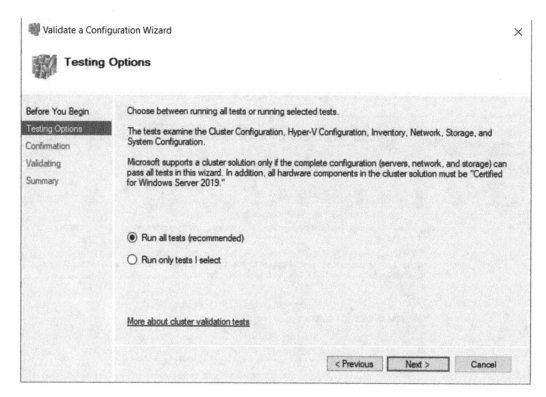

Figure 3-11.   *The Testing Options Page*

On the Confirmation page of the wizard, illustrated in Figure 3-12, you are presented with a summary of tests that will run and the cluster nodes that they will run against. The list of tests is comprehensive and includes the following categories:

- Inventory (such as identifying any unsigned drivers)

- Network (such as checking for a valid IP configuration)

- Storage (such as validating the ability to fail disks over, between nodes)

- System Configuration (such as validating the configuration of Active Directory)

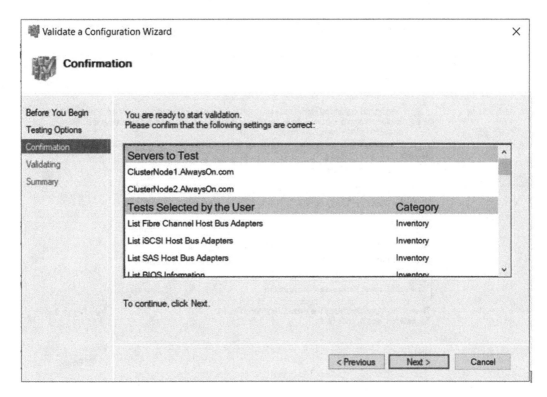

Figure 3-12. *The Confirmation Page*

The Summary page, shown in Figure 3-13, provides the results of the tests and also a link to an HTML version of the report. Make sure to examine the results for any errors or warnings. You should always resolve errors before continuing, but some warnings may be acceptable. For example, if you are building your cluster to host AlwaysOn Availability Groups, you may not have any shared storage. This will generate a warning but is not an issue in this scenario. Configuring AlwaysOn Availability Groups on Windows will be discussed in further detail in Chapters 5.

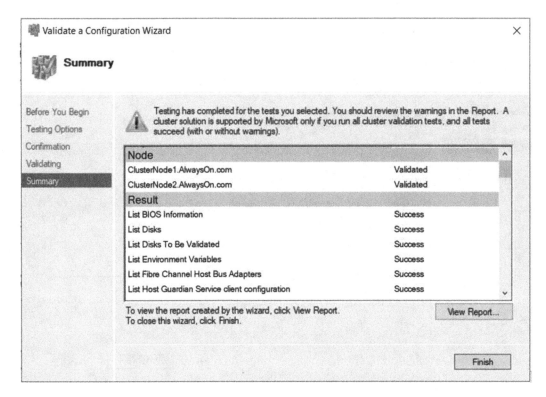

Figure 3-13. *The Summary Page*

The View Report button displays the full version of the validation report, as shown in Figure 3-14. The hyperlinks take you to a specific category within the report, where further hyperlinks are available for each test. These allow you to drill down to messages generated for the specific test, making it easy to identify errors.

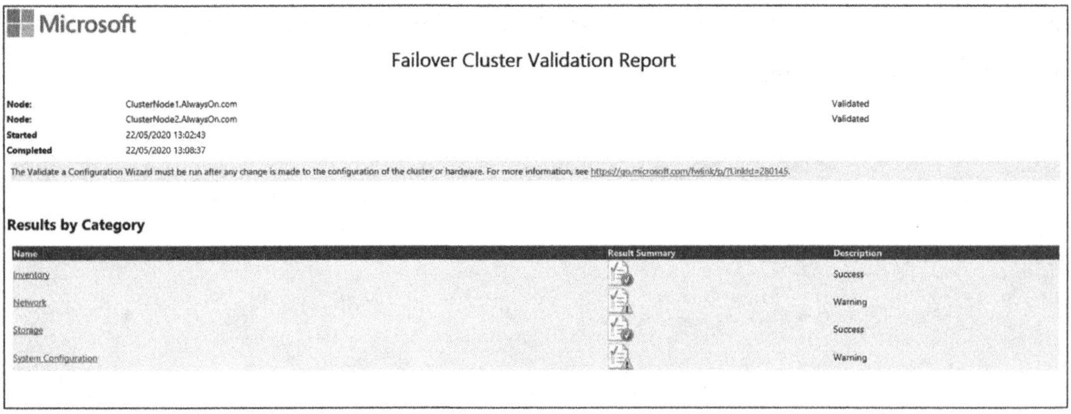

Figure 3-14. *The Failover Cluster Validation Report*

Clicking Finish on the Summary page returns you to the Create Cluster Wizard, where you are greeted with the Access Point for Administering the Cluster page. This screen is illustrated in Figure 3-15. On this page, you need to enter the virtual name of your cluster. We will name our cluster ALWAYSON-C. If the network card is configured to acquire an IP Address automatically, then an IP Address will be assigned using DHCP. Otherwise, you will be required to enter an IP Address manually. This is known as a static IP, as it will remain constant, whereas an IP Address assigned through DHCP may change. I strongly recommend using a static IP for cluster access points to avoid dynamic routing issues, but this can be changed after the cluster has been created.

Note   The virtual name and IP address are bound to whichever node is active, meaning that the cluster is always accessible in the event of failover.

In our case, the cluster resides within a simple domain, a single site, and a single subnet. If you are configuring a multi-subnet cluster, however, then the wizard detects this, and IP Addresses will be required for each subnet. In this scenario, you need to enter an IP address for each subnet.

Note   Each of the two NICs within a node is configured on a separate subnet so that the heartbeat between the nodes is segregated from the public network. However, a cluster is only regarded as multi-subnet if the data NICs of the cluster nodes reside in different subnets.

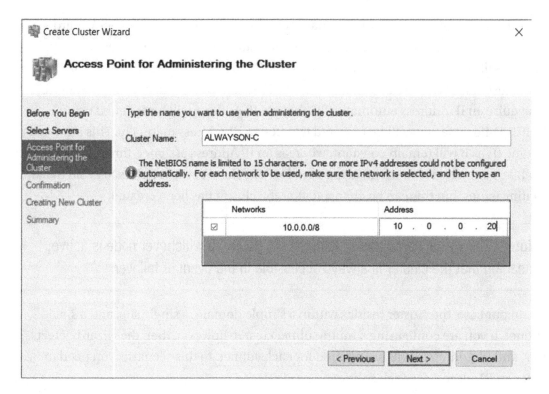

Figure 3-15. *The Access Point for Administering the Cluster Page*

Tip   If your cluster will reside within a domain, and if you do not have permissions to create AD (Active Directory) objects in the OU (organizational unit) that contains your cluster, then the VCO (virtual computer object) for the cluster must already exist and you must have the Full Control permission assigned.

The Confirmation page displays a summary of the cluster that is created. You can also use this screen to specify whether or not all eligible storage should be added to the cluster, which is generally a useful feature. This screen is displayed in Figure 3-16.

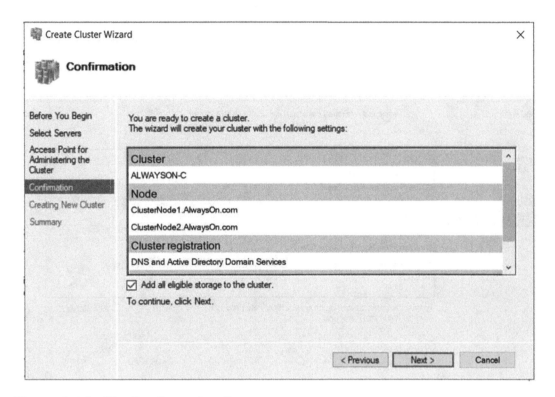

Figure 3-16. *The Confirmation Page*

After the cluster has been built, the Summary page shown in Figure 3-17 displays. This screen summarizes the cluster name, IP address, nodes, the quorum model that have been configured, and details of any warnings regarding the cluster. It also provides a link to an HTML (Hypertext Markup Language) version of the report.

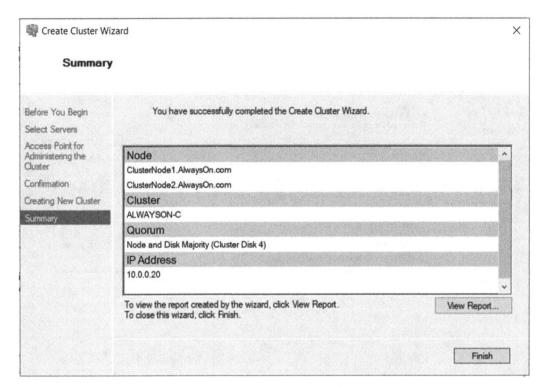

Figure 3-17. *The Summary Page*

The Create Cluster report displays a complete list of tasks that have been completed during the cluster build.

We could also have used PowerShell to create the cluster. The script in Listing 3-2 runs the cluster validation tests using the Test-Cluster cmdlet, before using the New-Cluster cmdlet to configure the cluster.

Listing 3-2. Validating and Creating the Cluster

```
#Run the validation tests

Test-Cluster -Node Clusternode1,Clusternode2

#Create the cluster

New-Cluster -Node ClusterNode1,ClusterNode2 -Name ALWAYSON-C
```

Configuring the Cluster

Many cluster configurations can be altered, depending on the needs of your environment. This section demonstrates how to change some of the more common configurations.

Changing the Quorum

If we examine our cluster storage in the Failover Cluster Manager, by drilling through ALWAYSON-C ➤ Storage ➤ Disks and highlighting the disk assigned to quorum, we can see that the witness has been correctly configured to use the Quorum volume. This is illustrated in Figure 3-18.

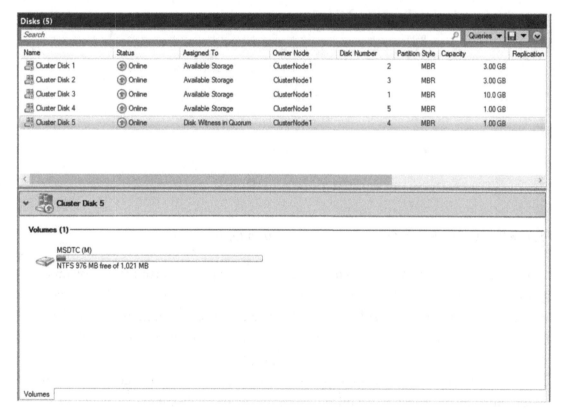

Figure 3-18. *Cluster Volumes*

We can modify this by entering the context menu of the cluster and by selecting More Actions ➤ Configure Cluster Quorum Settings, which causes the Configure Cluster Quorum Wizard to be invoked. On the Select Quorum Configuration Option page, shown in Figure 3-19, we choose the Select the Quorum Witness option.

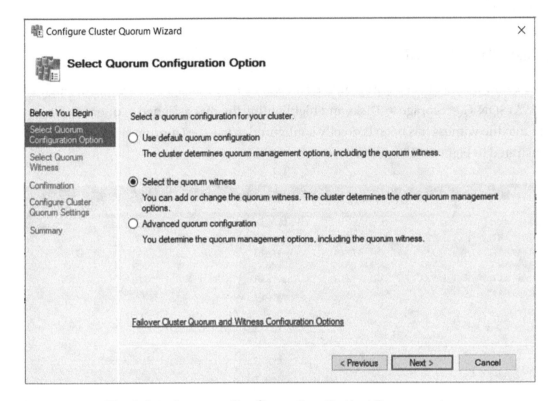

Figure 3-19. *The Select Quorum Configuration Option Page*

On the Select Quorum Witness page, we select the type of quorum that we want to configure. A disk witness is most appropriate when there are an even number of nodes in the cluster and all nodes reside in the same data center, or when there are an even number of nodes in the primary data center and another node in a secondary data center.

A file share witness is most appropriate when there are nodes split across two data centers, and you have access to a third data center, where a file share is available to act as a quorum. Windows Server 2019 supports file shares on any device that supports SMB 2.0 or above. This includes USB keys which can be attached to network routers.

A cloud witness is most appropriate when there are nodes spread across two data centers and there is not a third data center available to set up a file share witness. To use a cloud witness, you must have an Azure storage account, as the witness will be created in Azure BLOB storage.

It is most appropriate to not configure a witness, where there are an odd number of nodes in a single data center.

For our scenario, we will select the option to configure a disk witness. This is illustrated in Figure 3-20.

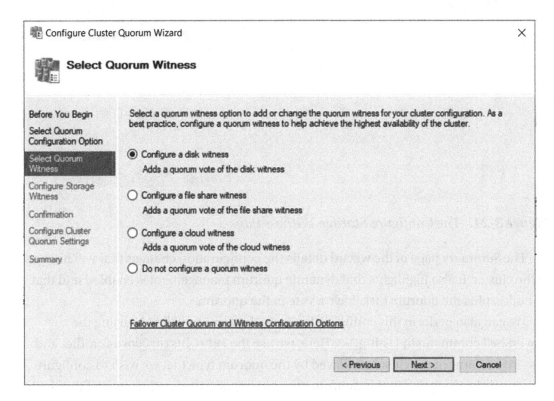

Figure 3-20. *The Select Quorum Witness Page*

On the Configure Storage Witness page of the wizard, we can select the correct disk to use as a quorum. In our case, this is Disk 4, as illustrated in Figure 3-21.

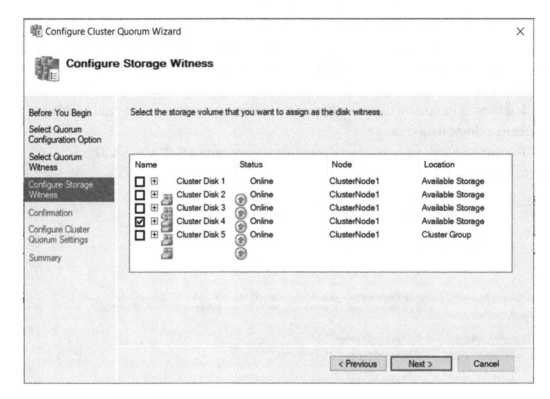

Figure 3-21. *The Configure Storage Witness Page*

The Summary page of the wizard details the configuration changes that will be made to the cluster. It also highlights that dynamic quorum management is enabled and that all nodes, plus the quorum disk, have a vote in the quorum.

We can also perform this configuration from the command line by using the PowerShell command in Listing 3-3. Here, we use the Set-ClusterQuorum cmdlet and pass in the name of the cluster, followed by the quorum type that we wish to configure. Because disk is included in this quorum type, we can also pass in the name of the cluster disk that we plan to use, and it is this aspect that allows us to change the quorum disk.

Tip   If following the demos using PowerShell, remember to change the disk number to match your own configuration.

Listing 3-3. Configuring the Quorum Disk

```
Set-ClusterQuorum -Cluster ALWAYSON-C -NodeAndDiskMajority "Cluster Disk 4"
```

Advanced Quorum Configuration

Recent versions of Windows Server allow you to configure advanced quorum configuration, such as voting weight and cluster witness. In this section, we will explore how to configure the vote weight of a node.

Node weight is generally useful if you have a *multi-subnet cluster*. In this scenario, it is recommended that you use a file share witness in a third site. This helps you avoid a cluster outage as a result of network failure between data centers. If you have an odd number of nodes in the quorum, however, then adding a file share witness leaves you with an even number of votes, which is dangerous. Removing the vote from one of the nodes in the secondary data center eliminates this issue.

You can also use node weight to temporarily remove the vote from a failed node, to avoid it impacting the quorum. I have also seen some people configure all nodes to have no vote, leaving the only vote with the disk witness. The idea here is to avoid having to dynamically changing the vote configuration should different nodes fail at different times. I would avoid this approach, however, as it introduces connectivity to the quorum disk as a single point of failure. If your quorum disk loses connectivity to the cluster, the cluster will become unavailable.

The vote weight of each node can be modified by using the Configure Cluster Quorum Wizard and choosing the Advanced Quorum configuration option on the Select Quorum Configuration Option page. This causes the Select Voting Configuration page to be displayed, as illustrated in Figure 3-22.

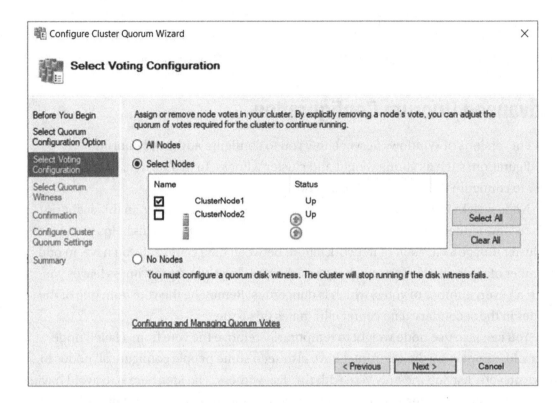

Figure 3-22. *Select Voting Configuration Page*

In this example, we have removed the vote from ClusterNode2, assuming that the node has failed and we do not want it to impact our quorum.

Note   To follow the rest of this example, you must have an Azure storage account. The account must be of the type "General Purpose" and should be configured on the standard performance tier and have locally redundant storage.

To change our disk witness to a cloud witness, we will then select the Configure a Cloud Witness option from the Configure Cluster Quorum page of the wizard, as shown in Figure 3-23.

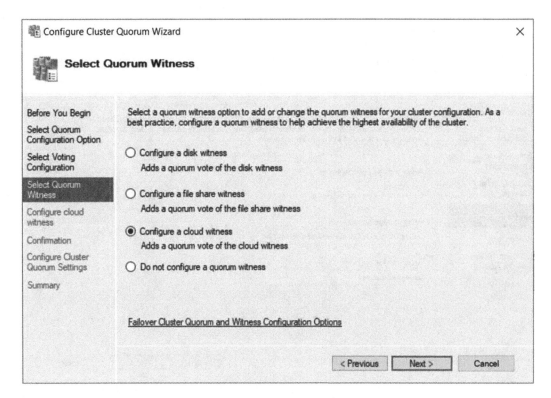

Figure 3-23. *Select Quorum Witness Page*

Because of our selection, we will next be presented with the Configure Cloud Witness page of the wizard, as illustrated in Figure 3-24. Here, we need to enter the name of our Azure storage account and primary access key of the storage account. The access key can be located in the Azure Portal, by drilling through Storage Accounts ➤ <Name of storage account> ➤ Access keys and copying Key 1. Generally, the service endpoint will remain with the default value; however, there are some occasions where you may need to change it. For example, Azure storage accounts in China use a different endpoint.

Note   The access key is not held within the cluster configuration. Instead, a SAS (shared access signature) is generated.

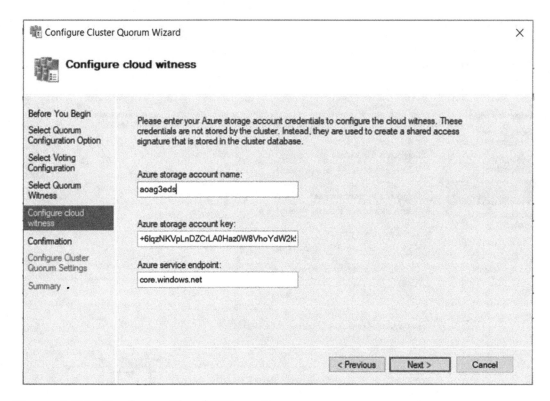

Figure 3-24. Configure Cloud Witness Page

The final page of the wizard (Figure 3-25) shows the Confirmation page. Here, you should check the details before choosing Next to apply the settings.

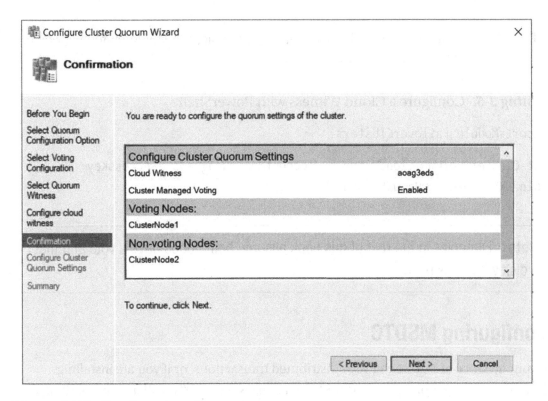

Figure 3-25. *Confirmation Page*

Tip   If you receive a generic error, asking you to confirm storage account details and connectivity over HTTPS, I have found that the most common reason is connectivity. The cloud witness requires Port 443 to be open, from all cluster nodes, to the Azure storage account.

To configure the node weight of a node, you can use the script in Listing 3-4.

Listing 3-4. Set Node Weight

```
Import-Module FailoverClusters

(Get-ClusterNode CLUSTERNODE2).NodeWeight = 0
```

To configure a cloud witness using PowerShell, use the script in Listing 3-5.

Tip   Make sure you change the account name and access key to match your own.

Listing 3-5. Configure a Cloud Witness with PowerShell

```
Import-Module FailoverClusters

Set-ClusterQuorum -CloudWitness -AccountName aoag3eds  -AccessKey
+6lqzNKVpLnDZCrLAOHazOW8VhoYdW2k==
```

Note   Examples in the rest of this book assume both nodes have a vote and that a disk witness is used.

Configuring MSDTC

If your instance of SQL Server uses distributed transactions, or if you are installing SQL Server Integration Services (SSIS), then it relies on MSDTC (Microsoft Distributed Transaction Coordinator). If your instance will use MSDTC, then you need to ensure that it is properly configured. If it is not, then setup will succeed, but transactions that rely on it may fail.

When installed on a cluster, SQL Server automatically uses the instance of MSDTC that is installed in the same role, if one exists. If it does not, then it uses the instance of MSDTC to which it has been mapped (if this mapping has been performed). If there is no mapping, it uses the cluster's default instance of MSDTC, and if there is not one, it uses the local machine's instance of MSDTC.

Many DBAs choose to install MSDTC within the same role as SQL Server; however, this introduces a problem. If MSDTC fails, it can also bring down the instance of SQL Server. Of course, the cluster attempts to bring both of the applications up on a different node, but this still involves downtime, including the time it takes to recover the databases on the new node, which takes a nondeterministic duration. For this reason, I recommend installing MSDTC in a separate role. If you do, the SQL Server instance still utilizes MSDTC, since it is the cluster's default instance, and it removes the possibility of MSDTC causing an outage to SQL Server. This is also preferable to using a mapped instance or the local machine instance since it avoids unnecessary configuration, and the MSDTC instance should be clustered when a clustered instance of SQL Server is using it.

To create an MSDTC role, start by selecting the Configure Role option from the Roles context menu in Failover Cluster Manager. This invokes the High Availability Wizard. On the Select A Role page of the wizard, select the Distributed Transaction Coordinator (DTC) role type, as shown in Figure 3-26.

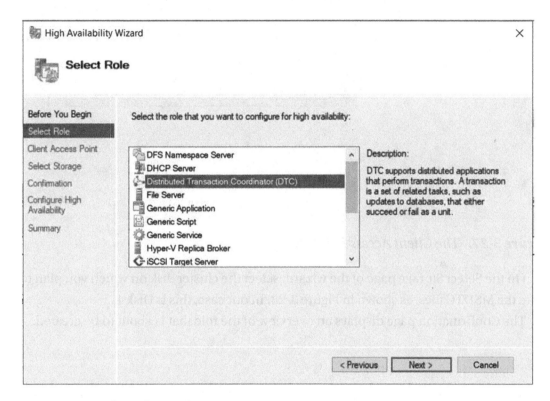

Figure 3-26. *The Select Role Page*

On the Client Access Point page, illustrated in Figure 3-27, you need to enter a virtual name and IP address for MSDTC. In our case, we name it ALWAYSON-MSDTC-C and assign 10.0.0.21 as the IP address. On a multi-subnet cluster, you need to provide an IP address for each network.

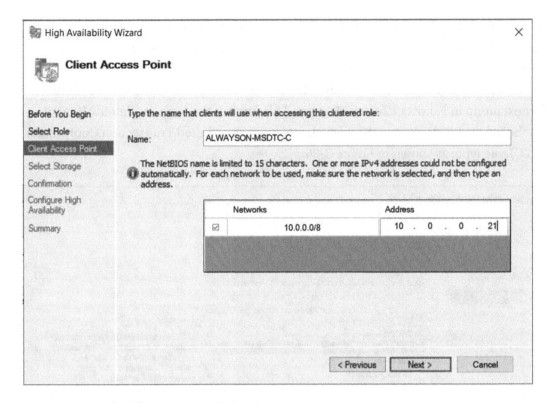

Figure 3-27. *The Client Access Point Page*

On the Select Storage page of the wizard, select the cluster disk on which you plan to store the MSDTC files, as shown in Figure 3-28. In our case, this is Disk 4.

The Confirmation page displays an overview of the role that is about to be created.

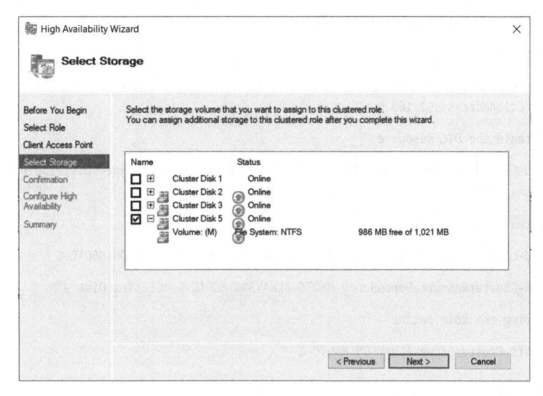

Figure 3-28. *The Select Storage Page*

Alternatively, we could create this role in PowerShell. The script in Listing 3-6 first uses the Add-ClusterServerRole cmdlet to create the role. We pass the virtual name to use for the role into the Name parameter, the name of the cluster disk to use into the Storage parameter, and the IP address for the role into the StaticAddress parameter.

We then use the Add-ClusterResource cmdlet to add the DTC resource. The Name parameter names the resource and the ResourceType parameter specifies that it is a DTC resource. We then need to create the dependencies between the resources within the role. We did not need to do this when using the GUI, as the dependencies were created for us automatically. Resource dependencies specify the resource or resources on which other resources depend. A resource failing propagates through the chain and could take a role offline. For example, in the case of our ALWAYSON-MSDTC-C role, if either the disk or the virtual name becomes unavailable, the DTC resource goes offline. Windows Server supports multiple dependencies with both AND and OR constraints. It is the OR constraints that make multi-subnet clustering possible, because a resource can be dependent on IP address A OR IP address B. Finally, we need to bring the role online by using the Start-ClusterGroup cmdlet.

Listing 3-6. Creating an MSDTC Role

```
#Create the Role

Add-ClusterServerRole -Name ALWAYSON-MSDTC-C -Storage "Cluster Disk 3"
-StaticAddress 192.168.0.50

#Create the DTC Resource

Add-ClusterResource -Name MSDTC-ALWAYSON-MSDTC-C -ResourceType "Distributed
Transaction Coordinator" -Group ALWAYSON-MSDTC-C

#Create the dependencies

Add-ClusterResourceDependency MSDTC-ALWAYSON-MSDTC-C ALWAYSON-MSDTC-C

Add-ClusterResourceDependency MSDTC-ALWAYSON-MSDTC-C "Cluster Disk 3"

#Bring the Role online

Start-ClusterGroup ALWAYSON-MSDTC-C
```

Configuring a Role

After creating a role, you may wish to configure it to alter the failover policy or configure nodes as preferred owners. To configure a role, select Properties from the role's context menu. On the General tab of the Properties dialog box, which is shown in Figure 3-29, you can configure a node as the preferred owner of the role. You can also change the order of precedence of node preference by moving nodes above or below others in the Preferred Owners window.

You can also select the priority for the role in the event that multiple roles fail over to another node at the same time. The options for this setting are as follows:

- High
- Medium
- Low
- No Auto Start

We will configure the ALWAYSON-MSDTC-C role to failover with High priority.

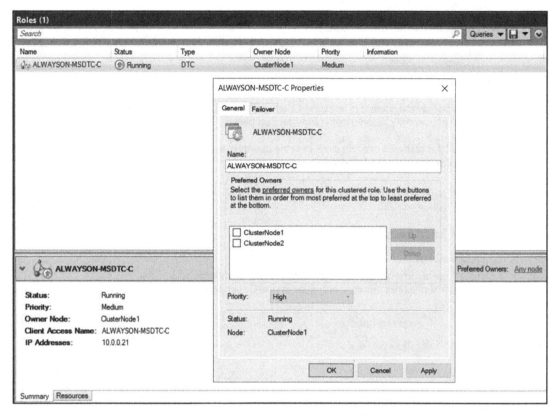

Figure 3-29. *The General Tab*

On the Failover tab of the Properties dialog box, you can configure the number of times that the role can fail over within a given period before the role is left offline. The default value for this is one failure within 6 hours. The issue with this is that if a role fails over, and after you fix the issue on the original node, you fail the role back, no more failovers are allowed within the 6-hour window. This is obviously a risk, and I generally advise that you change this setting. In our case, we have configured the role to allow a maximum of three failovers within a 24-hour time window, as illustrated in Figure 3-30. We have also configured the role to fail back to the most preferred owner if it becomes available again. Remember, when setting automatic failback, that failback also causes downtime in the same way that a failover does. If you aspire to a very high level of availability, such as five 9s, then this option may not be appropriate. We will configure the ALWAYSON-MSDTC-C Role to allow three failovers, within a 24-hour period. We will also configure the role to allow immediate failback.

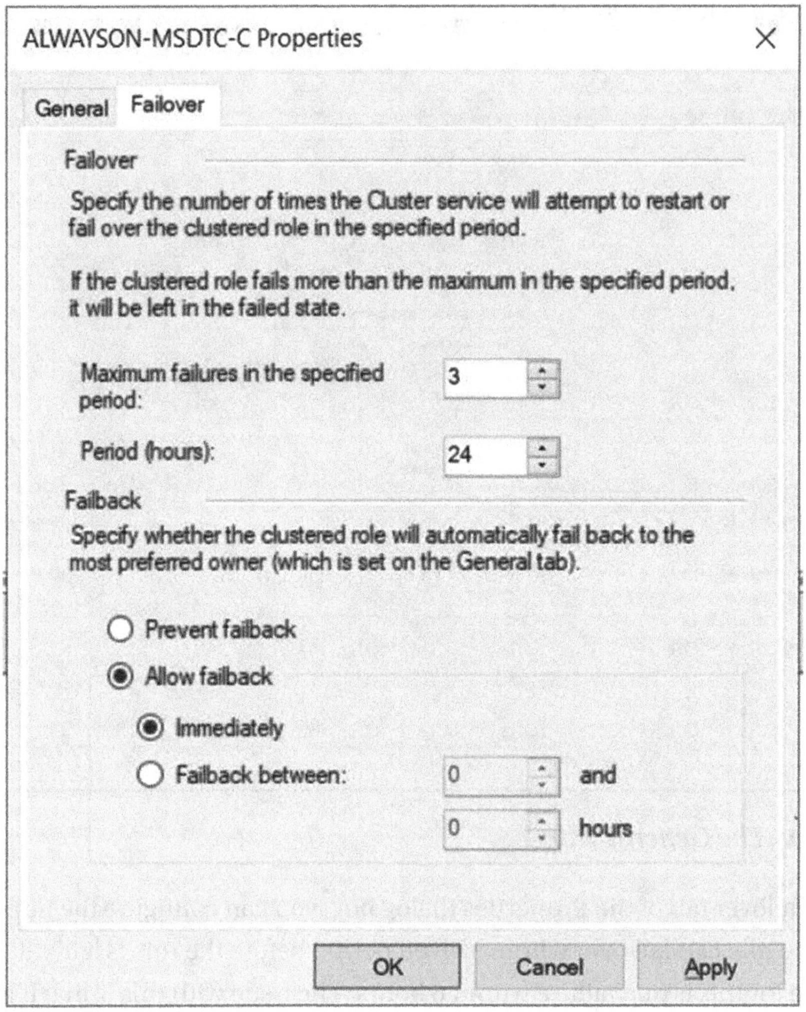

Figure 3-30. *The Failover Tab*

Summary

Before creating the cluster, the Microsoft Cluster Service (MCS) must be installed on all nodes. This can be achieved by installing the Cluster Feature, using the Add Roles and Features Wizard.

Once the cluster feature has been installed, clustering can be configured on each node by using the Create Cluster Wizard. Before building the cluster, this wizard will prompt you to run the Cluster Validation Wizard. The Cluster Validation Wizard will validate that environment meets the requirements for a cluster. If you find that your environment does not meet the requirements, you can continue to building the cluster, but the installation will not be supported by Microsoft.

Once the cluster has been built, it will also need to be configured. This will include configuring the quorum mode and may also include configuring MSDTC. After creating a role on the cluster, you may also wish to configure the role with failover policies or preferred owners.

CHAPTER 4

Implementing an AlwaysOn Failover Clustered Instance

Once the cluster has been built and configured, it is time to install the SQL Server AlwaysOn failover cluster instance. In our scenario, we want to build a clustered instance, which spans both nodes of the Windows cluster that we built in Chapter 3. We will also discuss how to build the failover clustered instance using PowerShell. To do this, we will need to use the Install a SQL Server Failover Cluster wizard on the primary node of the cluster. We will then need to run the Add Node wizard to allow the passive node to host the instance in the event of a failover. Therefore, in this chapter, we will perform the following tasks:

- Install a SQL Server failover clustered instance on the active cluster node.

- Configure the passive node of the wizard to support the failover clustered instance.

Building the Instance

An AlwaysOn Failover Clustered Instance can be built using the Install A SQL Server Failover Cluster wizard, which can be invoked by opening the SQL Server Installation Center, on the node hosting the cluster core resources, and selecting the New SQL Server Failover Cluster Installation option from the Installation. The Installation tab of the SQL Server Installation Center is illustrated in Figure 4-1.

© Peter A. Carter 2020

P. A. Carter, *SQL Server 2019 AlwaysOn*, https://doi.org/10.1007/978-1-4842-6479-9_4

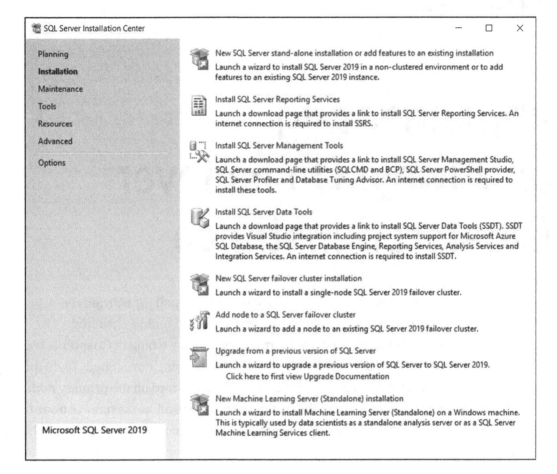

Figure 4-1. *SQL Server Installation Center – Installation Tab*

The Product Key page of the wizard is the first to be displayed and is illustrated in Figure 4-2. On this page of the wizard, you will either select one of the free versions of SQL Server to install, or enter a product key, or volume licensing key, which will automatically determine the correct version of SQL Server to install.

Tip   In SQL Server 2019, Developer Edition, which is functionally equivalent to Enterprise Edition, is free. Prior to SQL Server 2016, there was a nominal charge associated with this noncommercial license.

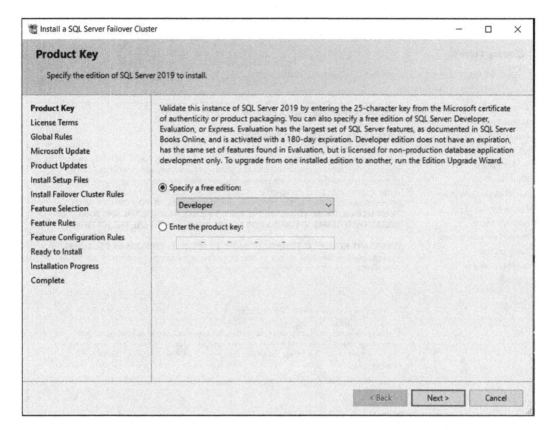

Figure 4-2. *Install a SQL Server Failover Cluster Wizard – Product Key Page*

On the License Terms page of the wizard (Figure 4-3), you will be invited to accept Microsoft's license terms, via a check box. The installation cannot proceed without agreement.

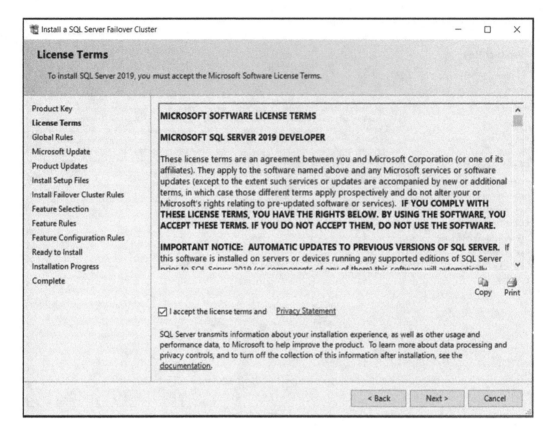

Figure 4-3. *Install a SQL Server Failover Cluster Wizard – License Terms Page*

Global Rules will now be checked to ensure that the setup support files can be successfully installed. When all checks are passed, the Microsoft Update page of the wizard, illustrated in Figure 4-4, will prompt you to choose if you want Windows Update to check for SQL Server patches and hotfixes. The choice here will depend on your organization's patching policy. Some organizations implement a ridged patching regime for the testing and acceptance of patches, followed by a patching cycle, which is often supported with software such as WSUS (Windows Server Update Services). If such a regime exists in your organization, then you should not select this option.

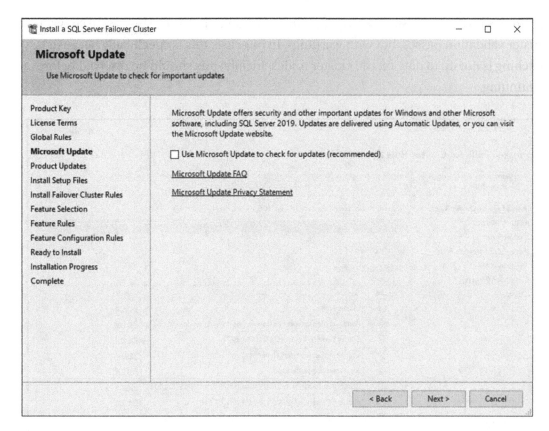

Figure 4-4. *Install a SQL Server Failover Cluster Wizard – Microsoft Update Page*

If you have chosen to check for updates, and if any available updates are discovered, then the Product Updates page of the wizard will list any available updates that have been found. You should confirm if they should be installed or not, using the check box.

After the setup support files and any product updates have been downloaded (if applicable), extracted, and installed, installation rules for the installation of a failover clustered instance will be checked and the results displayed on the Install Failover Cluster Rules page of the wizard, which is shown in Figure 4-5.

If you see a warning for Windows Firewall, this may simply because the Firewall is turned on. It does not indicate that the required ports are not open. For further information on configuring firewalls for SQL Server, I recommend the Apress book *Securing SQL Server 2nd Edition: DBAs Defending the Database*, which is available from www.apress.com/gb/book/9781484241608.

In this instance, we see a warning against cluster verification. This is caused when cluster validation passes, but with warnings. In our case, this is specifically because patching is not up to date on the cluster nodes. Ideally, this should be resolved before continuing.

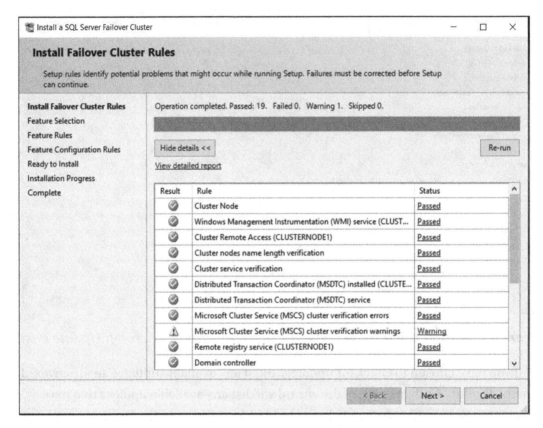

Figure 4-5. *Install a SQL Server Failover Cluster Wizard – Install Failover Cluster Rules*

On the Feature Selection page of the wizard, which is shown in Figure 4-6, you will select the features of the SQL Server 2019 product suite that you wish to install. For the purpose of this book, we will choose to install the Database Engine and SQL Server Integration Services (SSIS).

It is worthy of note that SSIS is not cluster-aware and is not designed to be clustered. There are some circumstances where you may decide to cluster the Integration Services service, and if this is the case, then you can work around the limitation, by creating a cluster role, with the Generic type, and adding the Integration Services service as a dependency. In most scenarios, however, the most appropriate way to manage SSIS on a clustered instance is simply to install the Integration Services service, as a stand-alone service, on each node of the cluster.

Additionally, the Feature Selection page of the wizard requires you to specify folder locations for the instance root folder and the shared features folder. You may want to move these to a different drive in order to leave the C:\ drive for the operating system. This may be a consideration for space reasons, or just to isolate the SQL Server binaries from other applications.

The instance root directory will typically contain a folder for each instance that you create on the server, and there will be separate folders for the Database Engine, SSAS, and SSRS installations. A folder associated with the Database Engine will be called MSSQL15.[InstanceName], where instance name is either the name of your instance or MSSQLSERVER for a default instance. The number 15 in the folder name relates to the version of SQL Server, which is 15 for SQL Server 2019.

This folder will contain a subfolder called MSSQL, which in turn will contain folders that will store files associated with your instance, including a folder called Binn, which will contain the application files, application extensions, and XML configurations associated with your instance; a folder called Backup, which will be the default location for backups of databases; and a folder called Data, which will be the default location of the system databases.

The default folders for TempDB, user databases, and backups can be modified later in the installation process, and splitting these databases into separate volumes is often a good practice, but may not be necessary (or even possible) if your data will be located on a SAN, as discussed in Chapter 3. Other folders will also be created here, including a folder called LOGS, which will be the default location for the files for both the Error Logs and the default Extended Event health trace.

If you are installing SQL Server in a 64-bit environment, you will be asked to enter folders for both 32-bit and 64-bit versions of the shared features directory. This is because some SQL Server components are always installed as 32-bit processes. The 32-bit and 64-bit components cannot share a directory, so for installation to continue, you must specify different folders for each of these options. The Shared Features directory becomes a root-level directory for features that are shared by all instances of SQL Server, such as SDKs and management tools.

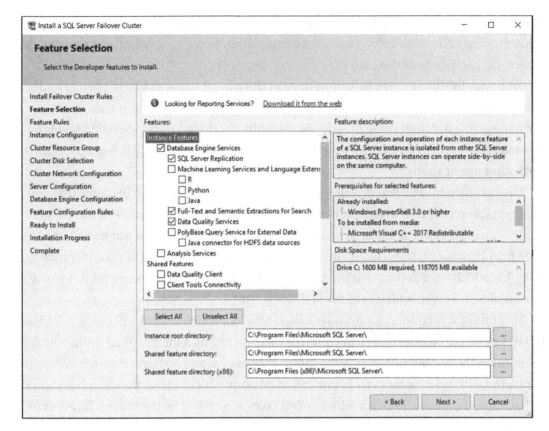

Figure 4-6. *Install a SQL Server Failover Cluster Wizard – Feature Selection Page*

The rules for installing the selected features are checked, and if all rules pass, then the Instance Configuration page will be displayed, as illustrated in Figure 4-7. On this page of the wizard, you will specify a name for the instance. Because the instance will be clustered, this page will also ask you to specify the network name for the instance. In this scenario, we will install a default instance of SQL Server, meaning that we do not need to specify an instance name. We will assign ALWAYSON-SQL-C as the network name.

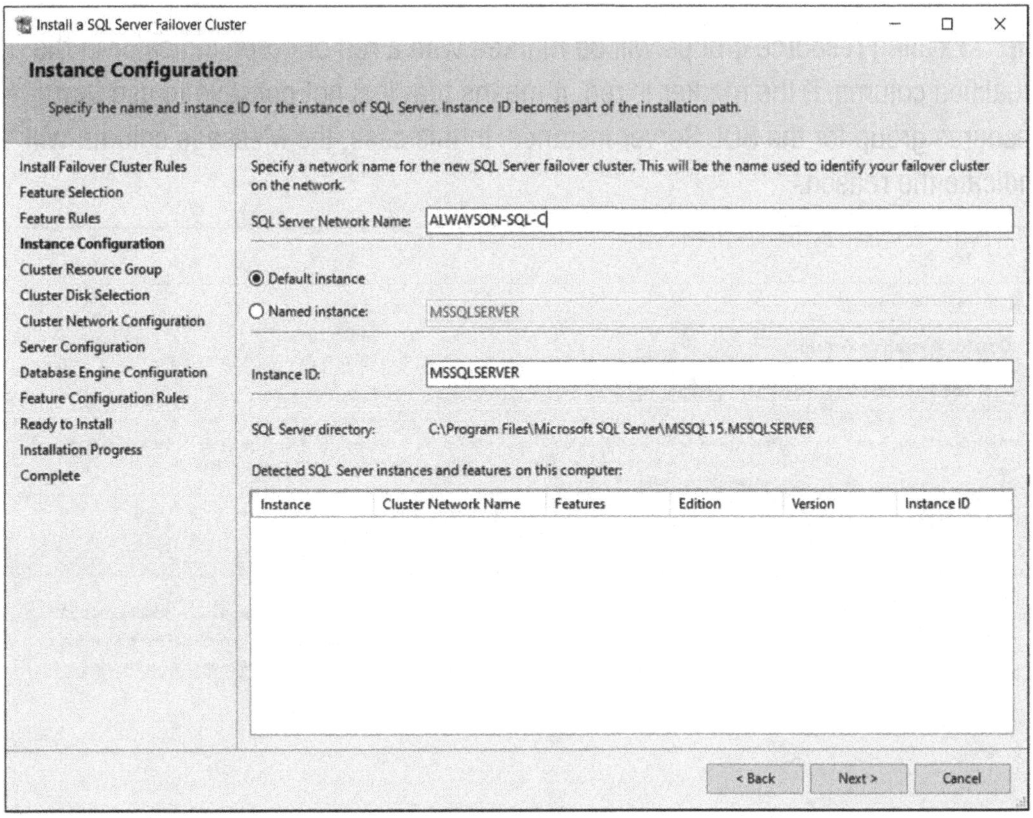

Figure 4-7. *Install a SQL Server Failover Cluster Wizard – Instance Configuration Page*

Tip   SQL Server uses the term cluster resource group to describe a cluster role. A cluster role is Microsoft's newer term, and within this chapter, the terms should be treated synonymously.

On the Cluster Resource Group page of the wizard, we have the option of either selecting an existing cluster resource group (which gives the option of a Windows administrator pre-creating the resource group) or entering the name of a new resource group, which will then be created by setup. In our case, we will specify ALWAYSON-SQL-C as a name for a new resource group. This is illustrated in Figure 4-8.

Tip   Existing resource groups will be marked with a red or green indicator in the
Qualified column. If the marker is red, it means that it is not possible to use that
resource group for the SQL Server instance. In this case, the Message column will
indicate the reason.

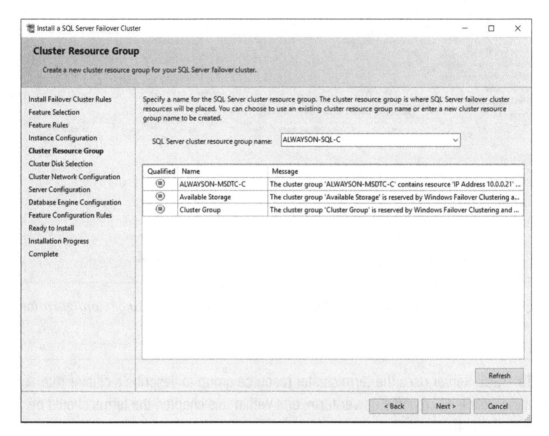

Figure 4-8.   *Install a SQL Server Failover Cluster Wizard – Cluster Resource Group*
Page

On the Cluster Disk Selection page, illustrated in Figure 4-9, you can select the disk
resources that should be associated with the resource group. The page will list all disks
that are associated with the cluster and indicate which disks can be selected with red or
green indicators in the Qualified column. Disks that are already associated with other
resource groups cannot be selected, because a disk can only be associated with a single
resource group. We will specify that all available disks (Data, Logs, and TempDB) should
be associated with the ALWAYSON-SQL-C resource group.

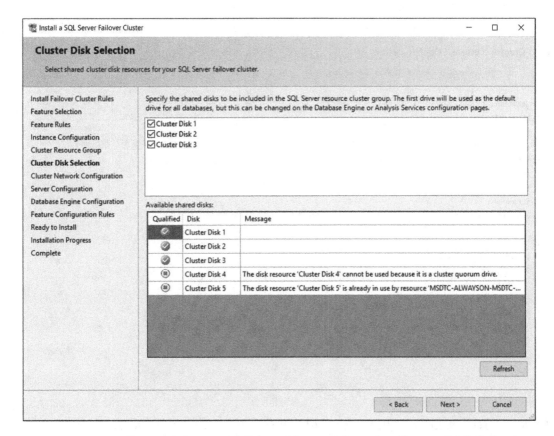

Figure 4-9. *Install a SQL Server Failover Cluster Wizard – Cluster Disk Selection Page*

On the Cluster Network Configuration page (Figure 4-10), we can configure the IP Address of the cluster role. We can either choose DHCP, which means that the IP address will be attained automatically, or we can specify a static IP address. In our case, we will specify a static IP address. If our cluster were a stretch cluster (spread across multiple subnets), we would need to specify an IP address for each subnet.

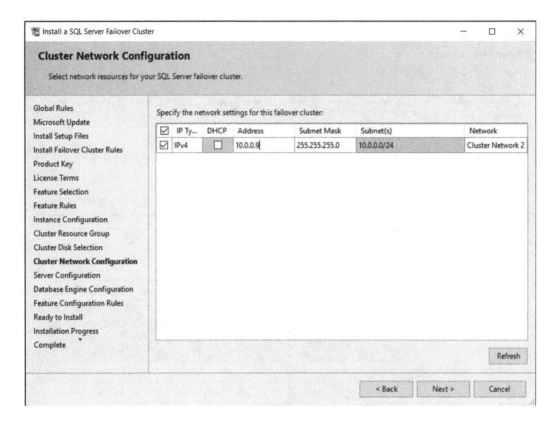

Figure 4-10. *Install a SQL Server Failover Cluster – Cluster Network Configuration Page*

The Server Configuration page has two tabs. The first tab is Service Accounts. On this tab, which is illustrated in Figure 4-11, we will specify the service account that will be used as the security context for each SQL Server service and also specify the startup mode for each of the services. This is worthy of note because when installing a stand-alone instance, you will usually set each service to start automatically. When installing a cluster, however, cluster-aware services should be configured to start manually. This is because they will be managed by the cluster service.

In recent versions of SQL Server, it is possible to enable Perform Volume Maintenance Tasks during setup, and this is implemented as a simple check box of the Service Accounts tab. The consideration here is security vs. performance. If you choose to perform volume maintenance tasks, then data files will not be zeroed out when they are created or expanded; however, an attacker with specialist software could potentially retrieve data that was previously stored on the allocated disk blocks. Perform Volume Maintenance Tasks does not apply to transaction log files.

Tip   For a full discussion on SQL Server security considerations, I recommend the Apress title *Securing SQL Server 2nd Edition: DBAs Defending the Database*, which can be purchased from www.apress.com/gb/book/9781484241608.

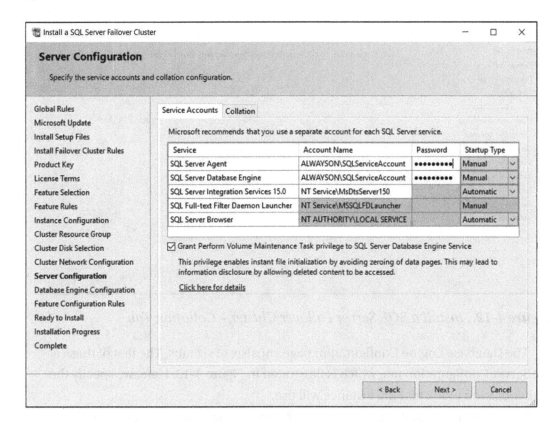

Figure 4-11. *Install a SQL Server Failover Cluster – Service Accounts Tab*

On the Collation tab, shown in Figure 4-12, you can specify the collation that will be configured for the instance. Wherever possible, it is a good idea to use a consistent collation throughout the enterprise or, at a minimum, throughout the instances that make up a data-tier application.

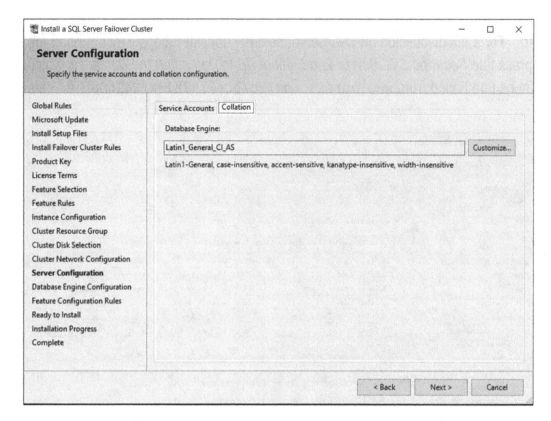

Figure 4-12. *Install a SQL Server Failover Cluster – Collation Tab*

The Database Engine Configuration page consists of six tabs. The first of these is the Server Configuration tab, which is illustrated in Figure 4-13. Here, we specify the authentication mode that the instance will use.

Windows Authentication Mode means that the credentials that a user supplies when logging into Windows will be passed to SQL Server, and the user does not require any additional credentials to gain access to the instance. With mixed mode, although Windows credentials can still be used to access the instance, users can also be given second-tier credentials. If this option is selected, then SQL Server will hold its own login names and passwords for login created inside the instance, and users can supply these, in order to gain access, even if their Windows identity does not have permissions.

For security best practice, it is a good idea to only allow Windows authentication to your instance. This is for two reasons. First, with Windows authentication only, if an attacker were to gain access to your network, then they would still not be able to access SQL Server, since they would not have a valid Windows account with the correct permissions. With mixed-mode authentication, however, once inside the network, attackers could use brute-force attacks or other hacking methodologies to attempt to gain access via a second-tier SQL Server Login. Second, if you specify mixed-mode authentication, then you are required to create an SA account. The SA account is a SQL Server user account that has administrative privileges over the instance. If the password for this account became compromised, then an attacker could gain administrative control over SQL Server. If mixed-mode authentication must be used, it is a good idea to disable the SA account.

Mixed-mode authentication is a necessity in some cases, however. For example, you may have a legacy application that does not support Windows authentication, or a third-party application that has a hard-coded connection that uses second-tier authentication. These would be two valid reasons why mixed-mode authentication may be required. Another valid reason would be if you have users that need to access the instance from a nontrusted domain.

Additionally, on the Server Configuration tab, you can specify Windows users that will be added to the sysadmin fixed server role, giving them unrestricted access to the instance. In our scenario, we will add the AlwaysOn\SQLAdmin user as an instance administrator and use Windows Authentication only.

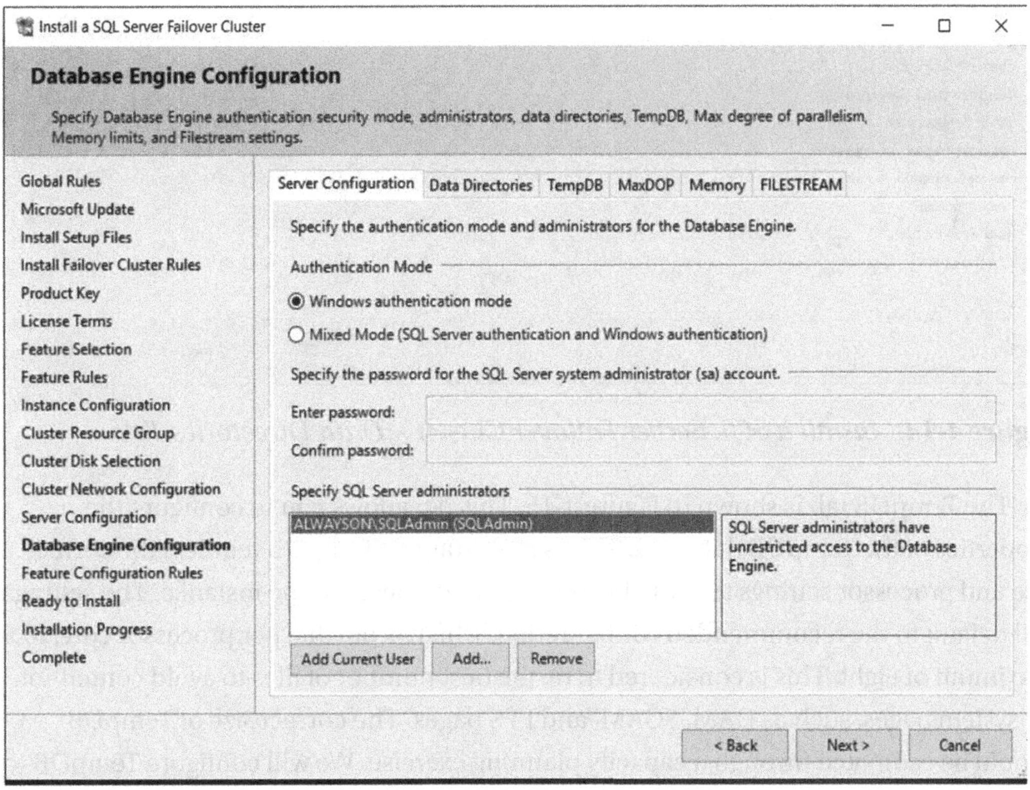

Figure 4-13. Install a SQL Server Failover Cluster – Server Configuration Tab

On the Data Directories tab, illustrated in Figure 4-14, you can alter the default location of the data root directory. On this screen, you can also change the default location for user databases and their log files. Finally, this tab allows you to specify a default location for backups of databases that will be taken. In our scenario, we must ensure that the data root is pointing at the Data volume, with log files pointing at the Logs volume.

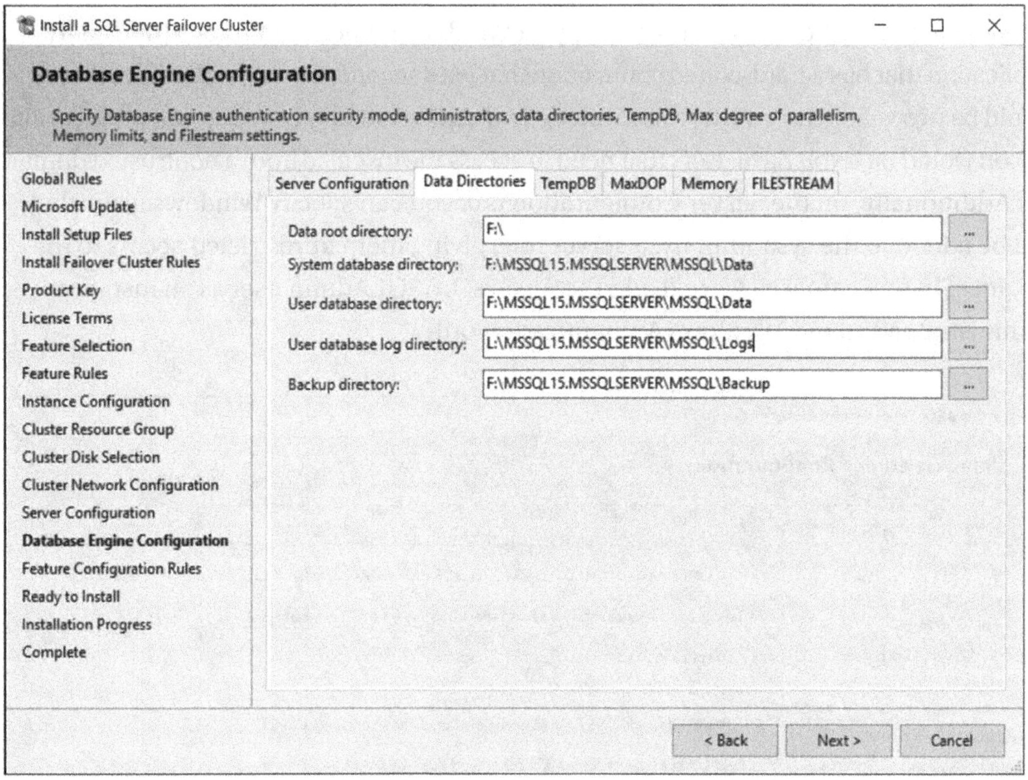

Figure 4-14. *Install a SQL Server Failover Cluster – Data Directories Tab*

The TempDB tab is shown in Figure 4-15. This tab allows you to configure the properties of the TempDB database. This is important as TempDB requires the correct size and processor settings to avoid becoming a bottleneck for the instance. The settings will default to the recommended configuration, which is one file per processor core, to a maximum of eight. This is considered to be the best number of files to avoid contention on system pages, such as GAM, SGAM, and PFS pages. The correct size of TempDB should be estimated through a capacity planning exercise. We will configure TempDB to have an initial size of 60MB per file (240MB in total). We have also configured TempDB to reside on the TempDB volume. In our scenario, we will also be setting the file location to point at our TempDB volume.

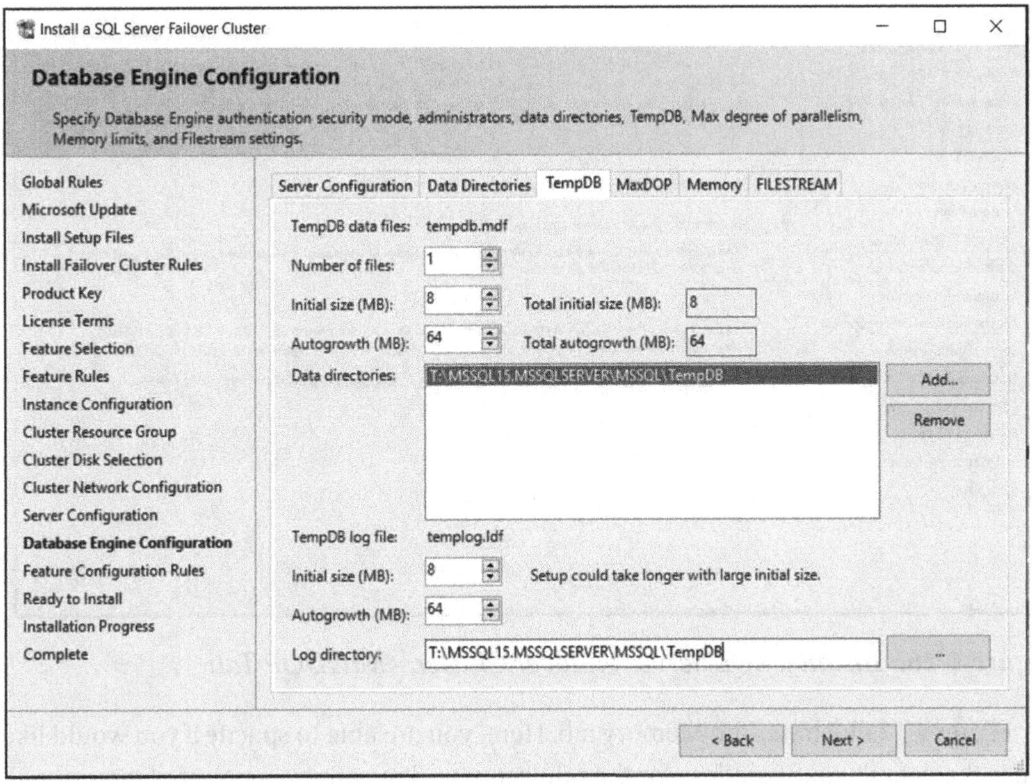

Figure 4-15. Install a SQL Server Failover Cluster – TempDB Tab

The MaxDOP tab, shown in Figure 4-16, allows you to configure the default Maximum Degree of Parallelism for queries run within the instance. The default value is calculated based on the number of cores available, to a maximum of eight. This can be overridden, if required, however. For example, for an instance hosting small databases with an OLTP (Online Transactional Processing) workload profile, where many small, simultaneous queries are running at the same time, it can sometimes be preferable to reduce the MaxDOP value.

Tip   Setting a MaxDOP of 0 allows all available processors to be used to process a query running with a parallel query plan.

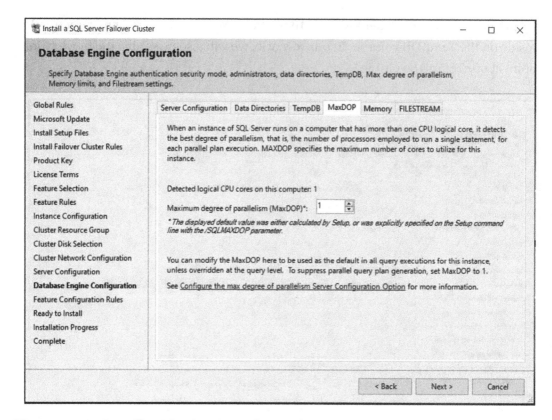

Figure 4-16. *Install a SQL Server Failover Cluster – MaxDOP Tab*

Figure 4-17 illustrates the Memory tab. Here, you are able to specify if you would like to use the default configuration, for the minimum and maximum amount of memory that can be allocated to the instance; use the recommended values, calculated by the setup wizard; or specify your own values. To specify your own preferred values, choose the recommended option, enter your values, and check the Click here to accept the recommended memory configurations for the SQL Server database engine check box. This check box must also be used, if you wish to adhere to the setup program's recommendations.

Tip   A full discussion of approaches for MaxDOP and Memory configuration can be found in the Apress title *Pro SQL Server 2019 Administration*, which can be purchased at www.apress.com/gb/book/9781484250884#otherversion= 9781484250891.

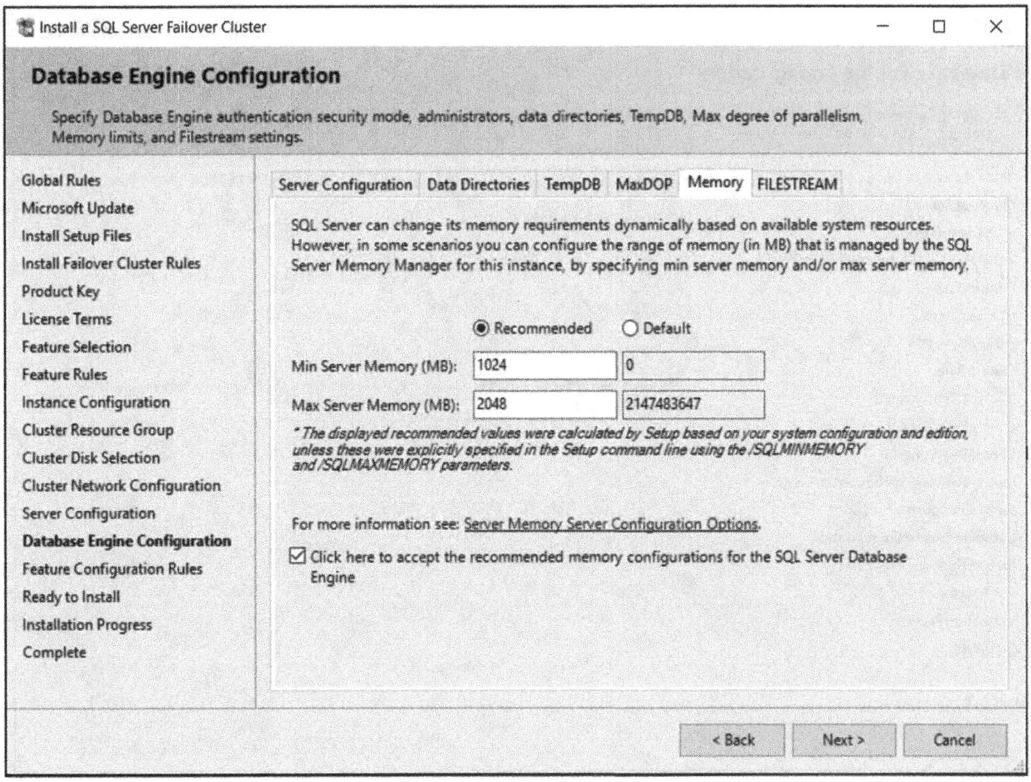

Figure 4-17. *Install a SQL Server Failover Cluster – Memory Tab*

The FILESTREAM tab of the Database Engine Configuration page allows you to enable and configure the level of access for SQL Server FILESTREAM functionality, as illustrated in Figure 4-18. FILESTREAM must also be enabled if you wish to use the FileTable feature of SQL Server. FILESTREAM and FileTable provide the ability to store data in an unstructured manner within the Windows folder structure, while retaining the ability to manage and interrogate this data from SQL Server.

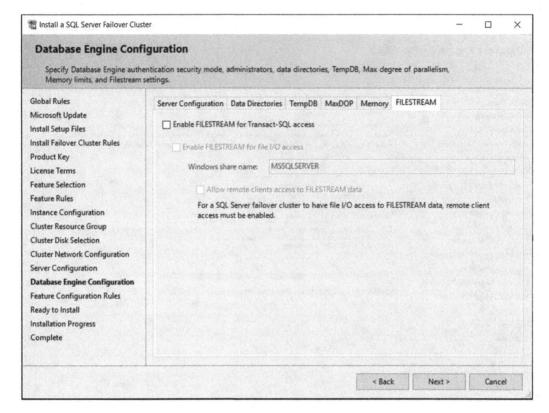

Figure 4-18. *Install a SQL Server Failover Clustered Instance – FILESTREAM Tab*

After the Feature Configuration Rules have been checked, the Ready to Install page of the wizard will be displayed. This page of the wizard provides a summary of actions that will be performed by the setup utility. Selecting Install on this page will cause the instance installation to begin. After installation is complete, the Complete page should be reviewed.

Installing the Instance with PowerShell

Of course, we can use PowerShell to install the AlwaysOn failover cluster instance instead of using the GUI. To install an AlwaysOn failover cluster instance from PowerShell, we can use SQL Server's `setup.exe` application with the `InstallFailoverCluster` action specified.

When you perform a command-line installation of a clustered instance, you need the parameters in Table 4-1, in addition to the parameters that are mandatory when you install a stand-alone instance of SQL Server.

Table 4-1. *Required Parameters for the Installation of a Clustered Instance*

Parameter	Usage
/FAILOVERCLUSTERIPADDRESSES	Specifies the IP address(s) to use for the instance in the format *<IP Type>;<address>;<network name>;<subnet mask>*. For multi-subnet clusters, the IP addresses are space delimited.
/FAILOVERCLUSTERNETWORKNAME	The virtual name of the clustered instance.
/INSTALLSQLDATADIR	The folder in which to place SQL Server data files. This must be a cluster disk.

The script in Listing 4-1 performs the same installation that has just been demonstrated when you run it from the root directory of the installation media.

Listing 4-1. Installing an AlwaysOn Failover Cluster Instance with PowerShell

```
.\SETUP.EXE /IACCEPTSQLSERVERLICENSETERMS /ACTION="InstallFailoverCluster"
/FEATURES=SQL,IS  /INSTANCENAME="MSSQLSERVER" /SQLSVCACCOUNT="ALWAYSON\
SQLServiceAccount" /SQLSVCPASSWORD="Pa$$w0rd" /AGTSVCACCOUNT="ALWAYSON\
SQLServiceAccount" /AGTSVCPASSWORD="Pa$$w0rd" /SQLSYSADMINACCOUNTS=
"ALWAYSO\SQLAdmin" /SQLMAXDOP="1" /FAILOVERCLUSTERIPADDRESSES="IPv4;10.0.0.9;
Cluster Network 2;255.255.255.0" /FAILOVERCLUSTERDISKS="Cluster Disk 1"
"Cluster Disk 2" "Cluster Disk 3" /FAILOVERCLUSTERNETWORKNAME=
"ALWAYSON-SQL-C" /INSTALLSQLDATADIR="F:\" /SQLUSERDBLOGDIR="L:\
MSSQL15.MSSQLSERVER\MSSQL\Logs" /SQLTEMPDBDIR="T:\MSSQL15.MSSQLSERVER\
MSSQL\TempDB" /SQLTEMPDBLOGDIR="T:\MSSQL15.MSSQLSERVER\MSSQL\TempDB"
/SQLMAXMEMORY="2048" /SQLMINMEMORY="1024" /qs
```

Adding a Node

The next step you should take when installing the cluster is to add the second node. Failure to add the second node results in the instance staying online, but with no high availability, since the second node is unable to take ownership of the role. To configure the second node, you need to log in to the passive cluster node and select the Add Node to SQL Server Failover Cluster option from the Installation tab of SQL Server Installation Center. This invokes the Add a Failover Cluster Node Wizard. The first page of this wizard is the Product Key page. Just like when you install an instance, you need to use this screen to provide the product key for SQL Server. Not specifying a product key only leaves you the option of installing the Evaluation Edition, and since this expires after 180 days, it's probably not the wisest choice for high availability.

The following License Terms page of the wizard asks you to read and accept the license terms of SQL Server. Additionally, you need to specify if you wish to participate in Microsoft's Customer Experience Improvement Program. If you select this option, then error reporting is captured and sent to Microsoft.

After you accept the license terms, a rules check runs to ensure that all of the conditions are met so you can continue with the installation. After the wizard checks for Microsoft updates and installing the setup files required for installation, another rules check is carried out to ensure that the rules for adding the node to the cluster are met.

On the Cluster Node Configuration page, illustrated in Figure 4-19, you are asked to confirm the instance name to which you are adding a node. If you have multiple instances on the cluster, then you can use the drop-down box to select the appropriate instance.

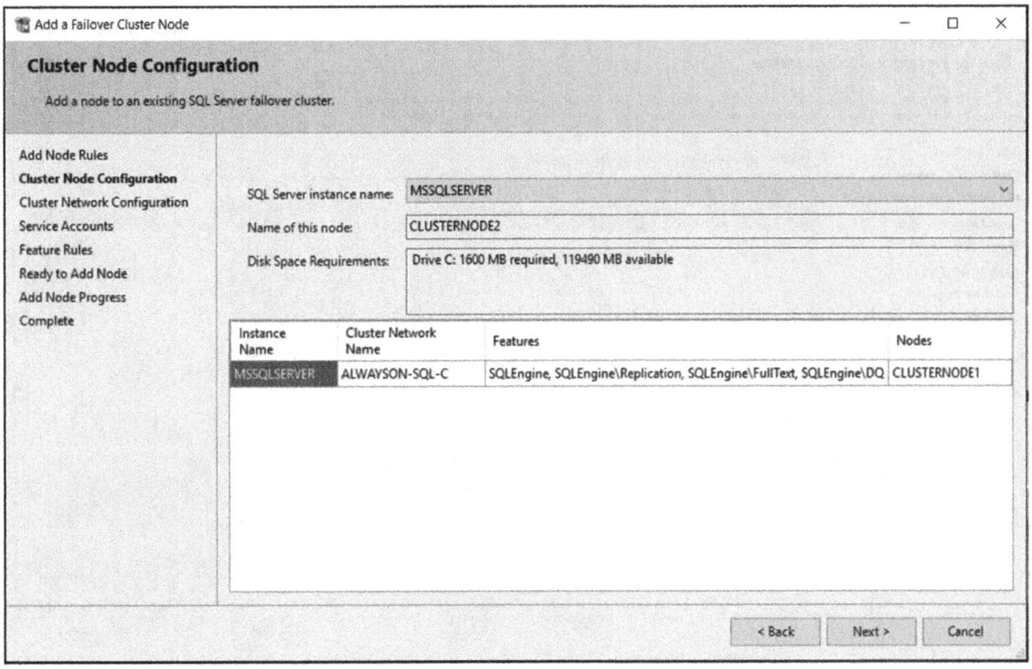

Figure 4-19. *Add a Failover Cluster Node Wizard – Cluster Node Configuration Page*

On the Cluster Network Configuration page, shown in Figure 4-20, you confirm the network details. These should be identical to the first node in the cluster, including the same IP address, since this is, of course, shared between the two nodes.

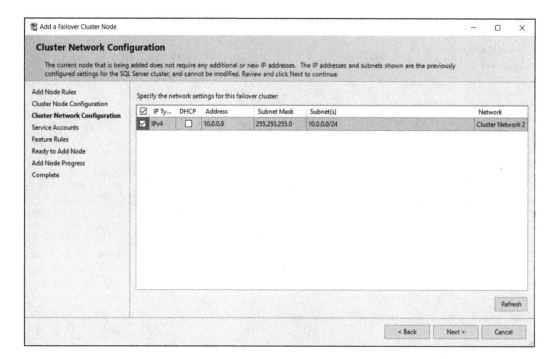

Figure 4-20. *The Cluster Network Configuration Page*

On the Service Accounts page of the wizard, most of the information is in read-only mode and you are not able to modify it. This is because the service accounts you use must be the same for each node of the cluster. You need to reenter the service account passwords, however. This page is shown in Figure 4-21.

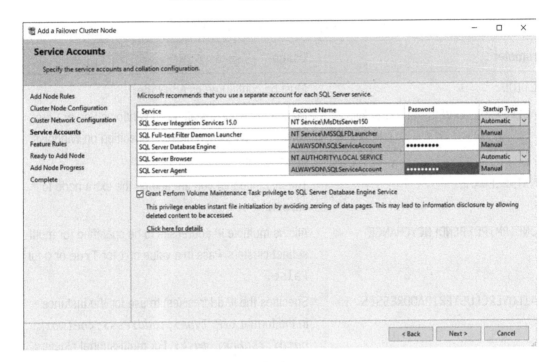

Figure 4-21. The Service Accounts Page

Now that the wizard has all of the required information, an additional rules check is carried out before the summary page displays. The summary page, known as the Ready to Add Node page, provides a summary of the activities that take place during the installation.

Adding a Node Using PowerShell

To add a node using PowerShell instead of the GUI, you can run SQL Server's `setup.exe` application with an `AddNode` action. When you add a node from the command line, the parameters detailed in Table 4-2 are mandatory.

Table 4-2. *Mandatory Parameters for the AddNode Action*

Parameter	Usage
/ACTION	Must be configured as AddNode.
/IACCEPTSQLSERVERLICENSETERMS	Mandatory when installing on Windows Server Core, since the /qs switch must be specified on Windows Server Core.
/INSTANCENAME	The instance that you are adding the extra node to support.
/CONFIRMIPDEPENDENCYCHANGE	Allows multiple IP addresses to be specified for multi-subnet clusters. Pass in a value of 1 for True or 0 for False.
/FAILOVERCLUSTERIPADDRESSES	Specifies the IP address(es) to use for the instance in the format *<IP Type>;<address>;<network name>;<subnet mask>*. For multi-subnet clusters, the IP addresses are space delimited.
/FAILOVERCLUSTERNETWORKNAME	The virtual name of the clustered instance.
/INSTALLSQLDATADIR	The folder in which to place SQL Server data files. This must be a cluster disk.
/SQLSVCACCOUNT	The service account that is used to run the Database Engine.
/SQLSVCPASSWORD	The password of the service account that is used to run the Database Engine.
/AGTSVCACCOUNT	The service account that issued to run SQL Server Agent.
/AGTSVCPASSWORD	The password of the service account that is used to run SQL Server Agent.

The script in Listing 4-2 adds ClusterNode2 to the role when you run it from the root folder of the install media.

Listing 4-2. Adding a Node Using PowerShell

```
.\setup.exe /IACCEPTSQLSERVERLICENSETERMS /ACTION="AddNode"
/INSTANCENAME="MSSQLSERVER" /SQLSVCACCOUNT="ALWAYSON\SQLServiceAccount"
/SQLSVCPASSWORD="Pa$$w0rd" /AGTSVCACCOUNT="ALWAYSON\SQLServiceAccount"
/AGTSVCPASSWORD="Pa$$w0rd" /FAILOVERCLUSTERIPADDRESSES="IPv4;10.0.0.9;
Cluster Network 2;255.255.255.0" /CONFIRMIPDEPENDENCYCHANGE=0 /qs
```

Summary

An AlwaysOn Failover Clustered Instance can be installed using SQL Server Installation Center or via PowerShell. When using the SQL Server Installation Center, the process is very similar to the installation of a stand-alone instance; however, you will need to specify additional details, such as the network name, IP Address, and resource group configuration.

When using PowerShell to install the Instance, you will use the InstallFailoverCluster action, specifying the /FAILOVERCLUSTERIPADDRESSES, /FAILOVERCLUSTERNETWORKNAME, and /INSTALLSQLDATADIR parameters, in addition to the parameters required for a stand-alone instance build.

CHAPTER 5

Implementing AlwaysOn Availability Groups On Windows

AlwaysOn Availability Groups provide a flexible option for achieving high availability, recovering from disasters, and scaling out read-only workloads. The technology synchronizes data at the database level, with health monitoring and quorum often provided by a Windows cluster, although a Windows cluster is not mandatory.

There are different variations of AlwaysOn Availability Groups. The traditional flavor sits on a Windows Failover Cluster, but if SQL Server is installed on Linux, then Pacemaker can be used. AlwaysOn Availability Groups can also be configured with no cluster at all. This is acceptable for offloading reporting but is not a valid high availability (HA) or disaster recovery (DR) configuration. When using SQL Server 2019 with Windows Server 2019, Availability Groups can even be configured for containerized SQL, with Kubernetes.

This chapter focuses on configuring Availability Groups on a Windows Failover Cluster, for the purpose of providing both HA and DR, and scaling read-only workloads. Availability Groups on Linux will be explored in Chapter 6.

© Peter A. Carter 2020
P. A. Carter, *SQL Server 2019 AlwaysOn*, https://doi.org/10.1007/978-1-4842-6479-9_5

Note   For the demonstrations in this chapter, we will use the cluster built in Chapter 3, but two additional nodes have been added to the cluster: CLUSTERNODE3 and CLUSTERNODE4. We will not use the Failover Clustered Instance that we configured in Chapter 4. Instead, stand-alone instances of SQL Server have been installed on each of the nodes, with the following names: CLUSTERNODE1\PROD, CLUSTERNODE2\SYNCHA, CLUSTERNODE3\ASYNCDR, and CLUSTERNODE4\READSCALE. Cluster nodes 1 and 2 sit within a subnet called Site1 and Cluster nodes 3 and 4 sit within a different subnet, called Site2. The instances are storing the Database data and log files on the C:\ volume. The shared storage within the cluster is not being used for these instances.

In this chapter, we will perform the following activities:

- Create Sales, Customers, Accounts, and HR Databases.

- Enable Availability Groups on our instances.

- Create an Availability group for the HR Database, using the New Availability Group wizard. This Availability Group will be configured for HA only.

- Create an Availability Group for the Sales and Customers database using the New Availability Group dialog box. This will be configured for HA, DR, and read-scaling.

- Create an Availability Group for the Accounts database using T-SQL. This Availability Group will be configured for HA and DR without any read-scaling.

- We will also discuss how PowerShell can be used to create Availability Groups.

Preparing to Implement AlwaysOn Availability Groups

Before implementing AlwaysOn Availability Groups, we first create four databases, which we will use during the demonstrations in this chapter. Each contains a single table, which we populate with data. Each database is configured with Recovery mode set to FULL. This is a hard requirement for a database to use AlwaysOn Availability Groups because data is synchronized via a log stream. The script in Listing 5-1 creates these databases.

Listing 5-1. Creating Databases

```
--Create Sales Database
CREATE DATABASE Sales ;
GO

USE Sales ;
GO

CREATE TABLE [dbo].[Orders](
        [OrderNumber] [int] IDENTITY(1,1) NOT NULL PRIMARY KEY CLUSTERED,
        [OrderDate] [date]  NOT NULL,
        [CustomerID] [int]  NOT NULL,
        [ProductID] [int]   NOT NULL,
        [Quantity] [int]    NOT NULL,
        [NetAmount] [money] NOT NULL,
        [TaxAmount] [money] NOT NULL,
        [InvoiceAddressID] [int] NOT NULL,
        [DeliveryAddressID] [int] NOT NULL,
        [DeliveryDate] [date] NULL,
) ;

DECLARE @Numbers TABLE
(
        Number        INT
)

--Populate ExistingOrders with data

;WITH CTE(Number)
AS
(
        SELECT 1 Number
        UNION ALL
```

```sql
        SELECT Number + 1
        FROM CTE
        WHERE Number < 100
)
INSERT INTO @Numbers
SELECT Number FROM CTE

INSERT INTO Orders
    SELECT
        (SELECT CAST(DATEADD(dd,(SELECT TOP 1 Number
                                 FROM @Numbers
                                 ORDER BY NEWID()),getdate())as DATE)),
        (SELECT TOP 1 Number -10 FROM @Numbers ORDER BY NEWID()),
        (SELECT TOP 1 Number FROM @Numbers ORDER BY NEWID()),
        (SELECT TOP 1 Number FROM @Numbers ORDER BY NEWID()),
        500,
        100,
        (SELECT TOP 1 Number FROM @Numbers ORDER BY NEWID()),
        (SELECT TOP 1 Number FROM @Numbers ORDER BY NEWID()),
        (SELECT CAST(DATEADD(dd,(SELECT TOP 1 Number - 10
    FROM @Numbers
        ORDER BY NEWID()),getdate()) as DATE))
FROM @Numbers a
CROSS JOIN @Numbers b ;

--SET FULL recovery mode on the database - required for Availability Groups

ALTER DATABASE Sales SET RECOVERY FULL ;
GO

--Create Customers Database

CREATE DATABASE Customers ;
GO

USE Customers ;
GO
```

```
CREATE TABLE dbo.Customers
(
    ID                  INT                 PRIMARY KEY         IDENTITY,
    FirstName           NVARCHAR(30),
    LastName            NVARCHAR(30),
    CreditCardNumber    VARBINARY(8000)
) ;
GO

--Populate the table

DECLARE @Numbers TABLE
(
    Number          INT
)

;WITH CTE(Number)
AS
(
    SELECT 1 Number
    UNION ALL
    SELECT Number + 1
    FROM CTE
    WHERE Number < 100
)
INSERT INTO @Numbers
SELECT Number FROM CTE

DECLARE @Names TABLE
(
    FirstName           VARCHAR(30),
    LastName            VARCHAR(30)
) ;

INSERT INTO @Names
VALUES('Peter', 'Carter'),
    ('Michael', 'Smith'),
    ('Danielle', 'Mead'),
```

```
        ('Reuben', 'Roberts'),
        ('Iris', 'Jones'),
        ('Sylvia', 'Davies'),
        ('Finola', 'Wright'),
        ('Edward', 'James'),
        ('Marie', 'Andrews'),
        ('Jennifer', 'Abraham'),
        ('Margaret', 'Jones')

INSERT INTO Customers(Firstname, LastName, CreditCardNumber)
        SELECT
            FirstName
          , LastName
          , CreditCardNumber
        FROM (
            SELECT
                (SELECT TOP 1 FirstName FROM @Names ORDER BY NEWID()) FirstName
              , (SELECT TOP 1 LastName FROM @Names ORDER BY NEWID()) LastName
              , (SELECT TOP 1 CONVERT(VARBINARY(8000), (
                    (SELECT TOP 1 CAST(Number * 100 AS CHAR(4))
                        FROM @Numbers
                            WHERE Number BETWEEN 10 AND 99
                            ORDER BY NEWID()
                    ) + '-' +
                    (SELECT TOP 1 CAST(Number * 100 AS CHAR(4))
                        FROM @Numbers
                        WHERE Number BETWEEN 10 AND 99 ORDER BY NEWID()
                    ) + '-' +
                    (SELECT TOP 1 CAST(Number * 100 AS CHAR(4))
                        FROM @Numbers
                        WHERE Number BETWEEN 10 AND 99 ORDER BY NEWID()
                    ) + '-' +
                    (SELECT TOP 1 CAST(Number * 100 AS CHAR(4))
                        FROM @Numbers
                        WHERE Number BETWEEN 10 AND 99 ORDER BY
                        NEWID())))
```

```
        FROM @Numbers a

    ) CreditCardNumber) d
CROSS JOIN @Numbers b
CROSS JOIN @Numbers c;

--SET FULL recovery mode on the database - required for Availability Groups

ALTER DATABASE Customers SET RECOVERY FULL ;
GO

--Create Accounts Database

CREATE DATABASE Accounts ;
GO

USE Accounts ;
GO

CREATE TABLE [dbo].[PurchaseOrders](
        [OrderNumber] [int] IDENTITY(1,1) NOT NULL PRIMARY KEY CLUSTERED,
        [OrderDate] [date]  NOT NULL,
        [CustomerID] [int]  NOT NULL,
        [ProductID] [int]   NOT NULL,
        [Quantity] [int]    NOT NULL,
        [NetAmount] [money] NOT NULL,
        [TaxAmount] [money] NOT NULL,
        [InvoiceAddressID] [int] NOT NULL,
        [DeliveryAddressID] [int] NOT NULL,
        [DeliveryDate] [date] NULL,
) ;

DECLARE @Numbers TABLE
(
        Number          INT
)

--Populate ExistingPurchaseOrders with data
```

```
;WITH CTE(Number)
AS
(
        SELECT 1 Number
        UNION ALL
        SELECT Number + 1
        FROM CTE
        WHERE Number < 100
)
INSERT INTO @Numbers
SELECT Number FROM CTE

INSERT INTO PurchaseOrders
    SELECT
        (SELECT CAST(DATEADD(dd,(SELECT TOP 1 Number
                                FROM @Numbers
                                ORDER BY NEWID()),getdate())as DATE)),
        (SELECT TOP 1 Number -10 FROM @Numbers ORDER BY NEWID()),
        (SELECT TOP 1 Number FROM @Numbers ORDER BY NEWID()),
        (SELECT TOP 1 Number FROM @Numbers ORDER BY NEWID()),
        500,
        100,
        (SELECT TOP 1 Number FROM @Numbers ORDER BY NEWID()),
        (SELECT TOP 1 Number FROM @Numbers ORDER BY NEWID()),
        (SELECT CAST(DATEADD(dd,(SELECT TOP 1 Number - 10
    FROM @Numbers
        ORDER BY NEWID()),getdate()) as DATE))
FROM @Numbers a
CROSS JOIN @Numbers b ;

--SET FULL recovery mode on the database - required for Availability Groups

ALTER DATABASE Accounts SET RECOVERY FULL ;
GO

CREATE DATABASE HR ;
GO
```

```
USE HR ;
GO

CREATE TABLE dbo.Employees
(
     ID                 INT                 PRIMARY KEY         IDENTITY,
     FirstName          NVARCHAR(30),
     LastName           NVARCHAR(30),
     EmployeeNumber     INT
) ;
GO

--Populate the table

DECLARE @Numbers TABLE
(
     Number        INT
)

;WITH CTE(Number)
AS
(
     SELECT 1 Number
     UNION ALL
     SELECT Number + 1
     FROM CTE
     WHERE Number < 100
)
INSERT INTO @Numbers
SELECT Number FROM CTE

DECLARE @Names TABLE
(
     FirstName          VARCHAR(30),
     LastName           VARCHAR(30)
) ;
```

```
INSERT INTO @Names
VALUES('Peter', 'Carter'),
       ('Michael', 'Smith'),
       ('Danielle', 'Mead'),
       ('Reuben', 'Roberts'),
       ('Iris', 'Jones'),
       ('Sylvia', 'Davies'),
       ('Finola', 'Wright'),
       ('Edward', 'James'),
       ('Marie', 'Andrews'),
       ('Jennifer', 'Abraham'),
       ('Margaret', 'Jones')

INSERT INTO Employees(Firstname, LastName, EmployeeNumber)
SELECT
       (SELECT TOP 1 FirstName FROM @Names ORDER BY NEWID()) FirstName
     , (SELECT TOP 1 LastName FROM @Names ORDER BY NEWID()) LastName
     , a.Number EmployeeNumber
FROM @Numbers a ;

--SET FULL recovery mode on the database - required for Availability Groups

ALTER DATABASE HR SET RECOVERY FULL ;
GO
```

Configuring SQL Server

The first step in configuring AlwaysOn Availability Groups is enabling this feature
on the SQL Server service. To enable the feature from the GUI, we open SQL Server
Configuration Manager, drill through SQL Server Services, and select Properties from the
context menu of the SQL Server service. When we do this, the service properties display
and we navigate to the Always On Availability Groups tab, shown in Figure 5-1.

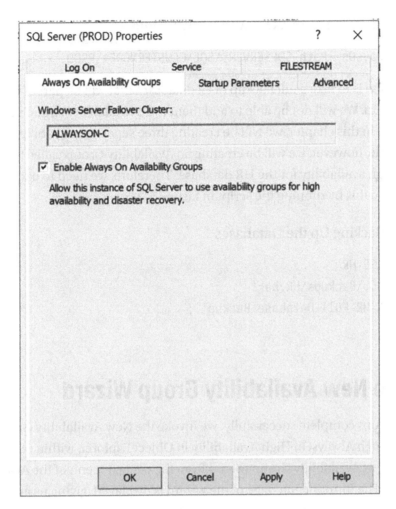

Figure 5-1. *The Always On Availability Groups Tab*

On this tab, we check the Enable AlwaysOn Availability Groups box and ensure that the cluster name displayed in the Windows Failover Cluster Name box is correct. We then need to restart the SQL Server service. Because AlwaysOn Availability Groups uses stand-alone instances, which are installed locally on each cluster node, as opposed to a failover clustered instance, which spans multiple nodes, we need to repeat these steps for each stand-alone instance hosted on the cluster.

We can also use PowerShell to enable AlwaysOn Availability Groups. To do this, we use the PowerShell command in Listing 5-2. The script assumes that CLUSTERNODE1 is the name of the server and that PROD is the name of the SQL Server instance.

Listing 5-2. Enabling AlwaysOn Availability Groups

```
Enable-SqlAlwaysOn -Path SQLSERVER:\SQL\CLUSTERNODE1\PROD
```

The next step is to take a full backup of all databases that will be part of the availability group. We will not be able to add them to an Availability Group until this has been done. In this chapter, we will be creating three separate availability groups. In the first example, however, we will be creating an Availability Group called HR, which will provide high availability for the HR database. Therefore, we need to back up the HR database. We do this by running the script in Listing 5-3.

Listing 5-3. Backing Up the Databases

```
BACKUP DATABASE HR
TO  DISK = N'C:\Backups\HR.bak'
WITH NAME = N'HR-Full Database Backup' ;
GO
```

Using the New Availability Group Wizard

When the backups complete successfully, we invoke the New Availability Group wizard by drilling through AlwaysOn High Availability in Object Explorer, within SSMS and selecting the New Availability Group wizard from the context menu of the Availability Groups folder. The Introduction page of the wizard is displayed, giving us an overview of the steps that we need to undertake.

On the Specify Name page (see Figure 5-2), we are prompted to enter a name for our availability group. We will also select Windows Server Failover Cluster as the Cluster Type. Other options for cluster type are external, which supports Pacemaker on Linux, and None, which is used for Clusterless Availability Groups. The Database Level Health Detection option will cause the Availability Group to fail over, should any database within the group go offline. The Per Database DTC Support option will specify if cross-database transactions are supported, using MSDTC (Microsoft Distributed Transaction Coordinator). A full discussion of configuring DTC is beyond the scope of this book, but further details can be found at https://docs.microsoft.com/en-us/previous-versions/windows/desktop/ms681291(v=vs.85).

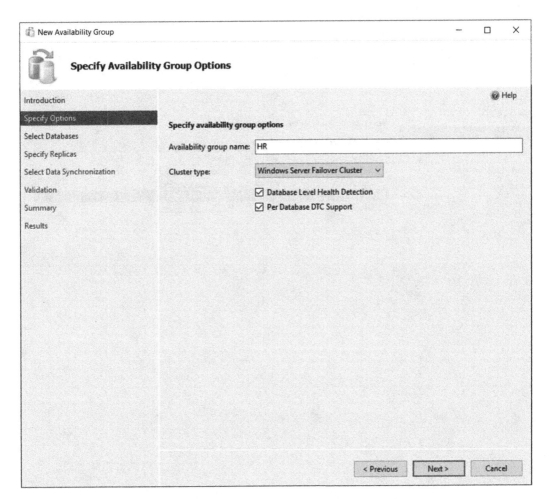

Figure 5-2. *The Specify Name Page*

On the Select Databases page, we are prompted to select the database(s) that we wish to participate in the availability group, as illustrated in Figure 5-3. On this screen, notice that we cannot select the Sales, Customers, or Accounts databases, because we have not yet taken a full backup of these databases.

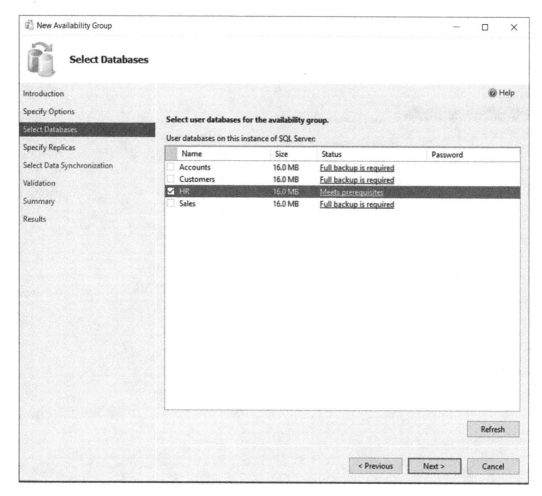

Figure 5-3. *The Select Database Page*

The Specify Replicas page consists of five tabs. We use the first tab, Replicas, to add the secondary replicas to the topology. Checking the Synchronous Commit option causes data to be committed on the secondary replica before it is committed on the primary replica. (This is also referred to as *hardening the log* on the secondary before the primary.) This means that, in the event of a failover, data loss is not possible, meaning that we can meet an SLA (service-level agreement) with an RPO (recovery point objective) of zero. It also means that there will be a performance degradation, however.

If we choose Asynchronous Commit, then the replica operates in Asynchronous Commit mode. This means that data is committed on the primary replica before being committed on the secondary replica. This stops us from suffering performance degradation, but it also means that, in the event of failover, the RPO is nondeterministic.

When we check the Automatic Failover option, the Synchronous Commit option is also selected automatically if we have not already selected it. This is because automatic failover is only possible in Synchronous Commit mode. We can set the Readable Secondary drop-down to No, Yes, or Read-intent. When we set it to No, the database is not accessible on replicas that are in a secondary role. When we set it to Read-intent, the Availability Group Listener can redirect read-only workloads to this secondary replica, but only if the application has specified `Application Intent=Read-only` in the connection string. Setting it to Yes enables the listener to redirect read-only traffic, regardless of whether the `Application Intent` parameter is present in the application's connection string. Although we can change the value of Readable Secondary through the GUI while at the same time configuring a replica for automatic failover without error, this is simply a quirk of the wizard. In fact, the replica is not accessible, since active secondaries are not supported when configured for automatic failover. The Replicas tab is illustrated in Figure 5-4. To meet our requirement of achieving high availability for the HR database, we have configured the secondary server within the same site as a synchronous replica. This means that the latency between data centers will not compound the performance degradation, which is associated with synchronous commits.

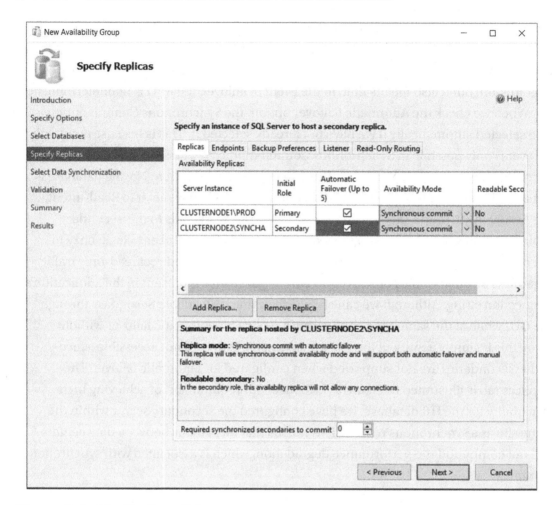

Figure 5-4. *The Replicas Tab*

On the Endpoints tab of the Specify Replicas page, illustrated in Figure 5-5, we specify the port number for each endpoint. The default port is 5022, but we can specify a different port if we need to. On this tab, we also specify if data should be encrypted when it is sent between the endpoints. It is usually a good idea to check this option, and if we do, then AES (Advanced Encryption Standard) is used as the encryption algorithm.

Optionally, you can also change the name of the endpoint that is created. Because only one database mirroring endpoint is allowed per instance, however, and because the default name is fairly descriptive, there is not always a reason to change it. Some DBAs choose to rename it to include the name of the instance, since this can simplify the management of multiple servers. This is a good idea if your enterprise has multiple availability groups, split across multiple instances on the same cluster.

The service account each instance uses is displayed for informational purposes. It simplifies security administration if you ensure that the same service account is used by both instances. If you fail to do this, you will need to grant each instance permissions to each service account. This means that instead of reducing the security footprint of each service account by using it for one instance only, you simply push the footprint up to the SQL Server level instead of the operating system level.

The endpoint URL specifies the URL of the endpoint that availability groups will use to communicate. The format of the URL is [Transport Protocol]://[Path]:[Port]. The transport protocol for a database mirroring endpoint is always TCP (Transmission Control Protocol). The path can either be the fully qualified domain name (FQDN) of the server, the server name on its own, or an IP address, which is unique across the network. I recommend using the FQDN of the server, because this is always guaranteed to work. It is also the default value populated. The port should match the port number that you specify for the endpoint.

Note   Availability groups communicate with a database mirroring endpoint. Although database mirroring is deprecated, the endpoints are not.

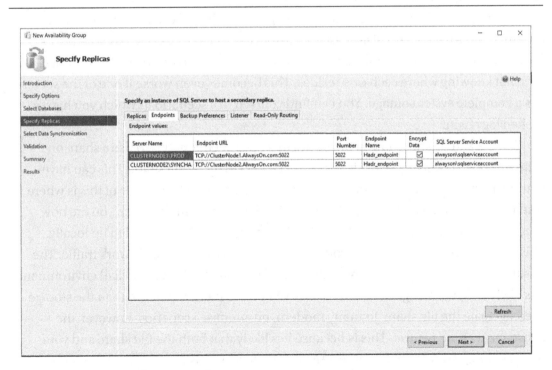

Figure 5-5. *The Endpoints Tab*

On the Backup Preferences tab (see Figure 5-6), we can specify the replica on which automated backups will be taken. One of the big advantages of AlwaysOn Availability Groups is that when you use them, you can scale out maintenance tasks, such as backups, to secondary servers. Therefore, automated backups can seamlessly be directed to active secondaries. The possible options are Prefer Secondary, Secondary Only, Primary, or Any Replica. It is also possible to set priorities for each replica. When determining which replica to run the backup job against, SQL Server evaluates the backup priorities of each node and is more likely to choose the replica with the highest priority.

Although the advantages of reducing IO on the primary replica are obvious, I, somewhat controversially, recommend against scaling automated backups to secondary replicas in many cases. This is especially the case when RTO (recovery time objective) is a priority for the application because of operational supportability issues. Imagine a scenario in which backups are being taken against a secondary replica and a user calls to say that they have accidently deleted all data from a critical table. You now need to restore a copy of the database and repopulate the table. The backup files, however, sit on the secondary replica. As a result, you need to copy the backup files over to the primary replica before you can begin to restore the database (or perform the restore over the network). This instantly increases your RTO.

Also, when configured to allow backups against multiple servers, SQL Server still only maintains the backup history on the instance where the backup was taken. This means that you may be scrambling between servers, trying to retrieve all of your backup files, not knowing where each one resides. This becomes even worse if one of the servers has a complete system outage. You can find yourself in a scenario in which you have a broken log chain.

The workaround for most of the issues that I just mentioned is to use a share on a file server and configure each instance to back up to the same share. This can have neutral, positive, or negative consequences. The negative consequence of this is where you have locally attached storage. By setting backups up in this manner, you are now sending all of your backups across the network rather than backing them up locally. This can increase the duration of your backups as well as increase network traffic. The positive consequence is if you are a cloud IaaS (Infrastructure as a Service) environment. It is likely that the storage attached to your VM will be more expensive than the storage used to create the file share. In many modern, on-premise scenarios, however, the consequences are neutral. This is because it is likely that both the file share and your server's storage reside on the same SAN or NAS device. This means that there is no difference in network traffic or latency if you configure backups in this way.

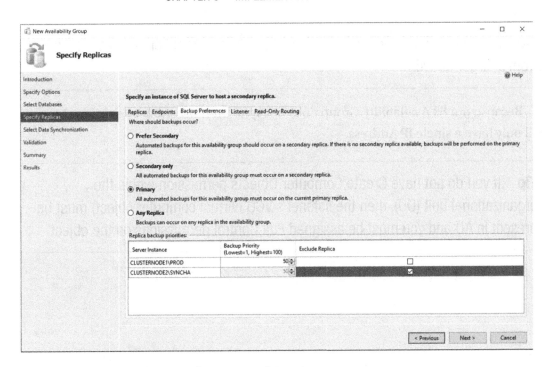

Figure 5-6. *The Backup Preferences Tab*

On the Listener tab, shown in Figure 5-7, we choose if we want to create an availability group listener or if we want to defer this task until later. If we choose to create the listener, then we need to specify the listener's name, the port that it should listen on, and the IP address(es) that it should use. We specify one address for each subnet, in multi-subnet clusters. The details provided here are used to create the client access point resource in the availability group's cluster role. You may notice that we have specified port 1433 for the listener, although our instance is also running on port 1433. This is a valid configuration, because the listener is configured on a different IP address than the SQL Server instance. It is also not mandatory to use the same port number, but it can be beneficial, if you are implementing AlwaysOn Availability Groups on an existing instance because applications that specify the port number to connect may need fewer application changes. Remember that the server name will still be different, however, because applications will be connecting to the virtual name of the listener, as opposed to the name of the physical server\instance. In our example, applications connect to HR instead of CLUSTERNODE1\PROD. Although connections via CLUSTERNODE1 are still permitted, they do not benefit from high availability or scale our reporting.

Tip   A subnet is a segment of a network containing a partition of IP Addresses from a larger network.

Because our HR Availability Group does not span multiple subnets, then our Listener will only have a single IP Address.

Tip   If you do not have Create Computer Objects permission within the organizational unit (OU), then the listener's VCO (virtual computer object) must be present in AD and you must be assigned Full Control permissions on the object.

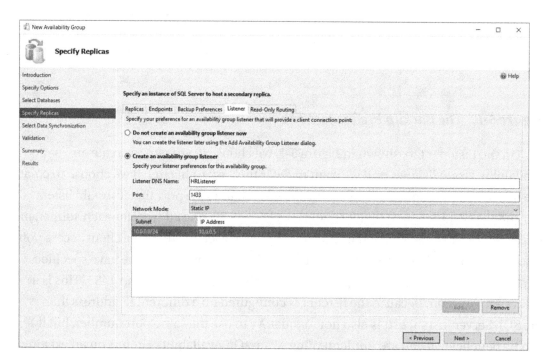

Figure 5-7.   *The Listener Tab*

Tip   Because the HR Availability Group will not be configured with readable secondaries, we do not need to configure the Read-Only Routing tab; however, we will explore read-only routing in the "Using the New Availability Group Dialog Box" section of this chapter.

On the Select Initial Data Synchronization screen, shown in Figure 5-8, we choose how the initial data synchronization of the replicas is performed. If you choose Full, then each database that participates in the availability group is subject to a full backup, followed by a log backup. The backup files are backed up to a share, which you specify, before they are restored to the secondary servers. The share path can be specified using either Windows or Linux formats, depending on your requirements. After the restore is complete, data synchronization, via log stream, commences.

If you have already backed up your databases and restored them onto the secondaries, then you can select the Join Only option. This starts the data synchronization, via log stream, on the databases within the availability group. Selecting Skip Initial Data Synchronization allows you to back up and restore the databases yourself after you complete the setup.

If you select the Automatic Seeding option, then an empty database is initially created on each Replica. The data is then seeding using VDI (Virtual Device Interface) over the log stream transport. This option is slower than initializing with a backup but avoid transferring large backup files between shares.

Tip   If your availability group will contain many databases, then it may be best to perform the backup/restore yourself. This is because the inbuilt utility will perform the actions sequentially, and therefore, it may take a long time to complete.

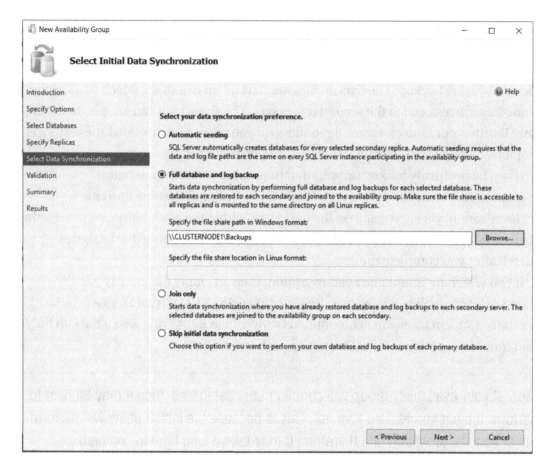

Figure 5-8. *The Select Data Synchronization Page*

On the Validation page, rules that may cause the setup to fail are checked. If any of the results come back as Failed, then you need to resolve them before you attempt to continue.

Tip   A common gotcha is discovered during the validation process, when you are using named instances. A requirement of availability groups is that the databases must reside in the same file path on all replicas. The default file location for SQL Server data files includes the name of the instance, however. This does not matter for default instances, because the instance name within the file path is always MSSQLSERVER. For named instances, however, ensure that the database files are stored in a file path that exists on all servers.

Once validation tests are complete and we move to the Summary page, we are presented with a list of the tasks that are to be carried out during the setup.

As setup progresses, the results of each configuration task display on the Results page. If any errors occur on this page, be sure to investigate them, but this does not necessarily mean that the entire availability group needs to be reconfigured. For example, if the creation of the availability group listener fails because the VCO had not been presented in AD, then you can re-create the listener without needing to re-create the entire availability group.

As an alternative to using the New Availability Group wizard, you can perform the configuration of the availability group using the New Availability Group dialog box, followed by the Add Listener dialog box. This method of creating an availability group is examined in the next section.

Using the New Availability Group Dialog Box

Now that we have successfully created our first availability group, let's create a second availability group for Sales. This availability group will contain the Sales and Customer databases. This time, we use the New Availability Group and Add Listener dialog boxes. We begin this process by backing up the two databases. Just like when we created the HR availability group, the databases are not selectable until we perform the backup. Unlike when we used the wizard, however, we have no way to make SQL Server perform the initial database synchronization using a backup/restore option. Therefore, we must either back up the database to the share that we created during the previous demonstration and then restore the backup, along with a transaction log backup, to the secondary instance, or use Automatic Seeding. In this example, we will use Automatic Seeding, so there is no need to restore the databases to the secondary Replicas in advance. The script in Listing 5-4 will perform the Full backup of the databases.

Tip   For Automatic Seeding to work, the Availability Group must be granted the CREATE ANY DATABASE permission on the secondary servers.

Listing 5-4. Backing Up and Restoring the Database

```
--Back Up Sales Database

BACKUP DATABASE Sales
TO  DISK = N'C:\Backups\Sales.bak'
WITH NAME = N'Sales-Full Database Backup' ;
GO

--Back Up Customers Database

BACKUP DATABASE Customers
TO  DISK = N'C:\Backups\Customers.bak'
WITH NAME = N'Customers-Full Database Backup' ;
GO
```

If we had not already created an availability group, then our next job would be
to create a TCP endpoint so the instances could communicate. We would then need
to create a login for the service account on each instance and grant it the connect
permissions on the endpoints. Because we can only ever have one database mirroring
endpoint per instance, however, we are not required to create a new one, and obviously
we have no reason to grant the service account additional privileges. Therefore, we
continue by creating the availability group. To do this, we drill through AlwaysOn High
Availability in Object Explorer and select New Availability Group from the context menu
of availability groups.

This causes the General tab of the New Availability Group dialog box to display, as
illustrated in Figure 5-9. On this screen, we type the name of the availability group in
the first field. Then, we click the Add button under the Availability Databases window
before we type the name of the database that we wish to add to the group. We then
need to click the Add button under the Availability Replicas window before we type the
server\instance name of the secondary replica in the new row. We have set Required
Synchronized Secondaries to Commit to 1, however. This setting, which was introduced
in SQL Server 2017, guarantees that the specified number of secondary replicas writes
the transaction data to log before the primary replica commits each transaction. In our
scenario, where we only have a single synchronous secondary, that in the event of a
failure on the Primary Replica, failover will happen automatically, but the Secondary
Replica will not allow user transactions to be written to the database, until the original
Primary Replica comes back online. This absolutely guarantees that there can be no data

loss in any circumstances. If we had left this setting as 0 (as we did in the first example in this chapter), then in the event that the Primary Replica failed and users wrote transactions to the Secondary Replica, before this Replica also failed, then data loss could occur, as the other Replicas are configured in asynchronous commit mode.

Now we can begin to set the replica properties. We discussed the Role, Availability Mode, Failover Mode, Readable Secondary, and Endpoint URL properties when we created the HR availability group. The Connection in Primary Role property defines what connections can be made to the replica if the replica is in the primary role. You can configure this as either Allow All Connections or Allow Read/Write connections. When Read/Write is specified, applications using the Application Intent = Read only parameter in their connection string will not be able to connect to the replica.

The Session Timeout property sets how long the replicas can go without receiving a ping from one another before they enter the DISCONNECTED state and the session ends. Although it is possible to set this value to as low as 5 seconds, it is usually a good idea to keep the setting at 60 seconds; otherwise, you run the risk of a false-positive response, resulting in unnecessary failover. If a replica times out, it needs to be resynchronized, since transactions on the primary will no longer wait for the secondary, even if the secondary is running in Synchronous Commit mode.

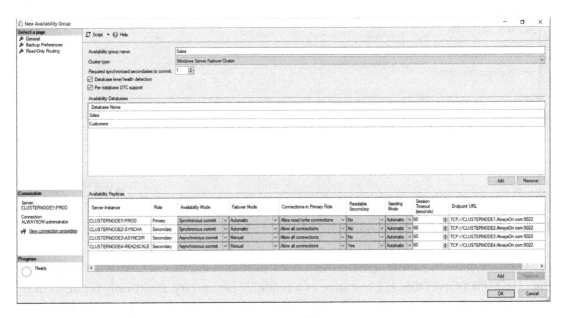

Figure 5-9. The New Availability Group Dialog Box

On the Backup Preferences tab of the dialog box, we define the preferred replica to use for automated backup jobs, as shown in Figure 5-10. Just like when using the wizard, we can specify Primary, or we can choose between enforcing and preferring backups to occur on a secondary replica. We can also configure a weight, between 0 and 100 for each replica, and use the Exclude Replica check box to avoid backups being taken on a specific node.

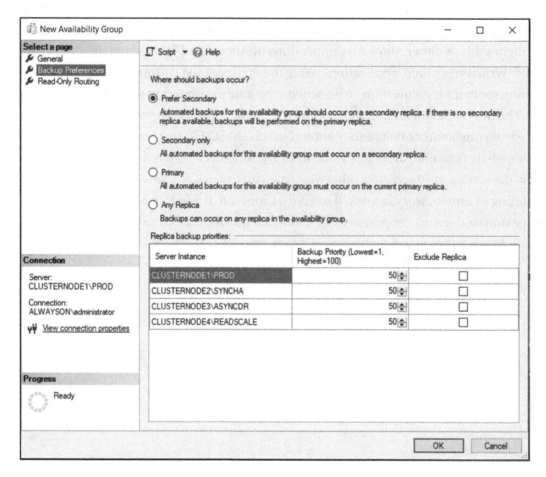

Figure 5-10. *The Backup Preferences Tab*

On the Read-Only Routing tab, which is illustrated in Figure 5-11, we will configure the CLUSTERNODE4\READSCALE instance as a readable secondary. Read-only requests that are sent to the listener will be redirected to this instance, instead of being sent to the primary replica, which will reside on one of the other three instances. The first step in this configuration is to add a Read-Only Routing URL for the readable secondary. This is similar to the Endpoint URL that we configured for each node, the difference is that this will service the read-only requests. The Read-Only URL can be an IP address or a FQDN and must include the port that the instance is listening on. This means you must ensure that the instance is listening on a static port, before performing this configuration.

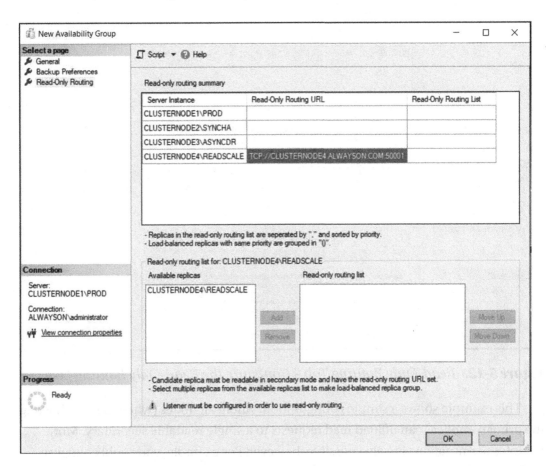

Figure 5-11. *Read-Only Routing Tab – Configure the Read-Only Routing URL*

Once the Read-Only routing URL has been added to each readable secondary that you plan to configure, the readable secondary will appear in the Available Replicas window in the lower section of the tab. You can now select the Read-Only Routing List cell for each replica that you wish to be able to route to the readable secondary and click the Add button in the lower half of the tab, to add it to the Read-Only Routing List, as shown in Figure 5-12.

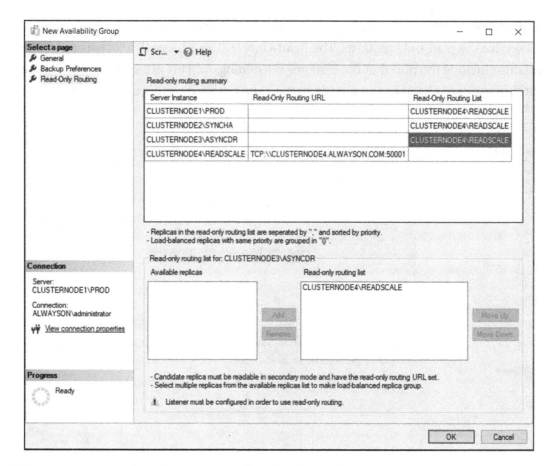

Figure 5-12. *Read-Only Routing Tab – Configure the Read-Only Routing List*

This example shows a simple configuration, where all nodes (when they are hosting the primary replica) can offload read requests to a single readable secondary. More complex permutations are also possible, however. For example, you could configure each node to route to an individual readable secondary. This could prove useful if your Availability Group is split between multiple sites and you want to ensure that each node will route read-only requests to a replica in the same site, improving redundancy for the read scale-out.

Alternatively, you could allow each node to route read-only requests to multiple readable secondaries. In this scenario, you have two options. The default implementation will always send read request to the first available replica, so you are simply adding redundancy for your readable secondaries. If this is the intention, then each readable secondary in the routing list will be separated by a comma. A more advanced implementation is to configure readable secondaries to load balance read-only requests. In this scenario, read-only requests will be routed across the load balanced set, using a round-robin approach. Nodes within the load balanced set will be separated with a comma and the set will be enclosed in parenthesis.

You can also configure multiple load balanced sets within the same routing list. Here, requests will be routed round-robin around the first load balanced set, unless the nodes within that set become unavailable, in which case, requests will be routed round-robin around the next set.

For example, imagine that you wanted read-only requests to be load balanced between ServerA and ServerB, but if those servers became unavailable, you wanted requests to be load balanced between ServerC and ServerD. Your read-only routing list would take the form: ((ServerA,ServerB),(ServerC,ServerD)).

Once we have created the availability group, we need to create the Availability Group Listener. To do this, we select New Listener from the context menu of the Sales Availability Group, which should now be visible in Object Explorer. This invokes the New Availability Group Listener dialog box, which can be seen in Figure 5-13.

In this dialog box, we start by entering the virtual name for the listener. We then define the port that it will listen on and the IP address that will be assigned to it.

Tip   We are able to use the same port for both of the listeners, as well as the SQL Server instance, because all three use different IP addresses.

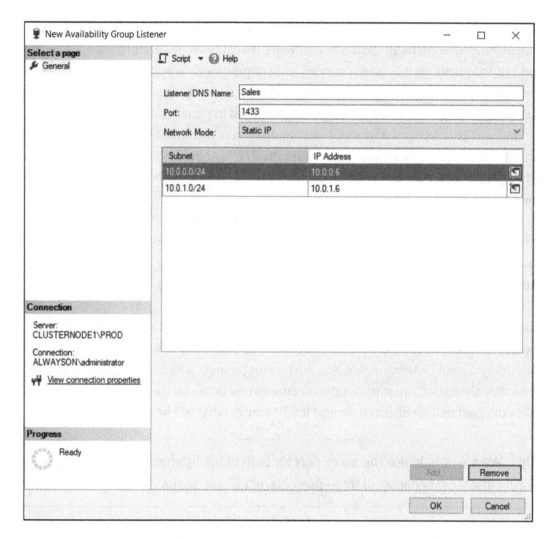

Figure 5-13. *The New Availability Group Listener Dialog Box*

Using T-SQL

Now that we have created Availability Groups using both GUI methods, in SSMS, let's see how to create an Availability Group using T-SQL. In this section, we will create an Availability Group called Accounts, which will provide both HA and DR for the Accounts database. As always, the first thing we need to do is to take a full backup of the database. We can achieve this using the script in Listing 5-5.

Listing 5-5. Backup the Accounts Database

```
BACKUP DATABASE HR
TO  DISK = N'C:\Backups\HR.bak'
WITH NAME = N'HR-Full Database Backup' ;
GO
```

To create the Availability Group, we will use the CREATE AVAILABLILITY GROUP T-SQL command. The WITH options supported by this command are detailed in Table 5-1.

Table 5-1. *CREATE AVAILABILITY GROUP with Options*

Option	Description
AUTOMATED_BACKUP_ PREFERENCE	Specifies which replica should be used for backups. Possible options are PRIMARY, meaning the Primary Replica will always be used; SECONDARY_ONLY, meaning that backup should never be performed on the Primary Replica; SECONDARY, meaning backups should not be taken on the Primary Replica, unless the Primary Replica is the only Replica online; and NONE, meaning that the role of each Replica will be ignored, when selecting which Replica to take the backup from.
FAILURE_CONDITION_LEVEL	Specifies the events that should cause an Availability Group to automatically fail over. Acceptable levels are 1–5*.
HEALTH_CHECK_TIMEOUT	Specified in milliseconds, the duration the cluster will wait for a response from the health check procedure, before assuming that the node is unresponsive and fails over.
DB_FAILOVER	When an Availability Group has multiple databases, determines if a single database within the Availability Group moving out of the ONLINE state triggers a failover.
DTC_SUPPORT	Specifies if cross-database transactions are supported within the Availability Group, using DTC (Distributed Transaction Coordinator). Acceptable values are PER_DB or NONE.
BASIC	Used to create a basic Availability Group. Basic Availability Groups are discussed in Chapter 7.

(continued)

Table 5-1. (*continued*)

Option	Description
DISTRIBUTED	Used to create a Distributed Availability Group. This is discussed in Chapter 7.
REQUIRED_SYNCHRONIZED_SECONDARIES_TO_COMMIT	Can be used to ensure a zero RPO, by enforcing a commit on secondary Replica(s) before proceeding. 0 indicates that transactions will be marked as NOT SYNCHRONIZED, but the Replica will continue to process transactions.
CLUSTER_TYPE	Specifies the type of cluster that the Availability Group resides on. Possible values are WSFC, indicating a Windows Failover cluster; EXTERNAL, indicating a non-Windows cluster, such as Linux Pacemaker; or NONE, indicating clusterless Availability Groups.

*Please see Table 5-2 for details of each failure level.

Table 5-2 details the events that will trigger an automatic failover, based on the failure condition level specified.

Table 5-2. *Failure Condition Levels*

Level	Events That Trigger Failover
1	• The SQL Server service is stopped. • The SQL Server instance's lease in the cluster has expired, because no acknowledgment has been received.
2	• Any Level 1 condition. • The SQL instance is not connected to the cluster and the health check threshold is exceeded. • The availability replica is in a FAILED state.
3 (Default)	• Any Level 1–2 condition. • Critical internal errors within the SQL Server instance.
4	• Any Level 1–3 condition. • Moderate internal errors within the SQL Server instance.
5	• Any Level 1–4 condition. • Any internal failure within the SQL Server instance.

When adding Replicas with the REPLICA ON clause, additional WITH OPTIONS are available. These are detailed in Table 5-3.

Table 5-3. *ON REPLICA WITH Options*

Option	Description
ENDPOINT_URL	The URL of the endpoint on the SQL Server instance that hosts the Replica.
FAILOVER_MODE	Specifies if the Replica should support automatic or manual failover.
AVAILABILITY_MODE	Specifies if transactions on the Replica should be committed synchronously or asynchronously. The availability mode can also be set to CONFIGURATION_ONLY mode, to support external cluster mode. This will be discussed in Chapter 6.
SESSION_TIMEOUT	Specifies the session timeout period in seconds.
BACKUP_PRIORITY	Provides a weighting for the Replica, which will be used to decide which Replica backups should be taken from. 0 indicates backups cannot be taken from the replica.
SEEDING_MODE	Specifies how the Replica is seeded. Acceptable values are AUTOMATIC and MANUAL.
PRIMARY_ROLE	Used to specify the ALLOW_CONNECTIONS setting and pass a READ_ONLY_ROUTING_LIST.
SECONDARY_ROLE	Used to specify a value for ALLOW_CONNECTIONS and pass a READ_ONLY_ROUTING_URL.

Therefore, the script in Listing 5-6 will create the Accounts Availability Group. Note that we have chosen to seed the replicas manually.

Listing 5-6. Create the Accounts Availability Group

```
CREATE AVAILABILITY GROUP Accounts
WITH (
     AUTOMATED_BACKUP_PREFERENCE = PRIMARY,
     DB_FAILOVER = OFF,
     DTC_SUPPORT = NONE,
     REQUIRED_SYNCHRONIZED_SECONDARIES_TO_COMMIT = 0
)
```

```
FOR
REPLICA ON
    'CLUSTERNODE1\PROD' WITH (
        ENDPOINT_URL = N'TCP://CLUSTERNODE1.AlwaysOn.com:5022',
        FAILOVER_MODE = AUTOMATIC,
        AVAILABILITY_MODE = SYNCHRONOUS_COMMIT,
        SESSION_TIMEOUT = 10,
        BACKUP_PRIORITY = 50,
        SEEDING_MODE = MANUAL,
        PRIMARY_ROLE(ALLOW_CONNECTIONS = ALL),
        SECONDARY_ROLE(ALLOW_CONNECTIONS = NO)
    ),
    'CLUSTERNODE2\SYNCHA' WITH (
        ENDPOINT_URL = N'TCP://CLUSTERNODE2.AlwaysOn.com:5022',
        FAILOVER_MODE = AUTOMATIC,
        AVAILABILITY_MODE = SYNCHRONOUS_COMMIT,
        SESSION_TIMEOUT = 10,
        BACKUP_PRIORITY = 50,
        SEEDING_MODE = MANUAL,
        PRIMARY_ROLE(ALLOW_CONNECTIONS = ALL),
        SECONDARY_ROLE(ALLOW_CONNECTIONS = NO)
    ),
    'CLUSTERNODE3\ASYNCDR' WITH (
        ENDPOINT_URL = N'TCP://CLUSTERNODE3.AlwaysOn.com:5022',
        FAILOVER_MODE = MANUAL,
        AVAILABILITY_MODE = ASYNCHRONOUS_COMMIT,
        SESSION_TIMEOUT = 10,
        BACKUP_PRIORITY = 50,
        SEEDING_MODE = MANUAL,
        PRIMARY_ROLE(ALLOW_CONNECTIONS = ALL),
        SECONDARY_ROLE(ALLOW_CONNECTIONS = NO)
    );
GO
```

Now that we have created the Accounts Availability Group, we will need to create an Availability Group Listener, so that the cluster knows where to direct requests. We will do this using the `ALTER AVAILABILITY GROUP` command with the `ADD LISTENER` clause. The ADD LISTENER clause has the WITH options specified in Table 5-4.

Table 5-4. *ADD LISTERNER WITH Options*

Option	Description
IP	Specify the IP Address(s) that the Listener will listen on, along with the subnet masks of the network relating to each IP address
PORT	The Port that the Listener will listen on

Because our `CLUSTERNODE3\ASYNCDR` instance is in a different subnet to `CLUSTERNODE1\PROD` and `CLUSTERNODE2\SYNCHA`, we need to specify two IP addresses, one for each subnet. Therefore, the script in Listing 5-7 will create the Availability Group Listener for the `Accounts` Availability Group.

Listing 5-7. Create an Availability Group Listener

```
ALTER AVAILABILITY GROUP Accounts
     ADD LISTENER 'Accounts' (
          WITH IP
               (
                    (N'10.0.0.8', N'255.255.255.0'),
                    (N'10.0.1.8', N'255.255.255.0')
               ),
          PORT=1433
     );
GO
```

Implementing Availability Groups with PowerShell

As you might expect, Microsoft offers PowerShell cmdlets that can be used to create and manage SQL Server Availability Groups and Availability Group Listeners. This is becoming increasingly important, as the world moves toward a DevOps culture, with PowerShell being the language of choice for many organizations looking to implement build automation.

The `sqlserver` PowerShell module is installed along with the SQL Server Management Studio, but can also be installed by using the command in Listing 5-8.

Listing 5-8. Install the sqlserver PowerShell Module

```
Install-Module sqlserver
```

Note   If this is the first time you have installed a PowerShell module on the server, then you will be prompted to install the NuGet provider.

Once the `sqlserver` module is installed, you will have access to cmdlets which allow you to create and manage Availability Groups via PowerShell. The New-AvailabilityReplica cmdlet allows you to create an object which specifies the properties for each Replica. These objects can then be passed to the `New-SqlAvailabilityGroup` cmdlet, which will create the Availability Group.

For example, imagine we want to create an Availability Group called Foo, which will contain the Foo database, with `CLUSTERNODE1\PROD` hosting the initial primary Replica and `CLUSTERNODE2\SYNCHA` hosting a secondary Replica, for high availability. We could achieve this using the script in Listing 5-9.

Listing 5-9. Create to Foo Availability Group

```
#Create connection to CLSUETERNODE1\PROD
$PrimaryServer = Get-Item "SQLSERVER:\SQL\CLUSTERNODE1\PROD" -Verbose

#Create connection to CLUSTERNODE2\SYNCHA
$SecondaryServer = Get-Item "SQLSERVER:\SQL\CLUSTERNODE2\SYNCHA"

#Set the properties of the primary Replica
$PrimaryReplicaOptions = @{
    Name             = "CLUSTERNODE1\PROD"
    EndpointUrl      = "TCP://CLUSTERNODE1.ALWAYSON.COM:5022"
    FailoverMode     = "Automatic"
    AvailabilityMode = "SynchronousCommit"
    Version          = ($PrimaryServer.Version)
}
```

```
#Create the primary Replica Object
$PrimaryReplica = New-SqlAvailabilityReplica @PrimaryReplicaOptions  -AsTemplate

#Set the properties of the secondary Replica
$SecondaryReplicaOptions = @{
    Name             = "CLUSTERNODE2\SYNCHA"
    EndpointUrl      = "TCP://CLUSTERNODE2.ALWAYSON.COM:5022"
    FailoverMode     = "Automatic"
    AvailabilityMode = "SynchronousCommit"
    Version          = ($SecondaryServer.Version)
}

#Create the secondary replica object
$SecondaryReplica = New-SqlAvailabilityReplica @SecondaryReplicaOption -As
Template

$AvailabilityGroupOptions = @{
    InputObject        = $PrimaryServer
    Name =             = "Foo"
    AvailabilityReplica = ($PrimaryReplica, $SecondaryReplica)
    Database           = @("Foo")
}
New-SqlAvailabilityGroup @AvailabilityGroupOptions
```

We could then create an Availability Group Listener by using the
New-SqlAvailabilityGroupListener cmdlet. This is demonstrated in Listing 5-10.

Listing 5-10. Create an Availability Group Listener

```
#Specify the options for the Listener

$ListenerOptions = @{
    Name = "Foo"
    StaticIp = "10.0.0.14/255.255.255.0"
    Path = "SQLSERVER:\Sql\CLUSTERNODE1\PROD\AvailabilityGroups\Foo"
}

#Create the Listener

New-SqlAvailabilityGroupListener @ListenerOptions
```

Summary

AlwaysOn Availability Groups can be implemented with up to eight secondary replicas, combining both Synchronous and Asynchronous Commit modes. When implementing high availability with availability groups, you always use Synchronous Commit mode, because Asynchronous Commit mode does not support automatic failover. When implementing Synchronous Commit mode, however, you must be aware of the associated performance penalty caused by committing the transaction on the secondary replica before it is committed on the primary replica. For disaster recovery, you will normally choose to implement Asynchronous Commit mode.

The availability group can be created via the New Availability Group wizard, through dialog boxes, through T-SQL, or even through PowerShell. If you create an availability group using dialog boxes, then some aspects, such as the endpoint and associated permissions, must be scripted using T-SQL or PowerShell.

If you implement disaster recovery with availability groups, then you need to configure a multi-subnet cluster. This does not mean that you must have SAN replication between the sites, however, since availability groups do not rely on shared storage. What you do need to do is add additional IP addresses for the administrative cluster access point and also for the Availability Group Listener. You also need to pay attention to the properties of the cluster that support client reconnection to ensure that clients do not experience a high number of timeouts.

CHAPTER 6

Implementing AlwaysOn Availability Groups On Linux

Since SQL Server 2017, it has been possible to install SQL Server on Linux as well as Windows. AlwaysOn Availability Groups can be configured on Linux with much of the same functionality, as when the instances are hosted on Windows. The installation and configuration of SQL Server on Linux is beyond the scope of this book, but full details can be found in the Apress title *Pro SQL Server 2019 Administration*, which can be found at www.apress.com/gb/book/9781484250884#otherversion=9781484250891.

This chapter focuses on configuring Availability Groups on Linux, for the purpose of providing high availability (HA). We will first have a brief overview of the technologies involved in implementing pacemaker clusters (Pacemaker is a Linux-based clustering technology), before configuring a two-node Availability Group, with automatic failover.

Note For the demonstrations in this chapter, we will use three servers, namely, LinuxProd, LinuxSyncHA, and LinuxConfig. A default instance of SQL Server 2019 is installed on each of the servers. The servers are built with the Ubuntu 18.04 operating system and are not joined to a domain.

In this chapter, we will perform the following activities:

- Create the Sales Databases.

- Enable Availability Groups on our instances and prepare the instances to support Availability Groups.

135

© Peter A. Carter 2020
P. A. Carter, *SQL Server 2019 AlwaysOn*, https://doi.org/10.1007/978-1-4842-6479-9_6

- Create an Availability group for the Sales database.

- Create the cluster.

- Configure the cluster.

Linux Cluster Technologies

The following sections will provide a high-level overview of the technologies that are used to configure a cluster in Linux. Before we begin, however, it is important to understand that unlike building Availability Groups on a Windows cluster, when building Availability Groups on a Linux pacemaker cluster, the Availability Group is not integrated with the cluster to the same degree. Specifically, the Availability Group is not aware of the cluster's state, or even existence. Therefore, failover operations must be performed at the cluster level. Additionally, while it is still possible to create a listener, the functionality is limited. You need to manually register the listener's name in DNS and there is no support for read-only routing.

Pcs

When you install pcs, the package will also install Pacemaker and Corosync. The pcs component itself, however, is a command-line utility, which is used to manage the Pacemaker cluster.

Pacemaker

Pacemaker is the heart of the cluster. It is responsible for managing cluster maintenance events, such as nodes being added and removed. It is also responsible for managing cluster events and moving resources between nodes to ensure the resources remain available after a failure occurs on a node.

Pacemaker supports all standard cluster configurations, including active/active, active/passive, N+1, and N+M. A discussion of advanced Pacemaker configurations is beyond the scope of this book; however, further details can be found in the Apress title *Pro Linux High Availability Clustering*, which can be found at www.apress.com/gp/book/9781484200803.

Corosync

Corosync provides the messaging layer for the cluster. It implements the quorum system by sending messages between nodes to check the health status and notifies Pacemaker if the quorum is lost.

STONITH

A supported configuration of a Pacemaker cluster must use fencing, which helps bring the cluster to a known good state, in the event of a node, or resources state being unknown. There are two types of fencing: resource fencing and node fencing. Resource fencing is used to prevent a resource from starting on a node. This can avoid data corruption, in the event of an outage while a resource is being configured. Node fencing prevents a node from running any resources. This is usually required if a node becomes unresponsive. Node fencing requires a fencing device and a fencing agent. The fencing device may be an uninterrupted power supply, a power distribution unit, or a management interface, such as lights-out device or blade power control device. The agent that interacts with these devices is STONITH (shoot the other node in the head). Because the implementation of STONITH is very specific to the fencing device you use, we will not configure it in this chapter. That is fine for development or testing purposes, but a production cluster should always have STONITH configured.

Preparing to Implement AlwaysOn Availability Groups

Before creating an Availability Group, there are several prerequisite tasks that need to be performed. Namely, we enable Availability Groups on the SQL Server instances and create and backup the database that we want to be made highly available, and because Linux servers cannot authenticate with each other, we will need to create certificates that can be used for authentication. The following sections demonstrate how to perform each of these tasks.

Enable Availability Groups

Just as is required in a Windows environment, the first step in configuring Availability Groups on Linux is to enable the feature at the service level. The script in Listing 6-1 demonstrates how to enable Availability Groups and then restart the service. This script needs to be executed on each server that will host a Replica.

Tip   sudo is used to elevate your permission when running a command.

Listing 6-1. Enable Availability Groups

```
sudo /opt/mssql/bin/mssql-conf set hadr.hadrenabled  1
sudo systemctl restart mssql-server
```

Create the Sales Database

The next step is to create the database that we wish to make highly available and take a backup of the database that can be used to seed the secondary. This can be achieved with the script in Listing 6-2.

Listing 6-2. Create the Sales Database

```
--Create Sales Database

CREATE DATABASE Sales ;
GO

USE Sales ;
GO

CREATE TABLE [dbo].[Orders](
        [OrderNumber] [int] IDENTITY(1,1) NOT NULL PRIMARY KEY CLUSTERED,
        [OrderDate] [date]  NOT NULL,
        [CustomerID] [int]  NOT NULL,
        [ProductID] [int]  NOT NULL,
        [Quantity] [int]  NOT NULL,
        [NetAmount] [money] NOT NULL,
```

```
        [TaxAmount] [money] NOT NULL,
        [InvoiceAddressID] [int] NOT NULL,
        [DeliveryAddressID] [int] NOT NULL,
        [DeliveryDate] [date] NULL,
) ;

DECLARE @Numbers TABLE
(
        Number          INT
)

--Populate ExistingOrders with data

;WITH CTE(Number)
AS
(
        SELECT 1 Number
        UNION ALL
        SELECT Number + 1
        FROM CTE
        WHERE Number < 100
)
INSERT INTO @Numbers
SELECT Number FROM CTE

INSERT INTO Orders
    SELECT
      (SELECT CAST(DATEADD(dd,(SELECT TOP 1 Number
                              FROM @Numbers
                              ORDER BY NEWID()),getdate())as DATE)),
      (SELECT TOP 1 Number -10 FROM @Numbers ORDER BY NEWID()),
      (SELECT TOP 1 Number FROM @Numbers ORDER BY NEWID()),
      (SELECT TOP 1 Number FROM @Numbers ORDER BY NEWID()),
     500,
     100,
      (SELECT TOP 1 Number FROM @Numbers ORDER BY NEWID()),
      (SELECT TOP 1 Number FROM @Numbers ORDER BY NEWID()),
      (SELECT CAST(DATEADD(dd,(SELECT TOP 1 Number - 10
```

```
      FROM @Numbers
            ORDER BY NEWID()),getdate()) as DATE))
FROM @Numbers a
CROSS JOIN @Numbers b ;

--SET FULL recovery mode on the database - required for Availability Groups

ALTER DATABASE Sales SET RECOVERY FULL ;
GO

--Backup the Sales Database

BACKUP DATABASE Sales
TO  DISK = N'/var/opt/mssql/data/Sales.bak'
WITH NAME = N'Sales-Full Database Backup' ;
GO
```

Create the Certificates

Because our Linux servers are not part of a domain and cannot authenticate with each other, using AD authentication, the next step is to create certificates, which can be used for instance authentication. You can create the certificates by connecting to the primary server and running the script in Listing 6-3. The script creates a certificate in the SQL Server instance and then backs it up to the operating system, so that we can copy it to the secondary server. Remember that you can connect to a SQL Server instance, running on Linux by using sqlcmd or by connecting from SSMS, installed on a Windows-based machine.

Listing 6-3. Create the Certificate

```
USE Master
GO

CREATE MASTER KEY
ENCRYPTION BY PASSWORD = 'Pa$$w0rd';
GO
```

```
CREATE CERTIFICATE aoag_certificate
WITH SUBJECT = 'AvailabilityGroups';
GO

BACKUP CERTIFICATE aoag_certificate
        TO FILE = '/var/opt/mssql/data/aoag_certificate.cer'
        WITH PRIVATE KEY (
            FILE = '/var/opt/mssql/data/aoag_certificate.pvk',
            ENCRYPTION BY PASSWORD = 'Pa$$w0rd'
        );
GO
```

We now need to copy the keys to the secondary server. To do this, we first need to grant the user permissions to the /var/opt/mssql/ data folder. We can do this with the command in Listing 6-4, which needs to be run on all servers that will participate in the Availability Group.

Listing 6-4. Grant Permissions

```
sudo chmod -R 777 /var/opt/mssql
```

The command in Listing 6-5, if run on the primary server, will use scp, a remote file copy program, to copy the public and private key of the certificate to the secondary server. For this command to work, SSH should be installed and configured on each server. SSH provides secure access to another machine, but a full discussion is beyond the scope of this book. A guide, however, can be found at http://ubuntuhandbook.org/ index.php/2014/09/enable-ssh-in-ubuntu-14-10-server-desktop/.

Tip   You should change the user and server names to match your own configuration.

Listing 6-5. Copy the Keys

```
scp /var/opt/mssql/data/aoag_certificate.* pete@linuxsyncha:/var/opt/mssql/data

scp /var/opt/mssql/data/aoag_certificate.* pete@linuxconfig:/var/opt/mssql/data
```

Tip   If you don't have a name server configured, you will need to specify an IP Address, rather than a server name.

We now need to create the certificate on the secondary server by importing the certificate and key from the file system. This can be achieved using the script in Listing 6-6.

Listing 6-6. Create the Certificate on the Secondary Server

```
CREATE MASTER KEY ENCRYPTION BY PASSWORD = 'Pa$$w0rd' ;
GO

CREATE CERTIFICATE aoag_certificate
    FROM FILE = '/var/opt/mssql/data/aoag_certificate.cer'
    WITH PRIVATE KEY (
            FILE = '/var/opt/mssql/data/aoag_certificate.pvk',
            DECRYPTION BY PASSWORD = 'Pa$$w0rd'
    ) ;
GO
```

Configuring the Availability Group

Now that our certificates are in place, we need to create the endpoints, which will be used for connections. The script in Listing 6-7 will create an endpoint called AOAG_ Endpoint, which listens on port 5022 and uses our certificate for authentication. This script should be run all instances that will participate in the Availability Group.

Listing 6-7. Create the Endpoints

```
CREATE ENDPOINT AOAG_Endpoint
STATE = STARTED
AS TCP (LISTENER_PORT = 5022)
FOR DATABASE_MIRRORING (
    ROLE = ALL,
    AUTHENTICATION = CERTIFICATE aoag_certificate,
    ENCRYPTION = REQUIRED ALGORITHM AES
);
```

Everything is now in place for us to create the Availability Group. We will perform these actions on the linuxprod server. We could use sqlcmd on the server, or connect to the server using SSMS on a management node, to allow us to use the GUI. Figure 6-1 illustrates the General page of the New Availability Group dialog box, running on a management node.

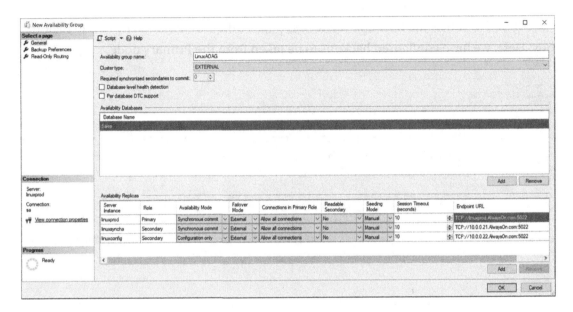

Figure 6-1. *New Availability Group Dialog Box – General Page*

There are two main differences to note in the configuration, compared to the Availability Groups that we configured in Chapter 5. Firstly, the Cluster Type and Failover mode is set to EXTERNAL. This indicates that the Availability Group will reside on a cluster that is not a Windows Failover Cluster. In this case, specifically, it will reside on a Pacemaker cluster. When building an Availability Group on Linux, we can choose to set the cluster type as EXTERNAL or NONE. If we select NONE, however, then it would not be suitable for high availability.

The second point of note is that the linuxconfig node is configured as configuration only. Because our Availability Group will not be running on a Windows Failover Cluster, then failover needs to be arbitrated by the Availability Group, instead of the cluster.

If we had three or more nodes, then a configuration-only node would not be required, as the failure of the primary node could still be arbitrated by the two (or more) secondaries. Because we only have a two-node cluster, however, a third node is required to act as a witness and maintain quorum in the event of a node failure.

The configuration-only node does not contain a copy of the user databases, but the Availability Group metadata is synchronized, using synchronous commit mode. The configuration-only node can use any version of SQL Server, including SQL Server Express edition, to avoid additional costs. A single instance can also act as the witness for multiple Availability Groups. However, a single Availability Group can only ever have a single configuration-only node.

Figure 6-2 shows the Backup Preferences page of the New Availability Group dialog box. Here, we have configured backups to be taken from the Primary node.

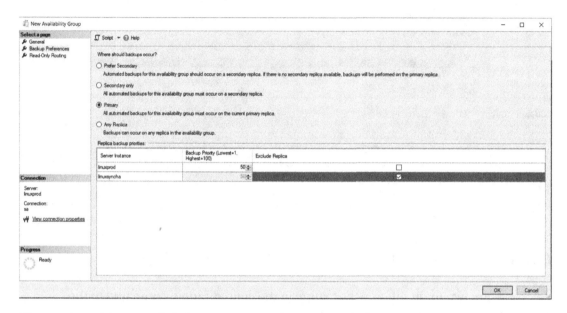

Figure 6-2. *New Availability Group Dialog Box – Backup Preferences Tab*

Because we are only configuring high availability, there is no need to configure the Read-only Routing. A discussion of Read-only Routing and other configuration options not discussed here can be found in Chapter 5, however.

Alternatively, we could create the Availability Group via T-SQL, using the script in Listing 6-8.

Listing 6-8. Create the Availability Group

```
USE master
GO
```

```
CREATE AVAILABILITY GROUP LinuxAOAG WITH (
     AUTOMATED_BACKUP_PREFERENCE = PRIMARY,
     DB_FAILOVER = OFF,
     DTC_SUPPORT = NONE,
     CLUSTER_TYPE = EXTERNAL,
     REQUIRED_SYNCHRONIZED_SECONDARIES_TO_COMMIT = 0
)
FOR DATABASE Sales
REPLICA ON
     'linuxconfig' WITH (
          ENDPOINT_URL = 'TCP://linuxconfig.AlwaysOn.com:5022',
          AVAILABILITY_MODE = CONFIGURATION_ONLY
     ),
     'linuxprod' WITH (
          ENDPOINT_URL = 'TCP://linuxprod.AlwaysOn.com:5022',
          FAILOVER_MODE = EXTERNAL,
          AVAILABILITY_MODE = SYNCHRONOUS_COMMIT,
          SESSION_TIMEOUT = 10,
          BACKUP_PRIORITY = 50,
          SEEDING_MODE = MANUAL,
          PRIMARY_ROLE(ALLOW_CONNECTIONS = ALL),
          SECONDARY_ROLE(ALLOW_CONNECTIONS = NO)
     ),
     'linuxsyncha' WITH (
          ENDPOINT_URL = 'TCP://linuxsyncha.AlwaysOn.com:5022',
          FAILOVER_MODE = EXTERNAL,
          AVAILABILITY_MODE = SYNCHRONOUS_COMMIT,
          SESSION_TIMEOUT = 10,
          BACKUP_PRIORITY = 0,
          SEEDING_MODE = MANUAL,
          PRIMARY_ROLE(ALLOW_CONNECTIONS = ALL),
          SECONDARY_ROLE(ALLOW_CONNECTIONS = NO)
     ) ;
GO
```

To manually seed the Sales database with a backup, you can copy the backup file to the secondary server by running the command in Listing 6-9 from the primary server.

Listing 6-9. Copy the Backup of the Sales Database

```
Scp /var/opt/mssql/data/sales.bak pete@linuxprod:/var/opt/mssql/data
```

The database can be restored using the command in Listing 6-10.

Listing 6-10. Restore the Sales Database

```
USE master
GO

RESTORE DATABASE Sales
FROM  DISK = '/var/opt/mssql/data/Sales.bak'
WITH
      FILE = 1,
      MOVE N'Sales' TO N'/var/opt/mssql/data/Sales.mdf',
      MOVE N'Sales_log' TO N'/var/opt/mssql/data/Sales_log.ldf',
      NORECOVERY ;

GO
```

Running the script in Listing 6-11 will join our secondary replica to the Availability Group and ensure that it has the appropriate permissions. This script needs to be run against all instances that will participate in the Availability Group.

Listing 6-11. Join the Secondary to the Availability Group

```
ALTER AVAILABILITY GROUP LinuxAOAG JOIN WITH (CLUSTER_TYPE = EXTERNAL) ;
GO

ALTER AVAILABILITY GROUP LinuxAOAG GRANT CREATE ANY DATABASE ;
GO
```

Configuring the Cluster

Before creating the cluster, we will need to create a login that will be used by the Pacemaker account and assign it the permissions that it requires, in each of the SQL Server instances that will be participating in the Availability Group. This can be achieved by using the script in Listing 6-12.

Listing 6-12. Configure the Pacemaker Login

```
CREATE LOGIN Pacemaker
WITH PASSWORD = 'Pa$$w0rd'
GO

GRANT ALTER, CONTROL, VIEW DEFINITION ON AVAILABILITY GROUP::LinuxAOAG
    TO Pacemaker ;

GRANT VIEW SERVER STATE TO Pacemaker
```

Next, we will need to configure the firewall. The ports that the cluster will require are detailed in Table 6-1.

Table 6-1. *Ports Required by Cluster*

Port	Description
TCP 2224	Required on all nodes. pcsd Web UI and node-to-node communication
TCP 3121	Required on all nodes if Pacemaker has remote nodes. Used for communication between the crmd and pacemaker_remoted daemons
TCP 21064	Required on all nodes. Used by resources requiring DLM
UDP 5405	Required on all nodes. Used by Corosync
TCP 1433	Required on all nodes. The examples in this chapter have the SQL instances listen on 1433; however, you should change this to match your own environment
TCP 5022	Required on all nodes. The examples in this chapter have the AlwaysOn endpoints on 5022; however, you should change this to match your own environment

Listing 6-13 provides an example of how to configure firewall rules in Ubuntu.

Listing 6-13. Configure Firewall Rules

```
sudo ufw allow 2224/tcp
sudo ufw allow 3121/tcp
sudo ufw allow 21064/tcp
sudo ufw allow 5405/udp

sudo ufw allow 1433/tcp
sudo ufw allow 5022/tcp

sudo ufw reload
```

Next, we will install the Pacemaker components. We can do this with the command in Listing 6-14. This command should be run on all server participating in the Availability Group.

Listing 6-14. Install Pacemaker Components

```
sudo apt-get install pacemaker pcs resource-agents
```

Caution   For a production system, be sure to also install `fence-agents` for node fencing.

During the installation of the pcs components, a `hacluster` will be created. You should set a password for this user using the passwd command, as shown in Listing 6-15. After running the command, you will be prompted to enter and then confirm the new password.

Note   It is important that you set the same password on each node.

Listing 6-15. Set hacluster Password

```
Sudo passwd hacluster
```

We can now enable the pcs and pacemarker services, using the script in Listing 6-16. You will notice that before enabling pacemaker, we issue a command to destroy any existing cluster. This is because a file called `/etc/cluster/corosync.conf` was created during the install of pcs, however, enabling pacemaker attempts to create this file. Using the `cluster destroy` command removes this file to avoid a failure when pacemaker is enabled.

Listing 6-16. Enable pcs and pacemarker

```
sudo systemctl enable pcsd
sudo systemctl start pcsd
sudo pcs cluster destroy
sudo systemctl enable pacemaker
```

Now that pacemaker is enabled, we can build the cluster. The process for this consists of running five `pcs cluster` commands. The first is `auth`. This is used to authenticate pcs to the pcs daemon on all of the nodes. The command expects a list of nodes, followed by the username and password of the pcs user that was created during install. Listing 6-17 demonstrates how to use the command in our scenario.

Listing 6-17. Authenticate Against pcs Daemon

```
sudo pcs cluster auth LinuxProd LinuxSyncHA LinuxConfig -u hacluster
```

Because we have not specified the -p parameter when you run this command, you will be prompted to enter the password for `hacluster`.

The second command is `set up`. This command is used to register the cluster name and each node within the cluster. The cluster name is specified using the -name parameter, followed by a node list. Listing 6-18 illustrates how to use the `setup` command in our scenario.

Tip   It is also possible to specify the –start parameter to start the cluster service, but we will choose to start the cluster using a separate command, to help illustrate the full process.

Listing 6-18. Set Up the Cluster

```
sudo pcs cluster setup --name LinuxCluster LinuxProd LinuxSyncHA
LinuxConfig
```

The next command is start. As you would expect, this is used to start the cluster service. The command either accepts the --all parameter to start the service on all nodes (demonstrated in Listing 6-19) or a node list of nodes where the cluster service should be started.

Listing 6-19. Start the Cluster Service

```
sudo pcs cluster start --all
```

After running this command, there can be a delay before the service is started. Therefore, you should run the status command before continuing to ensure that the cluster is up, as shown in Listing 6-20.

Listing 6-20. Check Cluster Status

```
Sudo pcs cluster status
```

Finally, we will configure the cluster service to run on startup, for each of the nodes. This can be achieved using the enable command, as shown in Listing 6-21. The command accepts either the --all parameter or a node list.

Listing 6-21. Enabling the Cluster Service

```
sudo pcs cluster enable --all
```

Now that the cluster has been created, we can install the SQL Server resource agent. This allows pacemaker to loosely integrate with Availability Groups. Specifically, it increments a sequence number in the sys.available_groups catalog view, each time configuration change, such as a failover or a new replica being added. It then interrogates this sequence number on failover, to identify if a node is up to date, before failover occurs. This allows the failover to be rejected if the sequence number is not the highest. Listing 6-22 demonstrates how to install the resource agent.

Listing 6-22. Install the Resource Agent

```
sudo apt-get install mssql-server-ha
```

Next, we need to give pacemaker permissions to the Availability Group. We created a login for pacemaker in Listing 6-12. Now we need to save the credentials in the operating system by running the script in Listing 6-23 on all nodes in the cluster.

Listing 6-23. Save the Pacemaker Credentials

```
echo 'pacemakerLogin' >> ~/pacemaker-passwd
echo 'Pa$$w0rd' >> ~/pacemaker-passwd
sudo mv ~/pacemaker-passwd /var/opt/mssql/secrets/passwd
sudo chown root:root /var/opt/mssql/secrets/passwd
sudo chmod 400 /var/opt/mssql/secrets/passwd
```

We now need to create cluster resources, both for the Availability Group and for the virtual IP Address. This can be achieved by running the script in Listing 6-24. The first command in the script creates an Availability Group resource for the LinuxAOAG Availability Group.

The second command in the script creates a resource for the IP Address that we wish to use. Notice that we specify both the IP Address and the network mask of the network. The network mask is specified using CIDR notation. CIDR notation is beyond the scope of this book, but a CIDR tutorial can be found at `www.controltechnology.com/Files/common-documents/application_notes/CIDR-Notation-Tutorial`.

Listing 6-24. Create the Cluster Resources

```
sudo pcs resource create LinuxAOAG ocf:mssql:ag ag_name=LinuxAOAG meta
failure-timeout=60s master meta notify=true
sudo pcs resource create VirtualIP ocf:heartbeat:IPaddr2 ip=10.0.0.25 cidr_
netmask=24
```

Caution   Because pacemaker does not have the concept of network name, the IP Address and desired name must be manually registered in DNS.

The decision of what node a resource should run on is based on scores, which are calculated at the resource level. This means that there is a risk that the virtual IP Address could be moved to a different node, to the availability group resource. To mitigate this risk, we need to add a colocation constraint, which ensures the resources are always on the same node. Constraints also have scores, with any number lower than infinity being a preference and infinite being a binding requirement. The command in Listing 6-25 will create the required constraint.

Listing 6-25. Create the Colocation Constraint

```
sudo pcs constraint colocation add VirtualIP LimuxAOAG INFINITY with-rsc-
role=Master
```

Because this command lists the virtual IP Address resource before the Availability Group resource, when resources are moved, the virtual IP Address will be moved and brought online, before the Availability Group resource is moved and brought online. This means that the virtual IP address could temporarily be pointing to the wrong node. This risk can be mitigated by adding an ordering constraint, which forces the Availability Group resource to be moved before the virtual IP Address is brought online. Listing 6-26 demonstrates how to configure this constraint.

Listing 6-26. Create Ordering Constraint

```
sudo pcs constraint order promote LinuxAOAG then start VirtualIP
```

Finally, we can create the Availability Group Listener. The Listener will use the IP Address of the virtual IP Address resource that we created in the Pacemaker cluster. It is important to remember that when Availability Groups are configured on a pacemaker cluster, the sole purpose of the Availability Group Listener is to provide an abstraction, with a single point of entry to the Replicas. It does not mask outages, because during failover, it will temporarily become unavailable while the virtual IP Address resource is started on another cluster node. We can create the Availability Group Listener by using the script in Listing 6-27.

Listing 6-27. Create the Availability Group Listener

```
USE master
GO

ALTER AVAILABILITY GROUP LinuxAOAG
ADD LISTENER 'LinuxAOListener' (
     WITH IP (
          (N'10.0.0.25', N'255.255.255.0')
     )
     , PORT=1433
);
GO
```

Summary

Availability Groups can be configured on Linux-based instances in a similar way to configuring Availability Groups on Windows-based instances. They can be configured without an underlying cluster or can make use of Linux-based clustering technology.

If high availability or disaster recovery is required, then a Linux clustering technology, such as pacemaker, must be used. A pacemaker cluster is made up of multiple components, including pcs, a command-line utility for managing pacemaker clusters; Corosync, which provides the heartbeat between the nodes; STONITH which is used for fencing; and then Pacemaker, the core cluster manager.

Availability Group Listeners are supported in a pacemaker cluster, but their functionality is limited. The IP Address resource temporarily goes offline when being moved to a new node. Therefore, the Availability Group Listener provides an abstraction, but does not mask the failure, as it will become inaccessible for a period.

CHAPTER 7

Atypical Availability Group Implementations

So far, we have discussed the typical, on-premise, enterprise workload scenarios for AlwaysOn Availability Groups and AlwaysOn Failover Clustered Instances. AlwaysOn is such a flexible suite of technologies, however, that there are many permutations that you may wish to take advantage of. Therefore, this chapter will provide an overview of some of the less typical AlwaysOn scenarios that you may need to support. This includes Basic Availability Groups, Availability Groups in Azure, Distributed Availability Groups, and creating Availability Groups without a cluster or a domain.

In this chapter, we will perform the following activities:

- Create an Availability Group in Azure IaaS.

- Create a Clusterless Availability Group.

- Create a domain-independent availability group.

- Create a distributed Availability Group.

Basic Availability Groups

All of the Availability Group demonstrations so far in this book have required SQL Server Enterprise Edition, but Availability Groups are also available in SQL Server Standard Edition. In Standard Edition, however, the functionality of Availability Groups is limited, hence why they are known as Basic Availability Groups.

The most noticeable limitation is that Basic Availability Groups only support two replicas. The replicas can, however, be configured as either in synchronous or asynchronous commit mode. This means that you can still achieve either high availability or disaster recovery.

155

© Peter A. Carter 2020
P. A. Carter, *SQL Server 2019 AlwaysOn*, https://doi.org/10.1007/978-1-4842-6479-9_7

> **Note**   Basic Availability Group on Linux supports a third, configuration-only replica, which is required to achieve high availability. Please see Chapter 6 for further details.

The secondary replica does not support read-only connections. This means that not only do Basic Availability Groups not support read-scaling, they also do not support backups or integrity checks being taken on the secondary.

Another limitation is that a Basic Availability Group can only contain a single database. This means that it is not possible to fail over multiple databases together, making administration of large instances far more difficult.

Other advanced Availability Group functionalities, such as Distributed Availability Groups, are also not supported, and once a Basic Availability Group has been built, it cannot be upgraded to a full-fat Availability Group. Instead, it must be destroyed and re-created.

To implement Basic Availability Groups, you can use the same syntax, as discussed earlier in this book, with the obvious exception being that you cannot implement unsupported features. The only syntax that is solely for Basic Availability Groups is the addition of the BASIC marker in the WITH clause, which reduces that available functionality. For example, the script in Listing 7-1 would create an Availability Group across two servers, named SQLStdProd and SQLStdSyncHA, and both servers have a default instance of SQL Server Standard Edition installed.

Listing 7-1. Create a Basic Availability Group

```
CREATE AVAILABILITY GROUP BasicAGAG
WITH (
    AUTOMATED_BACKUP_PREFERENCE = PRIMARY,
    BASIC,
    REQUIRED_SYNCHRONIZED_SECONDARIES_TO_COMMIT = 0
)
FOR DATABASE Sales
REPLICA ON 'SQLSTDPROD' WITH (
    ENDPOINT_URL = 'TCP://SQLSTDPROD.AlwaysOn.com:5022',
    FAILOVER_MODE = AUTOMATIC,
    AVAILABILITY_MODE = SYNCHRONOUS_COMMIT, 7
    SEEDING_MODE = AUTOMATIC
),
```

```
'SQLSTDSYNCHA' WITH (
    ENDPOINT_URL = N'TCP://SQLSTDSYNCHA.AlwaysOn.com:5022',
    FAILOVER_MODE = AUTOMATIC,
    AVAILABILITY_MODE = SYNCHRONOUS_COMMIT,
    SEEDING_MODE = AUTOMATIC
);

GO
```

Availability Groups on Azure IaaS

When migrating databases to the cloud, you have various options for the target. Azure SQL Database and Elastic Database Pools provide a database as a service offering, while Azure Managed Instances provide a SQL Server as a service. Both of these offerings provide high availability, based on Availability Groups. If your application requires access to the operating system, however, then you must use Azure VMs. With this solution, you must manually configure Availability Groups, as you would on-premise. In the following sections, we will look at some of the Azure Availability options that you should be aware of before designing your Availability Group topology, before exploring how to configure Availability Groups in Azure.

Azure Availability Concepts

A key principle of cloud is to design applications for failure. Therefore, implementing Availability Groups for SQL Server in cloud is a very important topic. Before discussing the implementation, you should be familiar with the concepts of Availability Sets, Availability Zones, and Regions. The following sections will provide an overview of each of these topics.

Availability Sets

Availability Sets are a construct that place VMs within the same data center on different fault domains and update domains. A fault domain indicates hardware that shares a common power supply and network switch. An Availability Set can be configured to stretch across three fault domains. Therefore, if you place three VMs in the same Availability Set, you know that each VM has a unique power supply and network switch to the other VMs in the Availability Set.

An update domain indicates physical hardware that is rebooted for either planned or unplanned maintenance. An Availability Set is split across five update domains by default, and this can be increased to a maximum of 20. If you place VMs in the same Availability Set, you know that they are on different hardware from each other and will not be rebooted at the same time.

Tip   When making use of Availability Sets, you should also ensure that you use Managed Disks. When using Managed Disks, the physical disks are split across fault domains that align with attached VMs, avoiding single points of failure.

Availability Zones

While an Availability Set protects against hardware issues and downtime within a data center, it does not protect against data center failure. To protect against data center failure, you must place your VMs in separate Availability Zones. Each Availability Zone is in a different building, with separate power, networking, and cooling.

Regions

Regions provide a mean of dispersing your servers geographical, in order to protect against a large-scale disaster that takes an entire Region offline. Regions within Azure are paired within a Geography, where a Geography is a political region. For example, Regions in the United States are paired with other regions physically located in the United States. The same applies for other territories, such as Europe and the United Kingdom. This allows you to protect against a disaster while still maintaining data sovereignty.

While I am aware of some companies, who have taken the stance that for DR, they only need to protect against the loss of a data center and have therefore decided to avoid the complexity and cost overhead of having a footprint in multiple regions, in cloud terms, you only have DR if your DR servers are in a different Region to your production servers.

Implementing Availability Groups in Azure

In this section, we will explore how to configure Availability Groups on Azure VMs. In this section, we will build an Availability Group for the Sales database across two Availability Zones, within the same region, for the purpose of providing high availability.

We will build each of the VMs on different subnets, within the same vnet. Before that, however, we will briefly discuss Availability Sets.

Creating an Availability Set

To create an Availability Set from the Azure Portal, navigate to the Availability Sets blade and use the Add button to launch the Create Availability Set page, which is illustrated in Figure 7-1. You will notice that we have selected the Subscription that we want the Availability Set to be created in and selected the Resource Group in which it should be created. We have also given it a name and selected the Region that it should be created in. Because we plan to have two servers within the Availability Set, then both Update Domains and Fault Domains have been configured as two. Each of the two servers will reside in a different Fault Domain and Update Domain. If we added additional servers to the Availability Set, then they would be allocated to Fault Domains and Update Domains in a round-robin fashion.

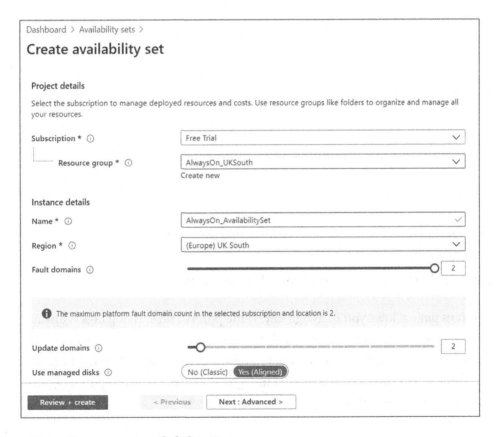

Figure 7-1. *Create an Availability Set*

On the Advanced page, illustrated in Figure 7-2, we have the option to assign a Proximity Placement Group to the Availability Group. A Proximity Placement Group helps ensure the lowest possible latency, by using hardware that is located physically close, within the data center. To use this option, you must create the Proximity Group before creating the Availability Set.

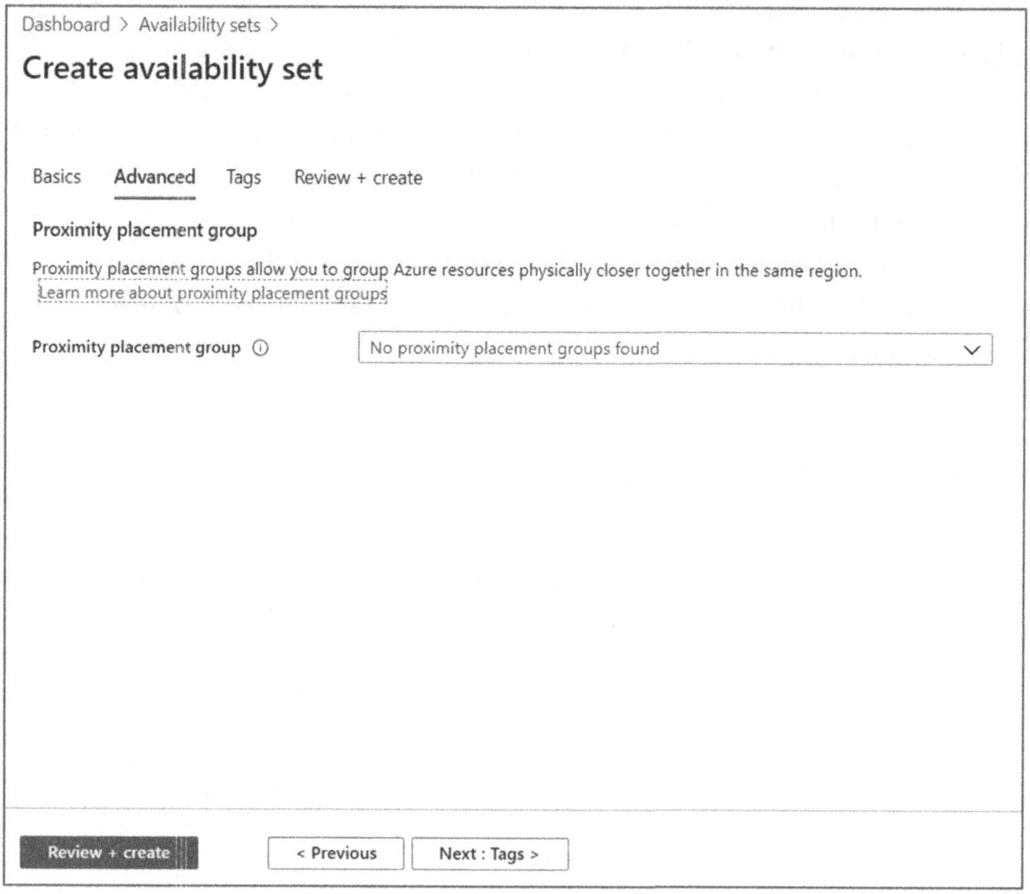

Figure 7-2. Create an Availability Set Advanced Page

The Tags page allows you to assign key/value pairs of tags. Using tags is always good practice for cloud as it helps not only with resource management but also with cost control, such as producing show-back or charge-back mechanisms to business divisions that consume cloud resources. As shown in Figure 7-3, we have configured tags for environment and application.

Tip   You can use Azure Policies to enforce specific tags are used when resources are created.

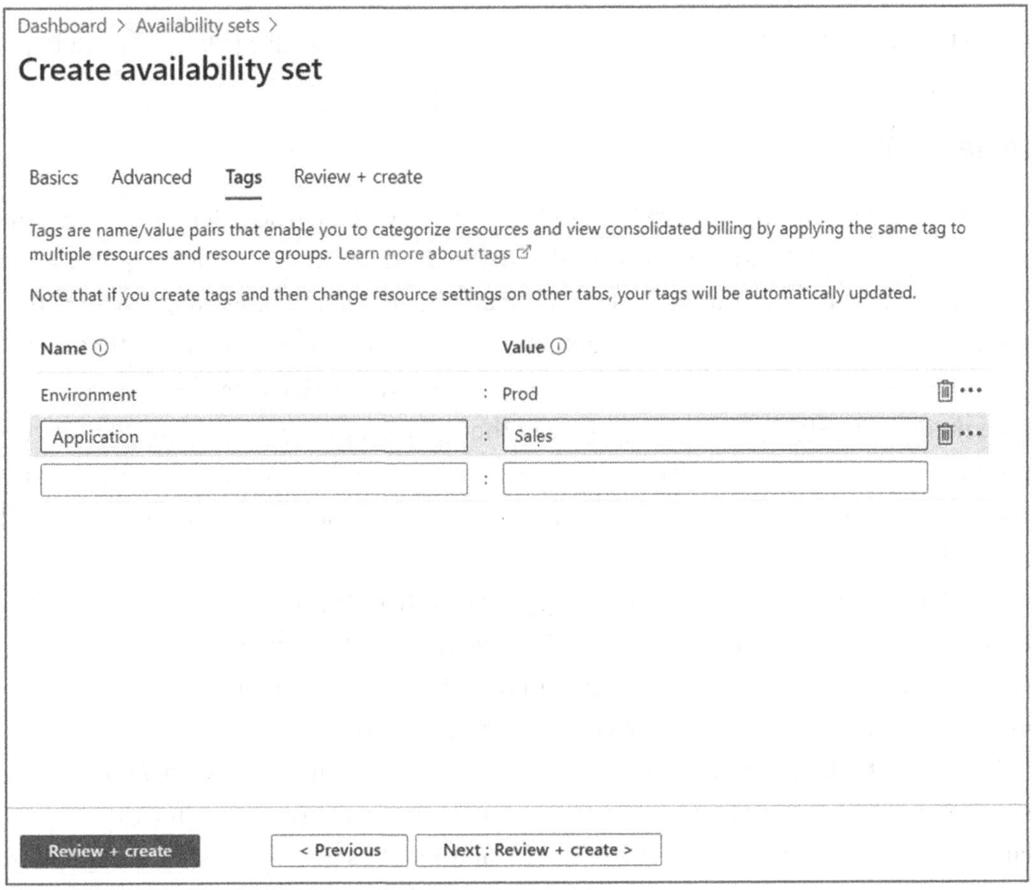

Figure 7-3.   *Create an Availability Set – Tags Page*

On the Review page, you have the opportunity to review the settings that you have configured, before creating the resource.

Create Availability Groups on Azure VMs

In the following sections, we will discuss building and configuring an Availability Group solution on Azure.

Note To follow demonstrations in the following sections, you will need an Azure subscription. This must be at least a pay-as-you-go subscription, as a free trial subscription will not give you enough cores to build the two servers. You will also need a vnet, with two subnets. The chapter also assumes that the either the vet contains a domain controller, or that you have configured Azure Domain Services.

Create the VMs

The first thing that we will require is three VMs, which will have SQL Server installed on them. There are various ways to achieve this in Azure, depending on your requirements. The first option is to go to the Azure Marketplace and find a machine image, with SQL Server installed. If you take this approach, then it is important to understand that there are two different types of license terms. The first is SPLA (Service Provide License Agreement). With SPLA licensing, the cost of the VM includes the cost of the SQL Server license. This means that your license is on a pay-as-you-go basis and avoids the upfront cost of license procurement, but does work out more expensive over time, if the VM will be long lived.

The second option type is BYOL (bring your own license). With this license model, the SQL Server license is not included in the cost of the VM. Instead, you must use an existing license that has already been procured. When you chose this option, then you must report your license usage to Microsoft within 10 days.

When you build a VM with SQL Server already installed, it arrives with a full installation of SQL Server, including all features. (Unless you choose an image marked Database Engine Only.) This is not ideal is most use cases, as it has a larger security footprint and resource utilization than installing just the features that you require. Therefore, if you use a VM image with SQL Server preinstalled (regardless of the licensing model), you should take the time to customize the image to meet your requirements.

Alternatively, you could simply build a VM from a vanilla Windows Server image and install SQL Server yourself. This is the most flexibly option, but if you take this approach, then you must bring your own license. No SPLA option will be available.

In this example, we will use the SQL Server 2019 on Windows Server 2019 image, with SPLA licensing. Figure 7-4 shows the Marketplace icon for this VM image.

Figure 7-4. *SQL Server 2019 on Windows Server 2019 VM Image*

In the first section of the Create Virtual Machine page, illustrated in Figure 7-5, we will specify the Subscription and Resource Group that the VM should be created in, before specifying a name for the server and the Region it should be created in.

We then go on to specify the Availability Options that we would like for the VM. This is critical when planning Availability Groups. In the Availability Options dialog box, we can choose between No infrastructure redundancy required, Availability Set, or Availability Zone. If we had chosen Availability Set, then we would have had the option either to use the Availability Set we created earlier or to create a new Availability Set. We have chosen Availability Zone, however, so we can specify which Availability Zone the server should be created in. Each Region has a minimum of three Availability Zones.

Caution   It is important to note, however, that the Availability Option cannot be changed after creating the VM. For example, you cannot create a VM with no availability option and then add it to an Availability Set later.

We then have the option to choose change the image that we are building from and specify if we want to use Spot instances. Spot instances are rarely suitable for SQL Server and never in a production environment. Spot instances are built from spare capacity within Azure and are very cost effective. However, Azure can terminate them at very short notice, if they need the capacity. Therefore, Spot instances are usually most applicable for stateless applications, within Scale Sets, or for stateless applications in test environments.

We also specify the size of VM that we would like to build. The monthly cost (based on the server being up 24x7) will be displayed to the right of the VMs size profile.

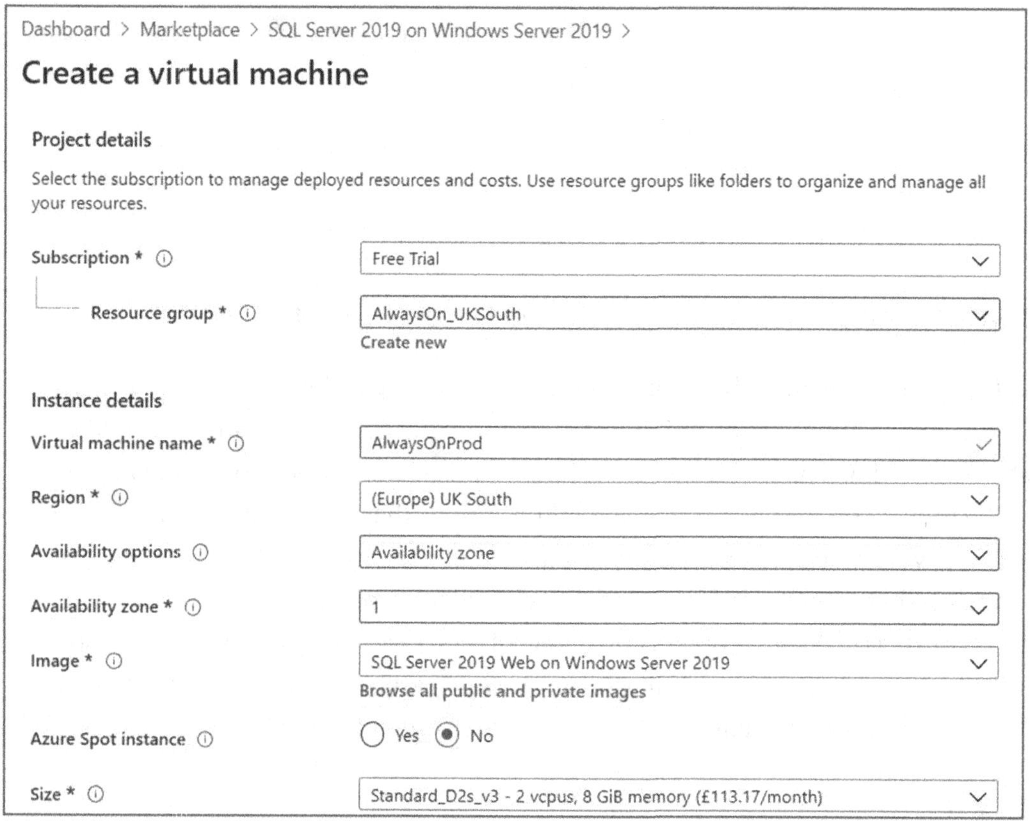

Figure 7-5. *Create a Virtual Machine (Part 1)*

We can now continue to populate the second half of the form, as shown in Figure 7-6. Here, we specify the username and password for the VMs Admin user and if ports should be opened on a public IP address for the server. If so, we can specify which ports should be open.

Caution   Public ports should only ever be opened for dev/test purposes and even then it is highly advisable to create a VPN, or use a Bastion instead.

Finally, we specify the licensing model we want to use. Note that this is just for the operating system, not for SQL Server, but we still have the same two options. We can either pay for the Windows license as we go or bring our own.

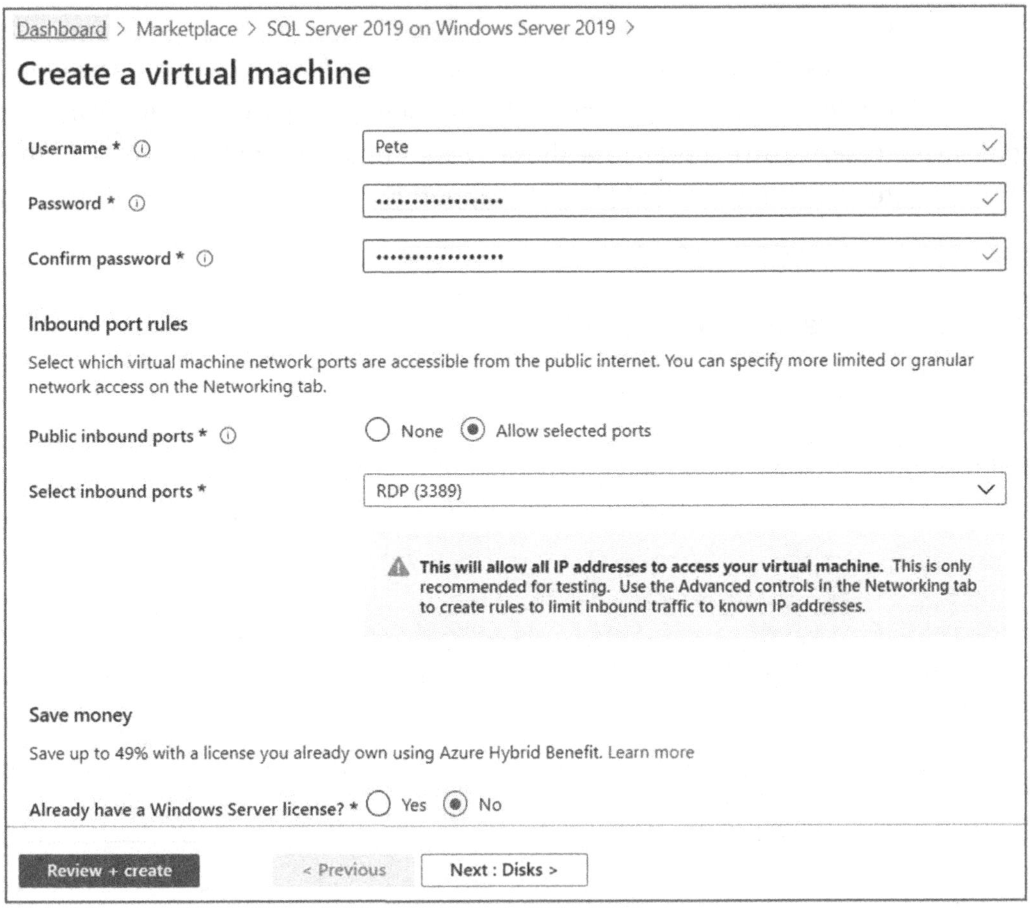

Figure 7-6. *Create a Virtual Machine (Part 2)*

On the Disks page, illustrated in Figure 7-7, we can configure the storage options for the VM. In the first section of the page, we can specify the storage tier that we want to use, from a choice of Standard HDD, Standard SSD. or Premium SSD. It will probably be unsurprising that I recommend using Premium SSD for VMs hosting SQL Server, although your choice may have other factors, such as company policy or budgetary constraints.

In the Advanced section of the page, we can specify if we want to use Managed or Unmanaged disks and if we want the OS disk to be ephemeral. Managed disks are usually recommended as they bring advantages such as automatically being split across Fault and Update domains. If your VM is being built on an Availability Set, these domains can also be aligned with the domains of the Availability Set. In our case, we must use Managed disks, as this is the only option when the Availability Option is configured as Availability Zone.

Ephemeral disks use very fast storage, which is not termination resistant. Therefore, they are applicable for stateless applications but not suitable for VMs running SQL Server. In our case, we do not even have the option to choose an ephemeral disk for the operating system, as our image is too large to support it.

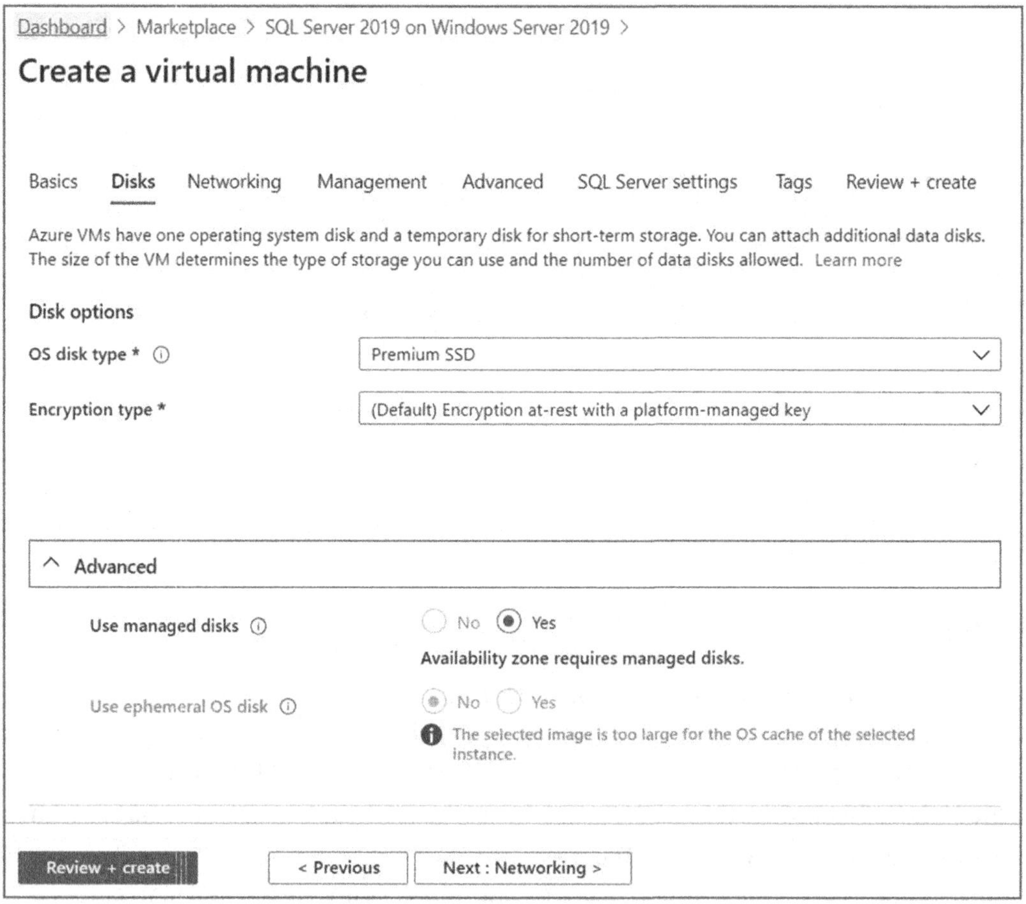

Figure 7-7. *Create a Virtual Machine – Disks Page*

On the Networking page (Figure 7-8), we can specify the vnet and subnet that the VM should be attached to, as well as configuring the public IP address and security groups that should be used. On this page, there are also options (unillustrated) that allow you to configure Accelerated Networking, which is a feature that allows low latency and high throughput to the VMs NIC (network interface card), but is only available for larger VMs, and also allows you to put the VM behind a preconfigured Load Balancer. This option is not suitable for SQL Server.

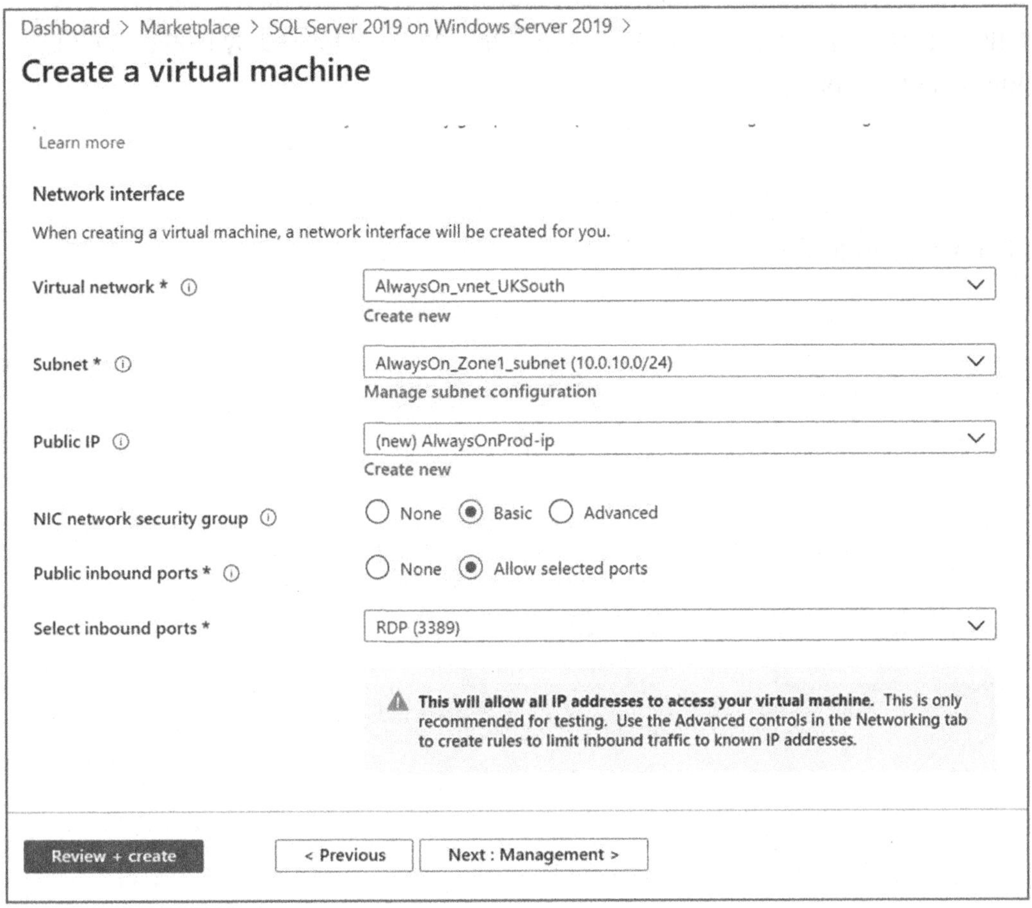

Figure 7-8. *Create a Virtual Machine – Networking*

On the Management page, shown in Figure 7-9, we can configure the diagnostic settings for the VM. Specifically, we can select if we want boot diagnostics and diagnostics from the guest operating system to be captured, alongside which storage account the diagnostics should be saved to.

We can also specify if we want a system-assigned managed identity to be used. If we select this option, then the VM can authenticate to native Azure services, such as Key

Vault, without the need to store the service credentials in code. Finally, we can specify if we want the VM to shut down at a specific time. If we select this option, then additional dialog boxes appear, allowing us to specify the shutdown schedule and if we want to be notified of the shutdown.

Tip When creating the VM, only a shutdown schedule can be added, but there is no option to create a startup schedule. This can be achieved by using an Azure Automation account.

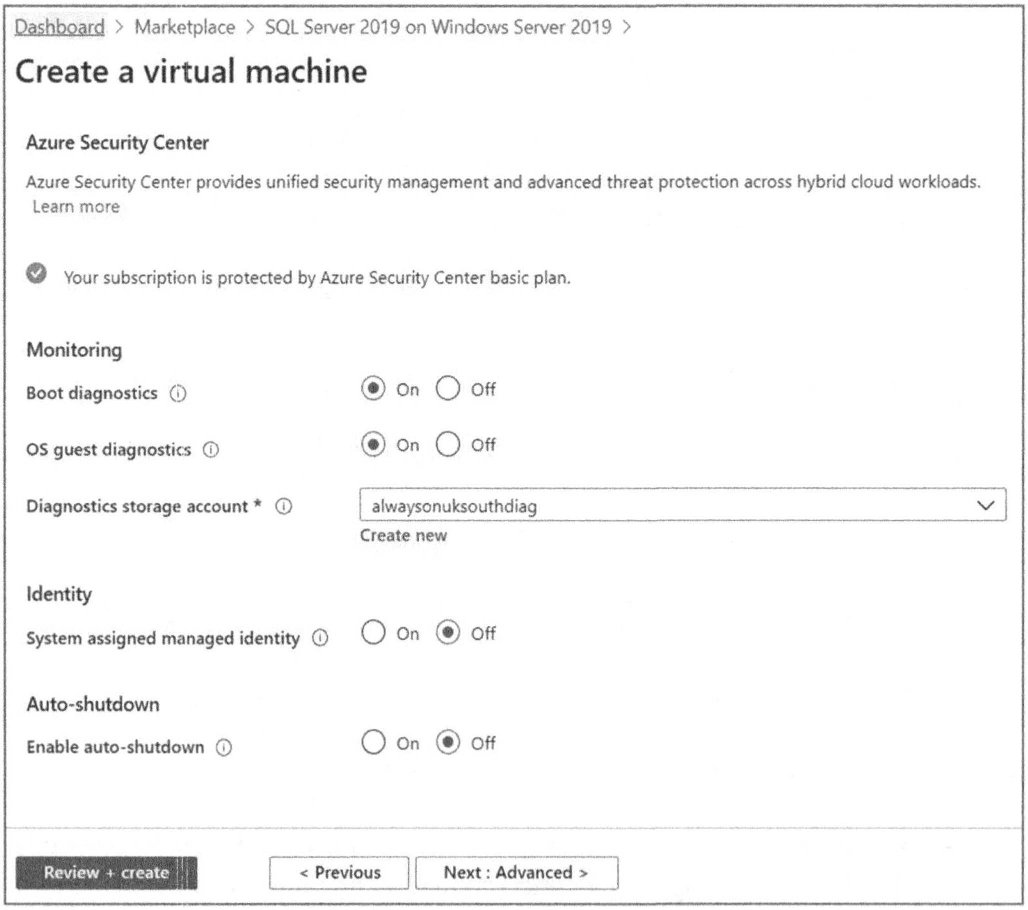

Figure 7-9. *Create a Virtual Machine – Management Page*

For our purposes, there is nothing that we need to configure on the Advanced page. However, this page can be used for passing configuration files to a known location within the VM, installing extensions of the VM, such as Puppet Agent, to allow for configuration management of the VM. If you want your VM to be placed on a Proximity Group, or you want it to reside on an existing dedicated host, then these options can also be configured on this page.

Because we are building a SQL Server VM, we have a page for SQL Server settings, which would not appear if we were building a VM from a standard Windows Server image. In the first part of this page (Figure 7-10), we can configure the SQL connectivity. This will give us the option of making the SQL Server instance available within the VM only, within our vnet, or publicly accessible on the Internet. It goes without saying that making an instance available to the Internet is undesirable, usually even in dev/test scenarios.

We can also specify the port that the instance should listen on and if we want SQL Server authentication to be enabled (instead of just Windows authentication). If we choose this option, we can then specify the username and password of our desired administrator account.

We can also select if we want the instance to be integrated with Azure Key Vault. If we choose this option, then we must provide the URL and credential information for the Key Vault service.

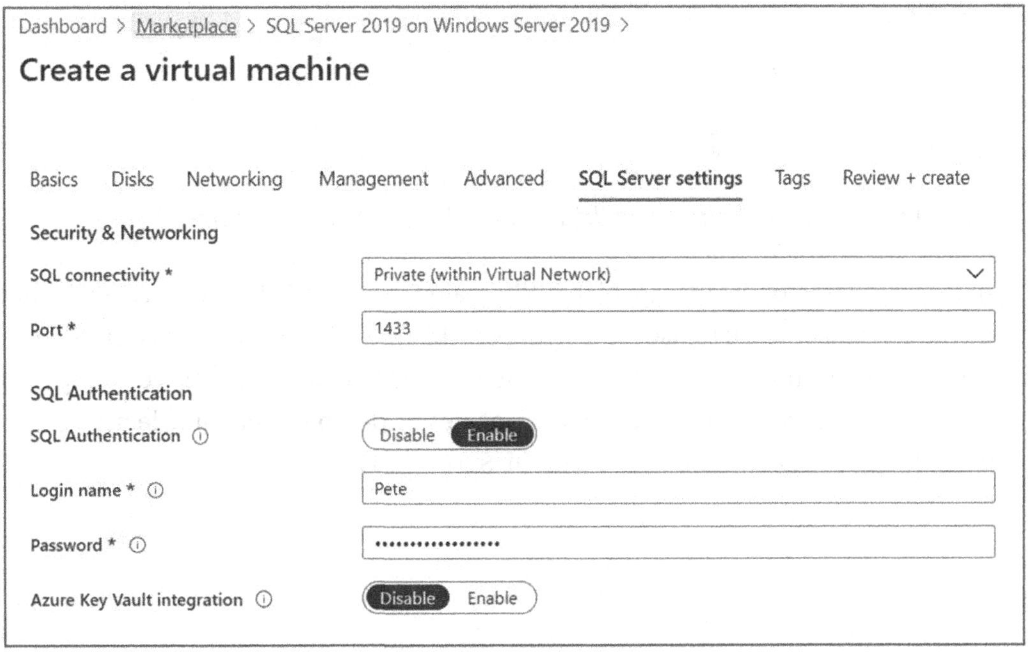

Figure 7-10. Create a Virtual Machine – SQL Server Settings (Part 1)

In the next section of the page, we are presented with the default storage options for SQL Server. Using the Change Configuration link will cause the Configure Storage page to be invoked, as shown in Figure 7-11. On this page, there are presets, for General, OLTP, and Data warehousing workload profiles, which can be customized to meet your requirements. You can specify if TempDB and log files should use the same drive or share the data drive. You can also specify the size and storage type of each disk.

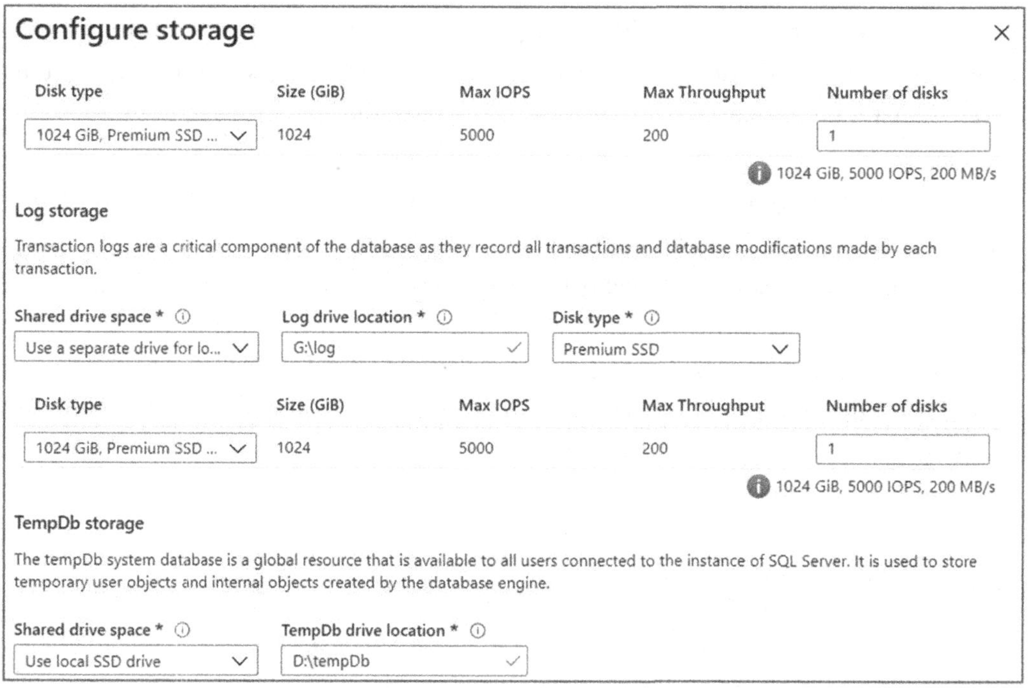

Figure 7-11. *Create a Virtual Machine – SQL Server Settings (Part 2)*

In the last section of the page, which is illustrated in Figure 7-12, we can specify the license model that we want to use for SQL Server (BYOL or SPLA), as well as specifying a patching window and choosing if we want automated backups. Finally, we can specify if we want R Services to be installed, which provides in-database machine learning features, which have been available since SQL Server 2017.

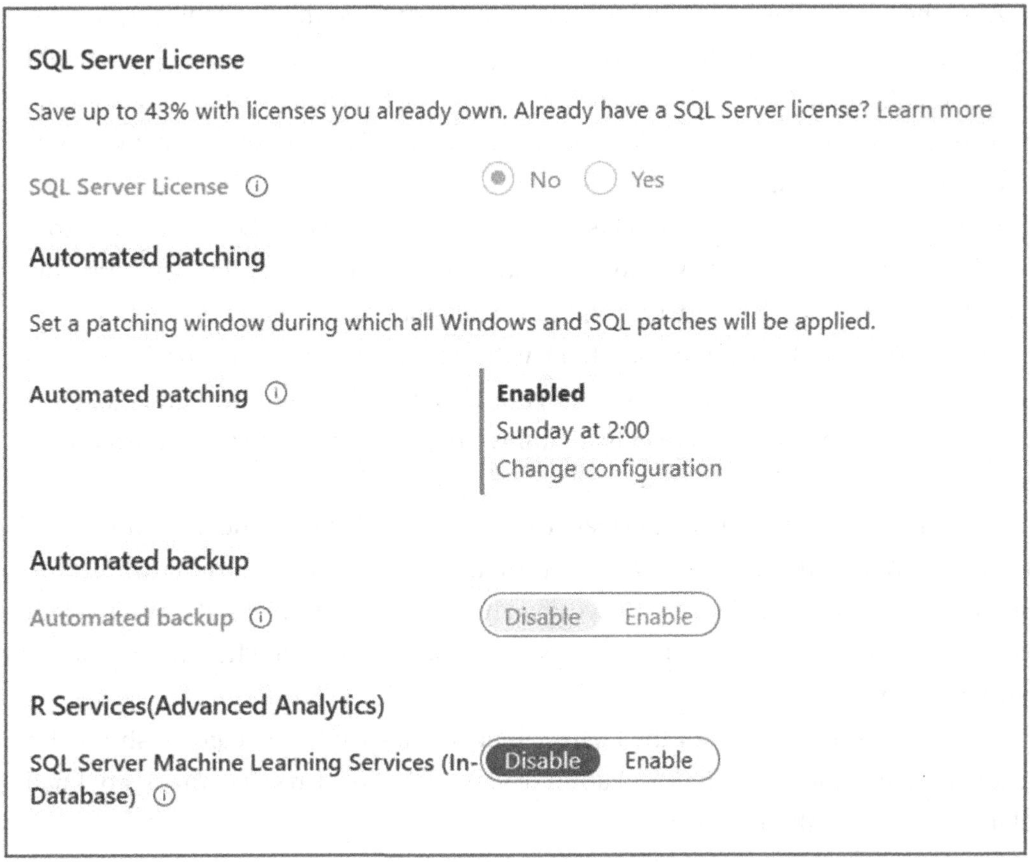

SQL Server License

Save up to 43% with licenses you already own. Already have a SQL Server license? Learn more

SQL Server License ⓘ   ⦿ No ◯ Yes

Automated patching

Set a patching window during which all Windows and SQL patches will be applied.

Automated patching ⓘ | **Enabled**
                               | Sunday at 2:00
                               | Change configuration

Automated backup

Automated backup ⓘ   (Disable   Enable)

R Services(Advanced Analytics)

SQL Server Machine Learning Services (In- (**Disable**   Enable)
Database) ⓘ

Figure 7-12. *Create a Virtual Machine – SQL Server Settings (Part 3)*

On the Tags page, we can add tags in key/value pairs, as described in the "Creating an Availability Set" section of this chapter. On the Review page, we can review our chosen configuration, before creating the virtual machine.

For our purposes, we should repeat this process to create a second VM, this time in Availability Zone 2 and residing on the other subnet within the vnet.

Configuring the Availability Group

Once the two servers have been built, you will need to join the servers to your domain and configure settings such as firewall rules. You can then create a cluster using the methods demonstrated in Chapter 3 of this book. Because we are implementing Availability Groups and not a Failover Clustered Instance, then there is no requirement for any shared storage in the Cluster.

After the Cluster has been configured, we can then build the Availability group by creating the Sales database, before configuring Availability Groups by using the methods discussed in Chapter 5 of this book. For the purpose of this exercise, the nodes should be configured with synchronous replication and automatic failover. Note that you should not create the Availability Group Listener at this point.

In Azure, the Availability Group Listener will require an Azure Load Balancer, to hold the IP Addresses for the Availability Group Listener and Failover Cluster. We should create the Load Balancer before creating the Availability Group Listener.

The Azure Load Balancer has two tiers, with differing functionality. Basic is the cheaper of the tiers, with more limited functionality, and Standard being the higher of the tiers. Because our servers are in Availability Zones, we must use a Standard Load Balancer.

To create the Load Balancer, navigate to the Load Balancers blade in Azure and select the Add button, to create a new Load Balancer. In the first section of the Create Load Balancer page, shown in Figure 7-13, we specify the Subscription and Resource Group that we want to create the Load Balancer in. This should match the Resource Group that your VMs are in.

We then provide a name for the Load Balancer and specify the region it should be created in. This should match the location of your VMs. We also select the tier of Load Balancer that we wish to create.

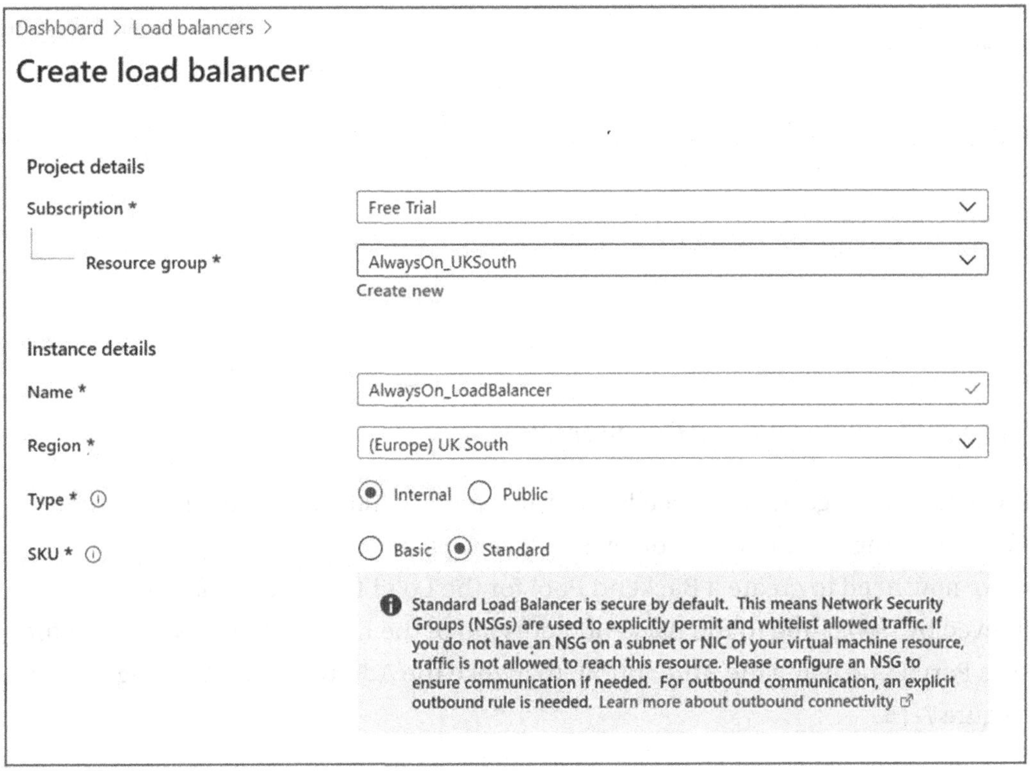

Dashboard > Load balancers >

Create load balancer

Project details

Subscription *

Free Trial

Resource group *

AlwaysOn_UKSouth

Create new

Instance details

Name *

AlwaysOn_LoadBalancer

Region *

(Europe) UK South

Type * ⓘ

◉ Internal ○ Public

SKU * ⓘ

○ Basic ◉ Standard

> ⓘ Standard Load Balancer is secure by default. This means Network Security
> Groups (NSGs) are used to explicitly permit and whitelist allowed traffic. If
> you do not have an NSG on a subnet or NIC of your virtual machine resource,
> traffic is not allowed to reach this resource. Please configure an NSG to
> ensure communication if needed. For outbound communication, an explicit
> outbound rule is needed. Learn more about outbound connectivity ⧉

Figure 7-13. *Create a Load Balancer (Part 1)*

In the next section of the page (Figure 7-14), we specify the network details for the
Load Balancer. Specifically, we specify the vnet that it should reside in, which should
match the vnet of your VMs. We also specify if it should use a static or dynamic IP
Address. For our purposes, we need a static IP Address, so we need to specify what
that address should be. Finally, we specify if the public IP address of the Load Balancer
should be created in an Availability Zone, or if it should use a zone-redundant path.

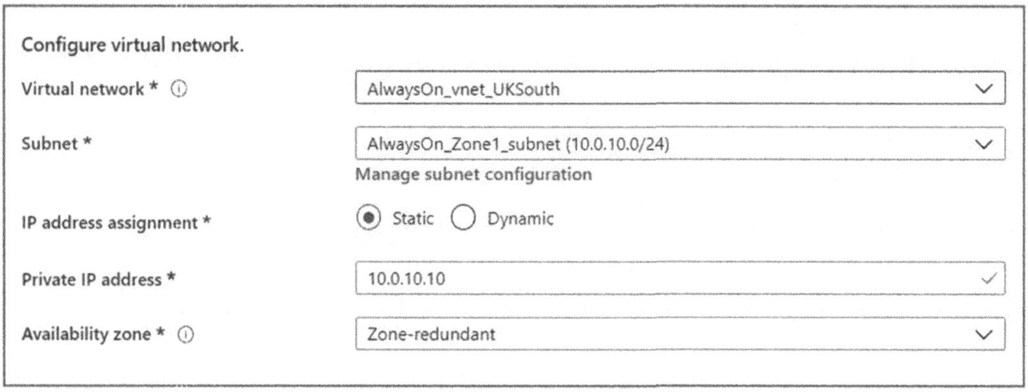

Configure virtual network.

Virtual network * ⓘ	AlwaysOn_vnet_UKSouth ⌄
Subnet *	AlwaysOn_Zone1_subnet (10.0.10.0/24) ⌄
	Manage subnet configuration
IP address assignment *	⦿ Static ◯ Dynamic
Private IP address *	10.0.10.10 ✓
Availability zone * ⓘ	Zone-redundant ⌄

Figure 7-14. *Create a Load Balancer (Part 2)*

On the Tags page, we can specify key/value pairs in line with company policies, before reviewing our configuration on the Review page.

We now need to create a Backend Pool for the Load Balancer. This can be achieved by navigating to the Backend Pools tab of the Load Balancer's blade in the Azure Portal and using the Add button, to invoke the Add Backend Pool page, shown in Figure 7-15.

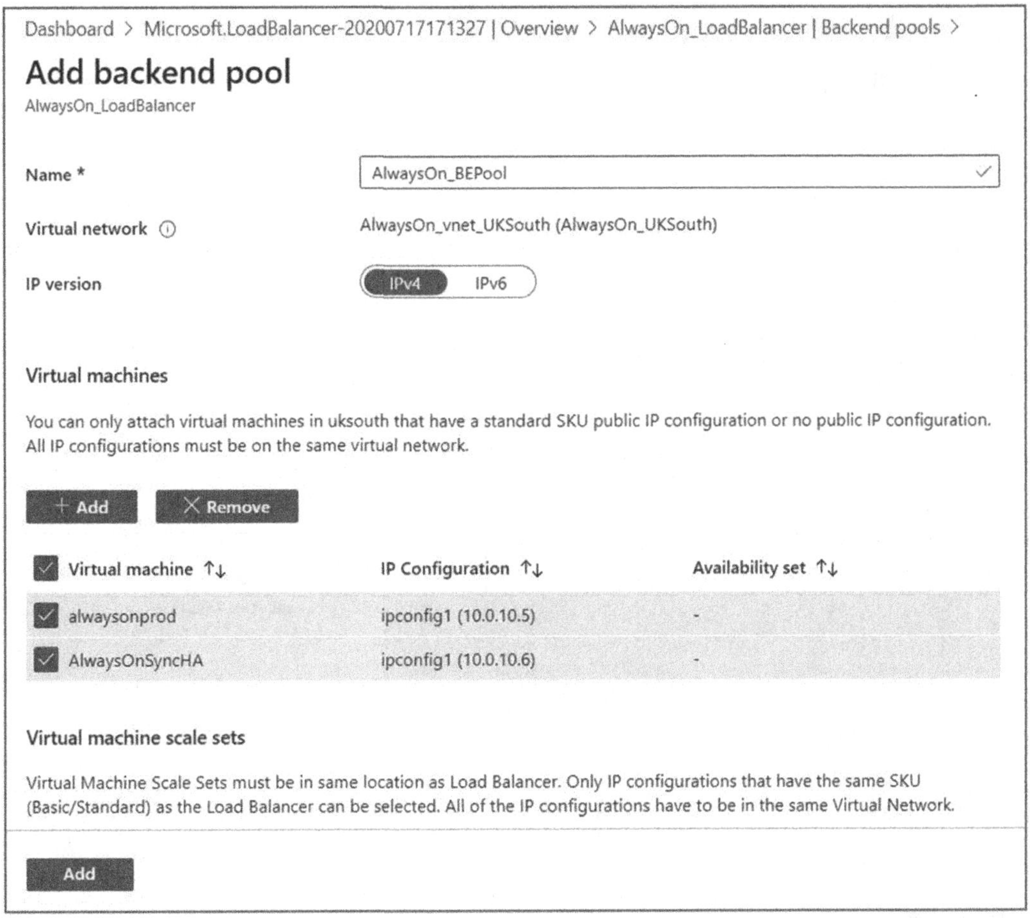

Dashboard > Microsoft.LoadBalancer-20200717171327 | Overview > AlwaysOn_LoadBalancer | Backend pools >

Add backend pool
AlwaysOn_LoadBalancer

Name *	AlwaysOn_BEPool ✓
Virtual network ⓘ	AlwaysOn_vnet_UKSouth (AlwaysOn_UKSouth)
IP version	(IPv4 IPv6)

Virtual machines

You can only attach virtual machines in uksouth that have a standard SKU public IP configuration or no public IP configuration. All IP configurations must be on the same virtual network.

[+ Add] [✕ Remove]

☑ Virtual machine ↑↓	IP Configuration ↑↓	Availability set ↑↓
☑ alwaysonprod	ipconfig1 (10.0.10.5)	-
☑ AlwaysOnSyncHA	ipconfig1 (10.0.10.6)	-

Virtual machine scale sets

Virtual Machine Scale Sets must be in same location as Load Balancer. Only IP configurations that have the same SKU (Basic/Standard) as the Load Balancer can be selected. All of the IP configurations have to be in the same Virtual Network.

[Add]

Figure 7-15. *Add a Backend Pool*

We can now create a Health Probe, which will perform connectivity checks to each node. We can do this by navigating to the Health Probes tab on the Load Balancer's blade, shown in Figure 7-16. Here, we are specifying a name for the probe and providing a protocol and unused port that the health check will use to connect to the nodes. We then specify how frequently the health check should run and how many concurrent failures result in a node as being marked unhealthy. If a node is marked as unhealthy, the Load Balancer will not send it any requests.

Dashboard > Microsoft.LoadBalancer-20200717171327 | Overview > AlwaysOn_LoadBalancer | Health probes >

Add health probe

AlwaysOn_LoadBalancer

Name *

AlwaysOn_HealthProbe

Protocol ⓘ

TCP

Port * ⓘ

50001

Interval * ⓘ

5

seconds

Unhealthy threshold * ⓘ

3

consecutive failures

OK

Figure 7-16. *Add a Health Probe*

Next, we will configure a new load balancing rule by using the Add button on the Load Balancer Rules tab of the Load Balancer blade. In the first section of this blade (Figure 7-17), we will specify a name for the rule, whether the Load Balancer should use IPv4 or IPv6. The Frontend IP address is the IP Address of the Load Balancer that we configured earlier. HA ports allow all ports on the backend pool to be load balanced, but we don't want to do this, so we will leave the box unchecked and select TCP as the protocol.

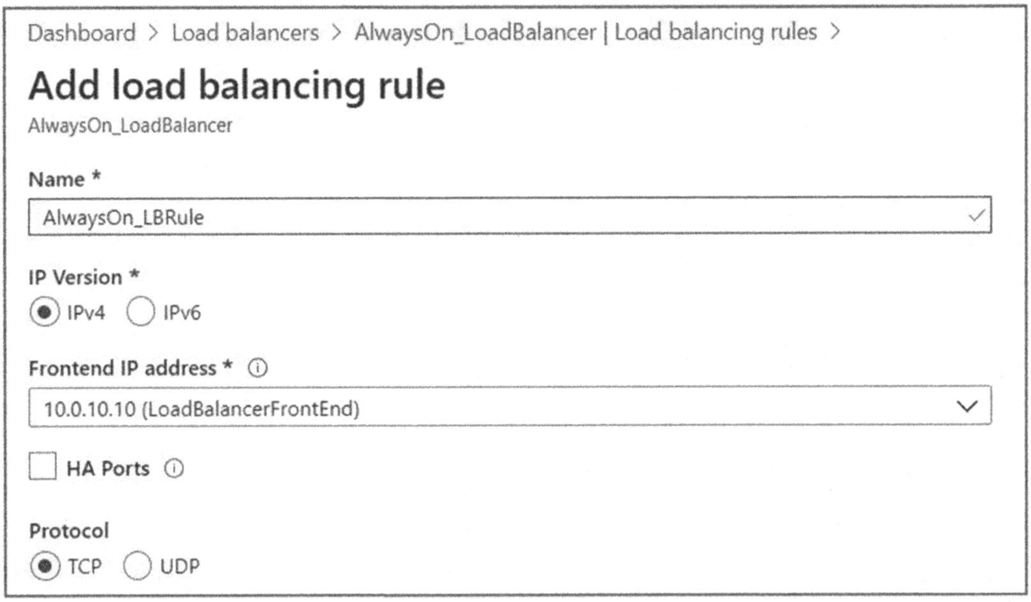

Dashboard > Load balancers > AlwaysOn_LoadBalancer | Load balancing rules >

Add load balancing rule

AlwaysOn_LoadBalancer

Name *

| AlwaysOn_LBRule | ✓ |

IP Version *

(•) IPv4   ( ) IPv6

Frontend IP address * ⓘ

| 10.0.10.10 (LoadBalancerFrontEnd) | ⌄ |

☐ HA Ports ⓘ

Protocol

(•) TCP   ( ) UDP

Figure 7-17. *Configure a Load Balancing Rule (Part 1)*

In the second section of this page, shown in Figure 7-18, we will configure the port that the Load Balancer will be listening on, followed by the port that the servers in the backend pool will be listening on. In our case, this will be port 1433 for both. We will choose the backend pool of servers and the health probe that we just created.

Session persistence specifies how successive requests from clients should be handled. If we select Client IP, then successive requests from the same IP address will be handled by the same server. If we choose Client IP and protocol, then successive requests from the same client will be handled by the same server, but only if the same protocol is used to connect. For Availability Groups, however, session persistence is not required, so we will choose None. This indicates that successive requests by the same client can be handled by any server in the backend pool.

The Idle Timeout indicates the minimum length of time that a connection will be kept open, without clients sending messages, and we will leave TCP reset disabled. Finally, we will select Floating IP, which changes the IP address mapping schema, allowing for multiple listeners, which is required for the Availability Group Listener.

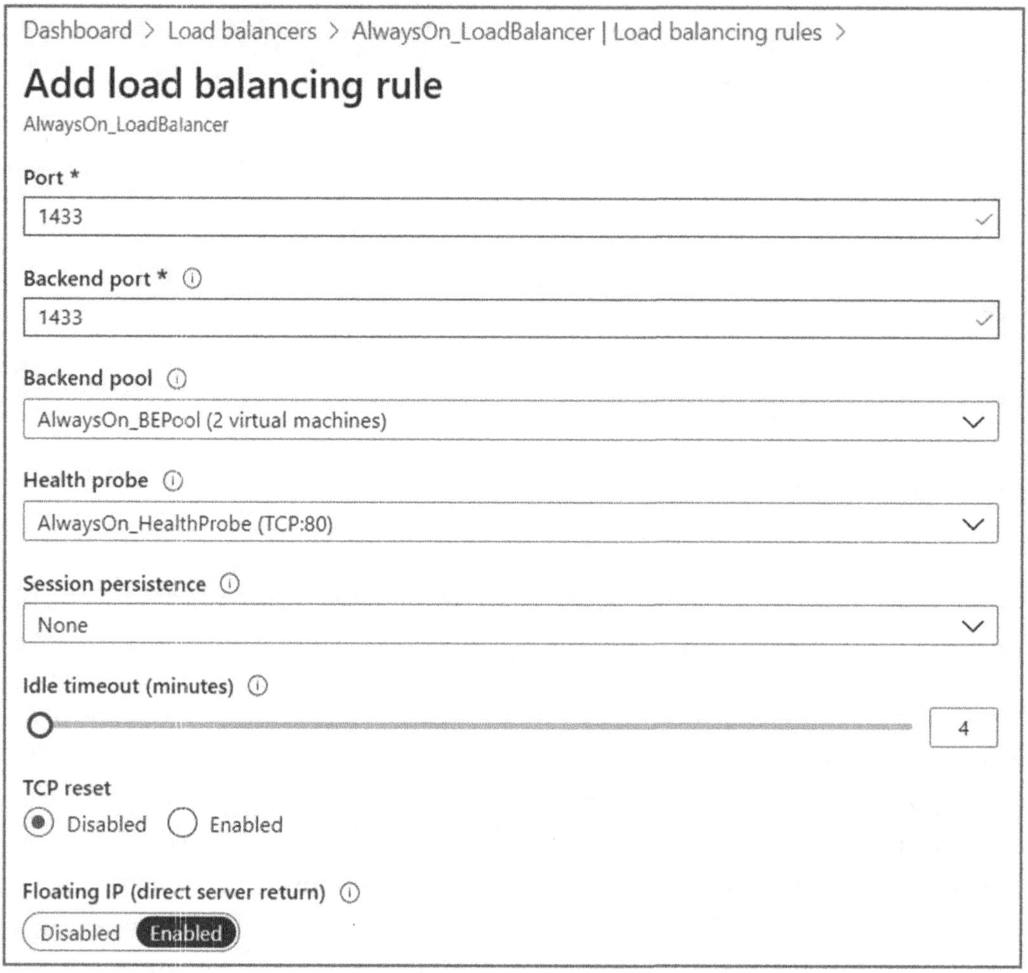

Dashboard > Load balancers > AlwaysOn_LoadBalancer | Load balancing rules >

Add load balancing rule
AlwaysOn_LoadBalancer

Port *

1433 ✓

Backend port * ⓘ

1433 ✓

Backend pool ⓘ

AlwaysOn_BEPool (2 virtual machines) ⌄

Health probe ⓘ

AlwaysOn_HealthProbe (TCP:80) ⌄

Session persistence ⓘ

None ⌄

Idle timeout (minutes) ⓘ

○━━━━━━━━━━━━━━━━━━━━━━━━━━━━━━━━━━━━ | 4 |

TCP reset

◉ Disabled ○ Enabled

Floating IP (direct server return) ⓘ

(Disabled **Enabled**)

***Figure 7-18.** Configure a Load Balancer Rule (Part 2)*

You should repeat this process to add a frontend port and load balancing rule for the core Cluster.

We will then be in a position where we can configure our Availability Group Listener. We will do this from within the Cluster Manager. From the context menu of the Sales Role, drill through Add Resource and choose Client Access Point. This will cause the New Resource Client Access Point wizard to be displayed. On the first page of this wizard, provide a name for the Client Access Point, and assign an IP Address. Because we created each VM on a different subnet, we will need to provide an IP Address for each subnet, as shown in Figure 7-19.

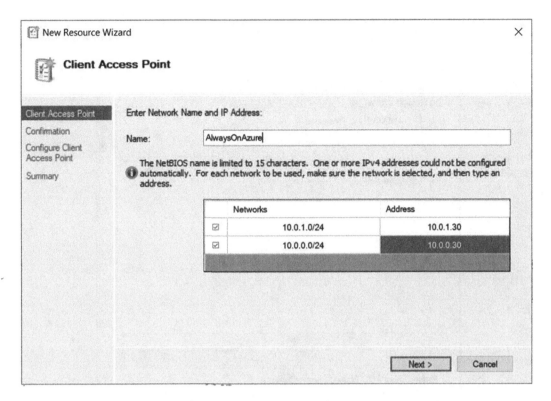

Figure 7-19. *Create New Client Access Point – Client Access Point Page*

When we move to the confirmation page of the wizard, our network settings will be validated. The Confirmation page displays a summary of what we are going to configure.

Once the Client Access Point has been created, we should use the Dependencies tab of Properties dialog box, of the Availability Group resource (shown under Other Resources in the Resource tab of the role) to add a dependency on the Client Access Point, as shown in Figure 7-20.

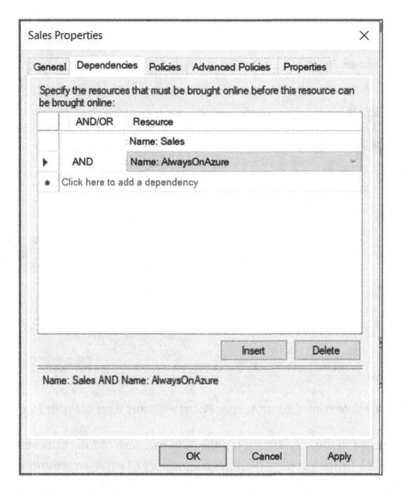

Figure 7-20. *Add a Dependency*

You should also repeat this process to make the Client Access Point dependent on the IP Address resources.

Next, we need to configure the Cluster to work with the Azure Load Balancer. We can do that using the script in Listing 7-2. This script updates each of the IP Address resources, with the Load Balancer IP and health probe port.

Note   Be sure to update the script to match your own configuration before running it.

Listing 7-2. Integrate the Cluster with the Load Balancer

```
$ClusterNetworkName = 'AlwaysOnAzure'
$LoadBalancerIP = '10.0.10.10'
[int]$LoadBalancerProbePort = 50001

Get-ClusterResource 'IP Address 10.0.0.35' | Set-ClusterParameter
-Multiple @{"Address"="$LoadBalancerIP";"ProbePort"=$LoadBalancerProbePort;"
SubnetMask"="255.255.255.0";"Network"="$ClusterNetworkName";"EnableDhcp"=0}

Get-ClusterResource 'IP Address 10.0.0.35' | Set-ClusterParameter
-Multiple @{"Address"="$LoadBalancerIP";"ProbePort"=$LoadBalancerProbePort;"
SubnetMask"="255.255.255.0";"Network"="$ClusterNetworkName";"EnableDhcp"=0}
```

Tip   After creating the Client Access Point, an Availability Group Listener will have been added to the Availability Group, with a default port of 1433. If you plan to use a different port, this can be updated in the Listener, in SQL Server Management Studio.

Clusterless Availability Groups

Clusterless Availability Groups appeared in SQL Server 2017, as a by-product of Linux support, but can also prove valuable to SQL Server DBAs supporting instances on Windows environments.

A clusterless implementation is not suitable for high availability scenarios. This is for several reasons. Firstly, because there is no cluster, there are no health checks. This means that there is no way to automatically arbitrate a failover. Secondly, although it is possible to use synchronous commit between the replicas, to failover without data loss, you will need to prepare the failover by taking the Availability Group offline on the primary Replica. This means that there will be an outage during failover. Finally, because there is no cluster, it is not possible to have a Listener. This means that applications connecting to the primary Replica will need to flip connection strings to point at the secondary Replica in the event of failover.

Tip   It is possible to create a C-NAME record in DNS that points to the Primary replica. You can then update the C-NAME record to point to the secondary replica at point of failover. While this is a manual process, usually involving teams external to the DBA function, it can avoid the need for a client to change its connection string.

Clusterless Availability Groups have most benefit in read-scale scenarios. For this reason, they are also known as Read-scale Availability Groups. Imagine a scenario where you have a SQL Server workload with a high read throughput, from multiple applications, but no HA requirement. You can remove the complexity of clustering while still keeping your databases synchronized. Some client applications can be configured to point to the primary Replica, while other client applications can be configured to point at secondary Replicas.

In this section, we will work on a scenario where we have two servers called Prod and ReadScale. Each server has a default instance of SQL Server 2019 Enterprise Edition installed. Both servers are in Site 1 and are both members of the AlwaysOn.com domain, but there is no cluster. We will configure an Availability Group to provide read-scaling for the Customers database, which is accessed by two applications, but one of the applications only performs read-only operations.

Preparing the Instances

As with all Availability Group scenarios, there are preparation tasks that we need to work through before configuring the Availability Group. The following sections describe how to prepare the instances.

Enable Availability Groups

As always, the first step in preparing an instance for Availability Groups is to enable Availability Groups on the database engine service. We can perform this task with PowerShell or SQL Server Configuration Manager, as demonstrated in Chapter 5. In this instance, we will use Configuration Manager, as shown in Figure 7-21. You will notice that because there is no underlying cluster, the dialog box informs us of this, rather than displaying the underlying cluster name. This task needs to be performed on all instances that will participate in the Availability Group.

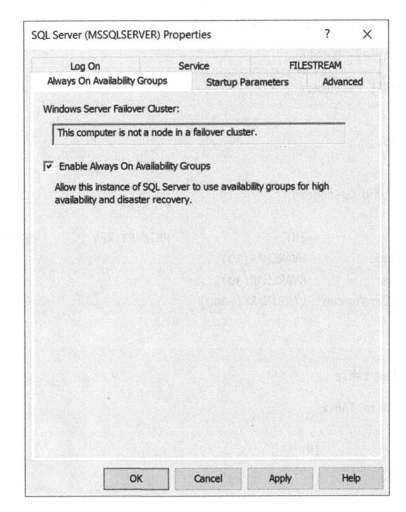

Figure 7-21. *Enable Availability Groups*

After enabling Availability Groups, the service needs to be restated for the change to take effect.

Create the Customers Database

The aim in this scenario is to provide read-scaling for the Customers database. Therefore, we can create the Customers database by using the script in Listing 7-3.

Listing 7-3. Create the Customers Database

```
--Create Customers Database

CREATE DATABASE Customers ;
GO

USE Customers ;
GO

CREATE TABLE dbo.Customers
(
    ID                INT            PRIMARY KEY        IDENTITY,
    FirstName         NVARCHAR(30),
    LastName          NVARCHAR(30),
    CreditCardNumber  VARBINARY(8000)
) ;
GO

--Populate the table

DECLARE @Numbers TABLE
(
    Number          INT
)

;WITH CTE(Number)
AS
(
    SELECT 1 Number
    UNION ALL
    SELECT Number + 1
    FROM CTE
    WHERE Number < 100
)
INSERT INTO @Numbers
SELECT Number FROM CTE
```

```sql
DECLARE @Names TABLE
(
        FirstName          VARCHAR(30),
        LastName           VARCHAR(30)
) ;

INSERT INTO @Names
VALUES('Peter', 'Carter'),
      ('Michael', 'Smith'),
      ('Danielle', 'Mead'),
      ('Reuben', 'Roberts'),
      ('Iris', 'Jones'),
      ('Sylvia', 'Davies'),
      ('Finola', 'Wright'),
      ('Edward', 'James'),
      ('Marie', 'Andrews'),
      ('Jennifer', 'Abraham'),
      ('Margaret', 'Jones')

INSERT INTO Customers(Firstname, LastName, CreditCardNumber)
    SELECT
                FirstName
            , LastName
            , CreditCardNumber
    FROM (
        SELECT
                (SELECT TOP 1 FirstName FROM @Names ORDER BY NEWID())
                FirstName
        , (SELECT TOP 1 LastName FROM @Names ORDER BY NEWID()) LastName
        , (SELECT TOP 1 CONVERT(VARBINARY(8000), (
            (SELECT TOP 1 CAST(Number * 100 AS CHAR(4))
                FROM @Numbers
                WHERE Number BETWEEN 10 AND 99
                ORDER BY NEWID()
            ) + '-' +
```

```
                    (SELECT TOP 1 CAST(Number * 100 AS CHAR(4))
                        FROM @Numbers
                        WHERE Number BETWEEN 10 AND 99 ORDER BY NEWID()
                    ) + '-' +
                    (SELECT TOP 1 CAST(Number * 100 AS CHAR(4))
                        FROM @Numbers
                        WHERE Number BETWEEN 10 AND 99 ORDER BY NEWID()
                    ) + '-' +
                    (SELECT TOP 1 CAST(Number * 100 AS CHAR(4))
                        FROM @Numbers
                        WHERE Number BETWEEN 10 AND 99 ORDER BY NEWID())))
            FROM @Numbers a

        ) CreditCardNumber) d
CROSS JOIN @Numbers b
CROSS JOIN @Numbers c;

--SET FULL recovery mode on the database - required for Availability Groups

ALTER DATABASE Customers SET RECOVERY FULL ;
GO
```

We also need to take a full backup of the database before it can be added to an Availability Group. We can achieve this using the script in Listing 7-4.

Listing 7-4. Back Up the Customers Database

```
--Back Up Customers Database

BACKUP DATABASE Customers
TO  DISK = 'C:\Program Files\Microsoft SQL Server\MSSQL15.MSSQLSERVER\
MSSQL\Backup\Customers.bak'
WITH NAME = 'Customers-Full Database Backup' ;
GO
```

Create Logins

Data synchronization will be performed by the service account(s) that are running the database engine services. Therefore, the service account(s) will require logins on all of the instances that will become Replicas in the Availability Group. In our scenario, both of the instance are running under the ALWAYSON\SqlServiceAccount domain account. Therefore, running the script in Listing 7-5 on all participating instances will create the required logins.

Listing 7-5. Create the Logins

```
CREATE LOGIN [ALWAYSON\SQLServiceAccount]
FROM WINDOWS ;
GO
```

Tip   If the servers were not members of the domain, then we could configure authentication using SQL logins and certificates.

Create and Configure the Availability Group

The first step in creating the Availability Group is to create the endpoint, which the Availability Group will use for sending messages between the Replicas. We also need to give the service account permissions to connect to the Endpoint. This can be achieved with the script in Listing 7-6.

Listing 7-6. Create the Endpoint

```
--Create the Endpoint

CREATE ENDPOINT ClusterlessEndpoint
    AS TCP (LISTENER_PORT = 5022)
    FOR DATA_MIRRORING (
        ROLE = ALL,
        ENCRYPTION = REQUIRED ALGORITHM AES
    ) ;
GO

--Start the Endpoint
ALTER ENDPOINT ClusterlessEndpoint STATE = STARTED ;
GO
```

```
--Grant Permissions to the Service Account
```

```
GRANT CONNECT ON ENDPOINT::ClusterlessEndpoint TO [ALWAYSON\
SQLServiceAccount];
GO
```

With the Endpoint in place, we can now go ahead and create the Availability Group. As always, we have a choice of using T-SQL, the New Availability Group wizard, or the New Availability Group dialog box. In this instance, we will use T-SQL by running the script in Listing 7-7. Note that the CLUSTER_TYPE option is set to NONE.

Listing 7-7. Create the Availability Group

```
USE master
GO

CREATE AVAILABILITY GROUP Customers_Clusterless
WITH (
      AUTOMATED_BACKUP_PREFERENCE = SECONDARY,
      CLUSTER_TYPE = NONE
)
FOR DATABASE Customers
REPLICA ON 'PROD' WITH (
      ENDPOINT_URL = 'TCP://PROD.AlwaysOn.com:5022',
      FAILOVER_MODE = MANUAL,
      AVAILABILITY_MODE = ASYNCHRONOUS_COMMIT,
      SEEDING_MODE = AUTOMATIC,
      SECONDARY_ROLE(ALLOW_CONNECTIONS = ALL)
),
'READSCALE' WITH (
      ENDPOINT_URL = 'TCP://READSCALE.AlwaysOn.com:5022',
      FAILOVER_MODE = MANUAL,
      AVAILABILITY_MODE = ASYNCHRONOUS_COMMIT,
      SEEDING_MODE = AUTOMATIC,
      SECONDARY_ROLE(ALLOW_CONNECTIONS = ALL)
) ;
GO
```

Finally, we can join the secondary Replica to the Availability Group by running the script in Listing 7-8, against the secondary instance.

Listing 7-8. Join the Secondary Replica to the Availability Group

```
ALTER AVAILABILITY GROUP Customers_Clusterless JOIN WITH (CLUSTER_TYPE =
NONE) ;
GO

ALTER AVAILABILITY GROUP Customers_Clusterless GRANT CREATE ANY DATABASE ;
GO
```

Another use case for clusterless Availability Groups is migrations. If you have a database that you need to migrate to a new server, you can easily configure a clusterless Availability Group to support a side-by-side migration.

Once the Availability Group is configured, users can check their application with read-only operations against the new instance while continuing to use their existing database. Once they are happy, the Availability Group can be failed over and the old instance decommissioned.

Domain-Independent Availability Groups

On the surface, domain-independent Clusters, also known as Workgroup Clusters and Availability Groups, may seem a little odd. If a company is large enough that it needs to run SQL Server Enterprise (or even Standard), then it is surely large enough and very likely to have a domain and the ability to create standard clusters. But if you think harder, there are many more use cases where enterprises may benefit from domain-independent high availability and disaster recovery. For example, imagine that you have a hybrid cloud environment. Instead of stretching your domain into Azure, or AWS, your company has decided to create a new domain in the cloud and form a trust relationship between the two. You then decide that you would like to use Availability Groups to synchronize a database between on-premise and the cloud, so that your databases supporting your online sales application are in the cloud, for the lowest latency, but you also want DR back to on-premise. Without domain-independent clusters or Availability Groups, this would only be possible using clusterless Availability Groups, meaning that you could not make use of the Listener.

In this section, we will explore how to create a domain-independent cluster and Availability Group. For networking simplicity, we will configure this between two servers in a workgroup within our Site1 subnet. In this scenario, there will be no domain. However, it is worthy of note that this method can also be used to create a cluster (and Availability Group) between two separate domains, or between a domain and a workgroup.

We will build the cluster and Availability Group across two nodes, named ClusterNode1 and ClusterNode2, in the same workgroup for the purpose of offloading read-only reporting. A default instance of SQL Server is installed on each node.

Preparing for the Cluster

It is a requirement that all nodes within the cluster need to add a common Primary DNS Suffix. This can be achieved by navigating to Control Panel ➤ System and Security ➤ System and selecting Change Settings in the Computer Name, Domain and Workgroup Settings area of the screen, to invoke the System Properties dialog box, where the Change button can be used to invoke the Computer Name/Domain Changes dialog box. You can now use the More button to invoke the DNS Suffix and NetBIOS Computer Name dialog box, shown in Figure 7-22. Here, we will enter our common DNS Suffix.

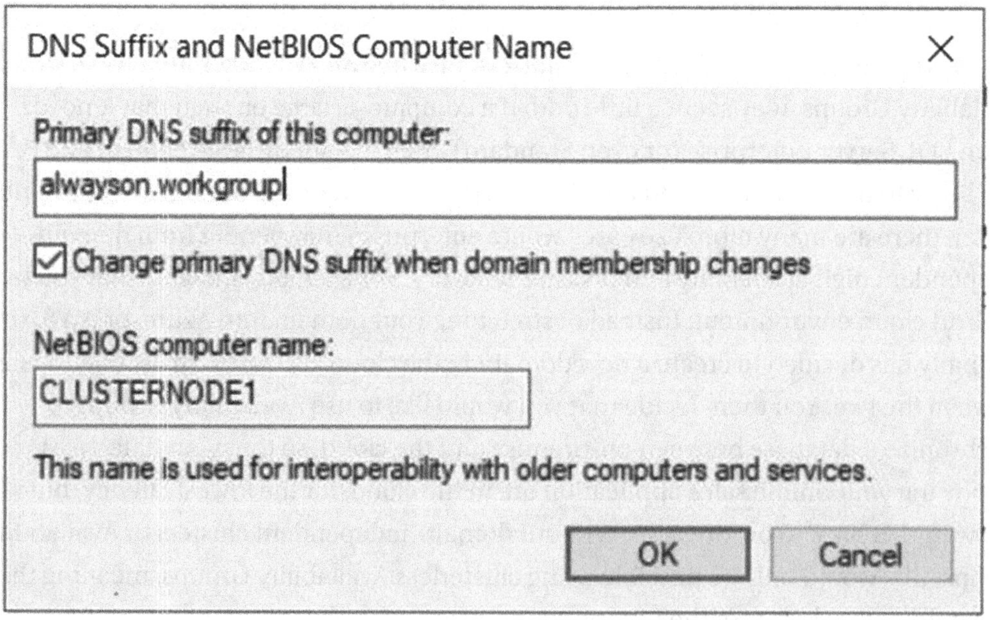

Figure 7-22. *DNS Suffix and NetBIOS Computer Name*

We also need to ensure that an account exists on all cluster nodes that has the same username and the same password and has local administrator permissions. In our scenario, we will use the built-in Administrator, but if we were to use any other account, then we must also set the value of LocalAccountTokenFilterPolicy to 1 in the registry. This can be achieved by using the PowerShell command in Listing 7-9.

Listing 7-9. Set LocalAccountTokenFilterPolicy

```
New-ItemProperty -path HKLM:\SOFTWARE\Microsoft\Windows\CurrentVersion\
Policies\System -Name LocalAccountTokenFilterPolicy -Value 1
```

Create the Cluster

We can now create the cluster by using the script in Listing 7-10. There are two interesting points to note here. Firstly, we are using the AdministrativeAccessPoint parameter, with a configuration value of DNS. This will create the Cluster Name Object but not attempt to create computer objects in Active Directory, which of course is not supported in a domain-independent cluster.

The second interesting point is that we have chosen to use a cluster disk as the witness. This is because a file share witness is not supported in domain-independent clusters.

Listing 7-10. Create the Cluster

```
New-Cluster -Name AOAGWorkGroupCluster -Node ClusterNode1,
ClusterNode2 -StaticAddress 10.0.0.52 -AdministrativeAccessPoint DNS

Set-ClusterQuorum -DiskWitness "Cluster Disk 1"
```

Preparing for the Availability Group

The first step in preparing for the Availability Group is to enable Availability Groups on the SQL Server service of all nodes that will participate. Information on how to do this can be found in the "Clusterless Availability Groups" section of this chapter.

Because there is no Active Directory authentication possible in this topology, the database_mirroring endpoints will require certificates to communicate with each other. We will also need SQL logins, which will be granted permissions to connect to the endpoint. Therefore, we will first need to create the certificates. This can be achieved using the script in Listing 7-11. Here, we first create a Database Master Key in the master database. We then create a certificate and back up that certificate to the operating system. This should be repeated on all nodes that will participate in the Availability Group, using a different certificate name for each instance.

Listing 7-11. Create the Certificates

```
USE master
GO

--Create the Database Master key

CREATE MASTER KEY ENCRYPTION BY PASSWORD = 'Pa$$w0rd';
GO

-- Create the certificate

CREATE CERTIFICATE Node1Cert
WITH SUBJECT = 'ClusterNode1 Certificate';
GO

--Back up the certificate

BACKUP CERTIFICATE Node1Cert
TO FILE = 'c:\Certificates\Node1Cert.cer';
GO
```

We now need to create a login for every node, which will be granted permissions to connect to the endpoint. We can achieve this using the script in Listing 7-12. These logins should be created on all instances that will participate in the Availability Group. Therefore, the script should be run against all instances.

Listing 7-12. Create the Logins

```
CREATE LOGIN ClusterNode1_AOAG
WITH PASSWORD = 'Pa$$w0rd';
GO
```

```
CREATE USER ClusterNode1_AOAG
FOR LOGIN ClusterNode1_AOAG;
GO

CREATE LOGIN ClusterNode2_AOAG
WITH PASSWORD = 'Pa$$w0rd';
GO

CREATE USER ClusterNode2_AOAG
FOR LOGIN ClusterNode2_AOAG;
GO
```

We can now copy the certificate for each instance to all other instances and restore them using the command in Listing 7-13. For each instance, you should change the certificate and usernames appropriately. This listing shows the command that should be run on CLUSTERNODE1, in our topology.

Listing 7-13. Restore the Certificates

```
CREATE CERTIFICATE Node2Cert
AUTHORIZATION ClusterNode2_AOAG
FROM FILE = 'C:\Certificates\Node2Cert.cer'
```

Finally, now that the certificates exist on each of the nodes, we can go ahead and create the database_mirroring endpoint, on each of the nodes. This can be achieved using the script in Listing 7-14. This script needs to be run on each of the nodes, with the certificate changed to match the node.

Listing 7-14. Create the Endpoint

```
--Create the endpoint
CREATE ENDPOINT AOAG_Endpoint
STATE = STARTED
AS TCP (
     LISTENER_PORT = 5022,
     LISTENER_IP = ALL
)
```

```
FOR DATABASE_MIRRORING (
    AUTHENTICATION = CERTIFICATE Node1Cert,
    ROLE = ALL
)

--Grant each user permissions to connect to the endpoint
GRANT CONNECT ON ENDPOINT::AOAG_Endpoint TO ClusterNode1_AOAG;
GO

GRANT CONNECT ON ENDPOINT::AOAG_Endpoint TO ClusterNode2_AOAG;
GO
```

You can now create an Availability Group using the techniques discussed in Chapter 5 of this book.

Distributed Availability Groups

Distributed Availability Groups (DAG) are an extension of Availability Groups, which allow for data to be synchronized between two separate Availability Groups. This is an exciting technology, with many different use cases. For example, it allows data synchronization between Windows- and Linux-based Availability Groups, it allows the number of readable secondary replicas to be extended beyond 8 (which is the limit for a standard Availability Group), and it allows cross-site replication, without the complexity of a stretch cluster. Distributed Availability Groups can also help server migrations by providing data synchronization when an in-place upgrade is not possible and a side-by-side migration is required. They can also be used as an alternative to domain-independent Availability Groups when you have servers in different domains.

While each side of the Distributed Availability Group can be a Windows Failover Cluster, this is not a requirement, as the focus is very much on maintaining the databases, and no cluster configuration occurs.

In this section, we will illustrate the technology by configuring DAGs for our HR Availability Group that we created in Chapter 5, between our ALWAYSON-C Cluster and a Linux-based Availability Group called Linux_AOAG which is hosted on two Linux servers, participating in a Pacemaker cluster.

The first step is to create the Distributed Availability Group on the Linux cluster. This can be achieved by using the script in Listing 7-15. Note the WITH (DISTRIBUTED) syntax, followed by the specifications of each Availability Group.

Note   Before starting, you should remove existing databases from the HR Availability Group; otherwise, it will not be able to join the Distributed Availability Group as the secondary Availability Group must be empty.

Listing 7-15. Create the Distributed Availability Group

```
CREATE AVAILABILITY GROUP DistributedAG
   WITH (DISTRIBUTED)
   AVAILABILITY GROUP ON
      'HR' WITH
      (
         LISTENER_URL = 'tcp://HRListener.alwayson.com:1433',
         AVAILABILITY_MODE = ASYNCHRONOUS_COMMIT,
         FAILOVER_MODE = MANUAL,
         SEEDING_MODE = AUTOMATIC
      ),
      'Linux_AOAG' WITH
      (
         LISTENER_URL = 'tcp://LinuxListener:5022',
         AVAILABILITY_MODE = ASYNCHRONOUS_COMMIT,
         FAILOVER_MODE = MANUAL,
         SEEDING_MODE = AUTOMATIC
      );
GO
```

We can now run the command in Listing 7-16, against the PROSQLADMIN-C cluster, to join it to the Distributed Availability Group.

Listing 7-16. Join the Second Availability Group

```
ALTER AVAILABILITY GROUP DistributedAG
    JOIN
    AVAILABILITY GROUP ON
        'HR' WITH
        (
            LISTENER_URL = 'tcp://HRListener.alwayson.com:1433',
            AVAILABILITY_MODE = ASYNCHRONOUS_COMMIT,
            FAILOVER_MODE = MANUAL,
            SEEDING_MODE = AUTOMATIC
        ),
        'Linux_AOAG' WITH
        (
            LISTENER_URL = 'tcp://LinuxListener:5022',
            AVAILABILITY_MODE = ASYNCHRONOUS_COMMIT,
            FAILOVER_MODE = MANUAL,
            SEEDING_MODE = AUTOMATIC
        ) ;
GO
```

Tip   Databases will need to be manually joined to secondary replicas within the secondary Availability Group.

Summary

Availability Groups offer a large amount of flexibility, enabling DBAs to configure high availability, disaster recovery, or read-scaling in almost any situation. Examples of atypical Availability Group topologies include configuring Availability Groups across Azure VMs, configuring Availability Groups with no underlying cluster, and configuring Availability Groups across domains, or with no domain at all.

When creating Availability Groups in Azure VMs, high availability can best be achieved by splitting the VMs across Availability Sets and Availability Zones, while DR can best be achieved by placing the DR node in a different Azure Region. In this scenario, data sovereignty can be maintained by using Azure paired regions, which are inside the same political geography while still geographically dispersing the solution.

Clusterless Availability Groups cannot be used to achieve high availability. This is because there is no cluster to perform node health checks. They are very well suited to read-scale scenarios, however, where the complexity of the clustering components can be avoided.

Domain-independent Availability Groups (also known as workgroup availability groups) allow for Availability Groups to be configured across multiple domains, or where there is no domain at all. They are especially well suited to hybrid cloud scenarios, where your organization has chosen to create a separate domain in the cloud, as opposed to stretching their on-premise domain.

Distributed Availability Groups can be used as an alternative to domain-independent Availability groups in hybrid cloud scenarios. Additionally, they provide the flexibility to distributed data across platforms. For example, data can be replicated between a Windows-based Availability Group and a Linux-based Availability Group.

Basic Availability Groups provide the option to configure Availability Groups on instances running SQL Server Standard Edition. If you choose to use this feature, however, then the functionality is limited. Only two replicas are supported and there can only be a single database per Availability Group. Additionally, there is no option to use read-only routing.

CHAPTER 8

Administering AlwaysOn

This chapter will discuss how to administer AlwaysOn features. We will first look at cluster maintenance, including rolling patch upgrades and removing an instance. We will then discuss managing Availability Groups, including how to fail over synchronously and asynchronously. We will also examine how to fail over a Distributed Availability Group.

Additional maintenance tasks, such as synchronizing instance-level objects, safe-stating an application, and adding multiple Listeners to an Availability Group will also be discussed. The chapter will end by discussing how to suspend data movement and how to remove a database from an Availability Group.

Managing a Cluster

Installing the cluster is not the end of the road from an administrative perspective. You still need to periodically perform maintenance tasks. The following sections describe some of the most common maintenance tasks.

Moving the Instance Between Nodes

Other than protecting against unplanned outages, one of the benefits of implementing high availability technologies is that doing so significantly reduces downtime for maintenance tasks, such as patching. This can be at the operating system level or the SQL Server level.

If you have a two-node cluster, apply the patch to the passive node first. Once you are happy that the update was successful, fail over the instance and then apply the patch to the other node. At this point, you may or may not wish to fail back to the original node,

© Peter A. Carter 2020
P. A. Carter, *SQL Server 2019 AlwaysOn*, https://doi.org/10.1007/978-1-4842-6479-9_8

depending on the needs of your environment. For example, if the overriding priority is the level of availability of the instance, then you may not wish to fail back, because this will incur another short outage.

To move an instance to a different node using Failover Cluster Manager, select Move ➤ Select Node from the context menu of the role that contains the instance. This causes the Move Clustered Role dialog box to display. Here, you can select the node to which you wish to move the role, as illustrated in Figure 8-1.

Figure 8-1. *The Move Clustered Role Dialog Box*

The role is then moved to the new node. If you watch the role's resources window in Failover Cluster Manager, then you see each resource move through the states of Online ➤ Offline Pending ➤ Offline. The new node is now displayed as the owner before the resources move in turn through the states of Offline ➤ Online Pending ➤ Online. The resources are taken offline and placed back online in order of their dependencies.

We can also fail over a role using PowerShell. To do this, we need to use the Move-ClusterGroup cmdlet. Listing 8-1 demonstrates this by using the cmdlet to fail over the MSDTC cluster role to ClusterNode2. We use the -Name parameter to specify the role that we wish to move and the -Node parameter to specify the node to which we wish to move it.

Listing 8-1. Moving the Role Between Nodes

```
Move-ClusterGroup -Name ALWAYSON-MSDTC-C -Node ClusterNode2
```

Rolling Patch Upgrade

If you have a cluster with more than two nodes, then consider performing a rolling patch upgrade when you are applying updates for SQL Server. In this scenario, you mitigate the risk of having different nodes, which are possible owners of the role, running different versions or patch levels of SQL Server.

The first thing that you should do is make a list of all nodes that are possible owners of the role. Then, select 50% of these nodes and remove them from the Possible Owners list. You can do this by selecting Properties from the context menu of the Name resource and then, in the Advanced Policies tab, unchecking the nodes in the possible owners list, as illustrated in Figure 8-2.

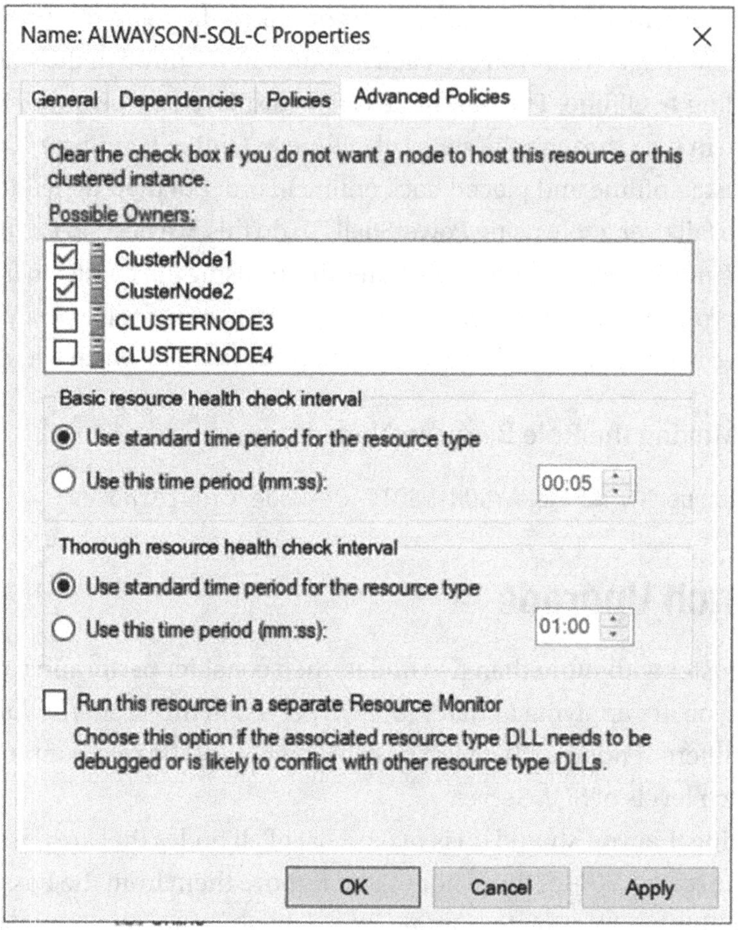

Figure 8-2. *Remove Possible Owners*

To achieve the same result using PowerShell, we can use the Get-Resource cmdlet to navigate to the name resource and then pipe in the Set-ClusterOwnerNode to configure the possible owners list. This is demonstrated in Listing 8-2. The possible owners list is comma separated in the event that you are configuring multiple possible owners.

Listing 8-2. Configuring Possible Owners

```
Get-ClusterResource "SQL Network Name (ALWAYSON-SQL-C)" |
Set-ClusterOwnerNode -Owners clusternode1
```

Once 50% of the nodes have been removed as possible owners, you should apply the update to these nodes. After the update has been verified on this half of the nodes, you should reconfigure them to allow them to be possible owners once more.

The next step is to move the role to one of the nodes that you have upgraded. After failover has successfully completed, remove the other half of the nodes from the preferred owners list before applying the update to these nodes. Once the update has been verified on this half of the nodes, you can return them to the possible owners list.

Tip   The possible owners can only be set on a resource. If you run `Set-ClusterOwnerNode` against a role using the `-Group` parameter, then you are configuring preferred owners rather than possible owners.

Removing a Node from the Cluster

Note   Do not follow the demonstration in this section, if you wish to follow the subsequent demonstrations in this book.

If you wish to uninstall an AlwaysOn failover cluster instance, then you cannot perform this action from Control Panel as you would a stand-alone instance. Instead, you must run the Remove Node Wizard on each of the nodes of the cluster. You can invoke this wizard by selecting Remove Node from a SQL Server Failover Cluster option from the Maintenance tab in SQL Server Installation Center.

The wizard starts by running a global rules check, followed by a rules check for removing a node. Then, on the Cluster Node Configuration page shown in Figure 8-3, you are asked to confirm the instance for which you wish to remove a node. If the cluster hosts multiple instances, you can select the appropriate instance from the drop-down box.

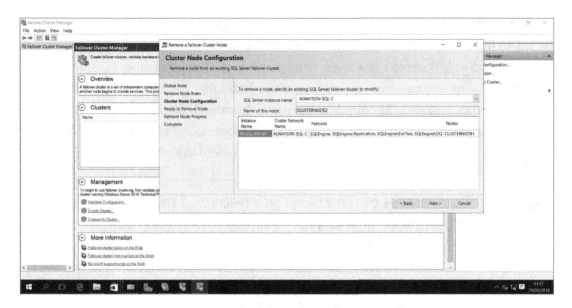

Figure 8-3. *The Cluster Node Configuration Page*

On the Ready to Remove Node page, you are given a summary of the tasks that will be performed. After confirming the details, the instance is removed. This process should be repeated on all passive nodes and then finally on the active node. When the instance is removed from the final node, the cluster role is also removed.

To remove a node using PowerShell, we need to run SQL Server's `setup.exe` application, with the action parameter configured as `RemoveNode`. When you use PowerShell to remove a node, the parameters in Table 8-1 are mandatory.

Table 8-1. *Mandatory Parameters When Removing a Node from a Cluster*

Parameter	Usage
`/ACTION`	Must be configured as `RemoveNode`.
`/INSTANCENAME`	The instance that you are adding the extra node to support.
`/CONFIRMIPDEPENDENCYCHANGE`	Allows multiple IP addresses to be specified for multi-subnet clusters. Pass in a value of `1` for `True` or `0` for `False`.

The script in Listing 8-3 removes a node from our cluster when we run it from the root directory of the SQL Server installation media.

Listing 8-3. Removing a Node

```
.\setup.exe /ACTION="RemoveNode" /INSTANCENAME="ALWAYSON-SQL-C"
/CONFIRMIPDEPENDENCYCHANGE=0 /qs
```

Managing AlwaysOn Availability Groups

Once the initial setup of your availability group is complete, you still need to perform administrative tasks. These include failing over the availability group, monitoring, and on rare occasions, adding additional listeners. These topics are discussed in the following sections.

Failover

If a replica is in Synchronous Commit mode and is configured for automatic failover, then the availability group automatically moves to a redundant replica in the event of an error condition being met on the primary replica. There are occasions, however, when you will want to manually fail over an availability group. This could be because of DR testing, proactive maintenance, or because you need to bring up an asynchronous replica following a failure of the primary replica or the primary data center.

Synchronous Failover

If you wish to fail over a replica that is in Synchronous Commit mode, launch the Failover Availability Group wizard by selecting Failover from the context menu of your availability group in Object Explorer. After moving past the Introduction page, you find the Select New Primary Replica page (see Figure 8-4). On this page, check the box of the replica to which you want to fail over. Before doing so, however, review the Failover Readiness column to ensure that the replicas are synchronized and that no data loss will occur.

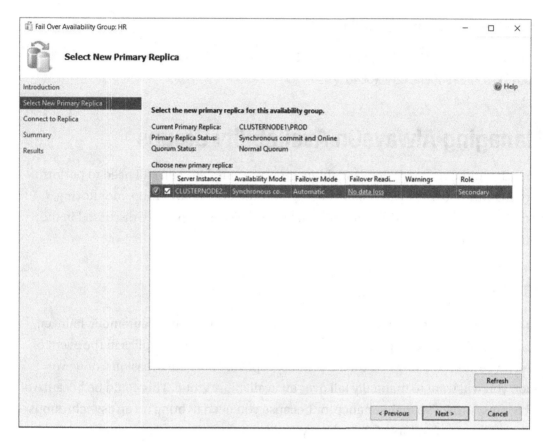

Figure 8-4. *The Select New Primary Replica Page*

On the Connect to Replica page, illustrated in Figure 8-5, use the Connect button to establish a connection to the new primary replica.

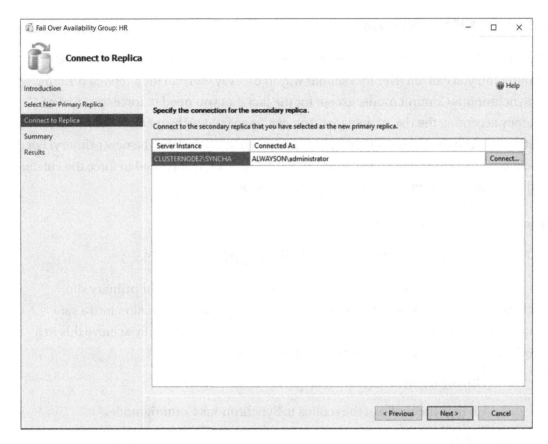

Figure 8-5. *The Connect to Replica Page*

On the Summary page, you are given details of the task to be performed, followed by a progress indicator on the Results page. Once the failover completes, check that all tasks were successful, and investigate any errors or warnings that you receive.

We can also use T-SQL to fail over the availability group. The command in Listing 8-4 achieves the same results. Make sure to run this script from the replica that will be the new primary replica. If you run it from the current primary replica, use SQLCMD mode and connect to the new primary within the script.

Listing 8-4. Failing Over an Availability Group

```
ALTER AVAILABILITY GROUP HR FAILOVER ;
GO
```

Asynchronous Failover

If your availability group is in Asynchronous Commit mode, then from a technical standpoint, you can fail over in a similar way to the way you can for a replica running in Synchronous Commit mode, except for the fact that you need to force the failover, thereby accepting the risk of data loss. You can force failover by using the command in Listing 8-5. You should run this script on the instance that will be the new primary. For it to work, the cluster must have quorum. If it doesn't, then you need to force the cluster online before you force the availability group online.

Listing 8-5. Forcing Failover

```
ALTER AVAILABILITY GROUP HR FORCE_FAILOVER_ALLOW_DATA_LOSS ;
```

From a process perspective, you should only ever do this if your primary site is completely unavailable. If this is not the case, first put the application into a safe state. This avoids any possibility of data loss. The way that I normally achieve this in a production environment is by performing the following steps:

1. Disable logins.

2. Change the mode of the replica to Synchronous Commit mode.

3. Fail over.

4. Change the replica back to Asynchronous Commit mode.

5. Enable the logins.

You can perform these steps with the script in Listing 8-6. When run from the DR instance, this script places the databases in HR into a safe state before failing over, and then it reconfigures the application to work under normal operations.

Listing 8-6. Safe-Stating an Application and Failing Over

```
--DISABLE LOGINS

DECLARE @AOAGDBs TABLE
(
DBName NVARCHAR(128)
) ;
```

```
INSERT INTO @AOAGDBs
SELECT database_name
FROM sys.availability_groups AG
INNER JOIN sys.availability_databases_cluster ADC
        ON AG.group_id = ADC.group_id
WHERE AG.name = 'HR' ;

DECLARE @Mappings TABLE
(
    LoginName NVARCHAR(128),
    DBname NVARCHAR(128),
    UserName NVARCHAR(128),
    AliasName NVARCHAR(128)
) ;

INSERT INTO @Mappings
EXEC sp_msloginmappings ;

DECLARE @SQL NVARCHAR(MAX)

SELECT DISTINCT @SQL =
(
        SELECT 'ALTER LOGIN [' + LoginName + '] DISABLE; ' AS [data()]
        FROM @Mappings M
        INNER JOIN @AOAGDBs A
                ON M.DBname = A.DBName
        WHERE LoginName <> SUSER_NAME()
        FOR XML PATH ('')
)

EXEC(@SQL)
GO

--SWITCH TO SYNCHRONOUS COMMIT MODE

ALTER AVAILABILITY GROUP HR
MODIFY REPLICA ON N'CLUSTERNODE3\ASYNCDR' WITH (AVAILABILITY_MODE =
SYNCHRONOUS_COMMIT) ;
GO
```

```
--FAIL OVER

ALTER AVAILABILITY GROUP HR FAILOVER
GO

--SWITCH BACK TO ASYNCHRONOUS COMMIT MODE

ALTER AVAILABILITY GROUP HR
MODIFY REPLICA ON N'CLUSTERNODE3\ASYNCDR' WITH (AVAILABILITY_MODE =
ASYNCHRONOUS_COMMIT) ;
GO

--ENABLE LOGINS

DECLARE @AOAGDBs TABLE
(
DBName NVARCHAR(128)
) ;

INSERT INTO @AOAGDBs
SELECT database_name
FROM sys.availability_groups AG
INNER JOIN sys.availability_databases_cluster ADC
        ON AG.group_id = ADC.group_id
WHERE AG.name = 'HR' ;

DECLARE @Mappings TABLE
(
    LoginName NVARCHAR(128),
    DBname NVARCHAR(128),
    Username NVARCHAR(128),
    AliasName NVARCHAR(128)
) ;

INSERT INTO @Mappings
EXEC sp_msloginmappings

DECLARE @SQL NVARCHAR(MAX)
```

```
SELECT DISTINCT @SQL =
(
        SELECT 'ALTER LOGIN [' + LoginName + '] ENABLE; ' AS [data()]
        FROM @Mappings M
        INNER JOIN @AOAGDBs A
                ON M.DBname = A.DBName
        WHERE LoginName <> SUSER_NAME()
        FOR XML PATH ('')
) ;

EXEC(@SQL)
```

Failing Over a Distributed Availability Group

Distributed availability groups do not support automatic failover; only manual failover is supported. When you need to fail over to a secondary Availability Group, within a Distributed Availability Group, you should perform the following steps:

- Set the synchronization mode to synchronous commit.

- Wait for the secondary Availability Group to become synchronized.

- Set the primary Availability Group to take the role of the secondary.

- Force Failover.

The script in Listing 8-7 will force failover for the Distributed Availability Group discussed in Chapter 6.

Listing 8-7. Fail Over a Distributed Availability Group

```
--Set the secondary Availability Group to synchronous commit mode

ALTER AVAILABILITY GROUP DistributedAG
MODIFY
AVAILABILITY GROUP ON
'HR' WITH
  (
   LISTENER_URL = 'tcp://HRListener.alwayson.com:1433',
   AVAILABILITY_MODE = ASYNCHRONOUS_COMMIT,
   FAILOVER_MODE = MANUAL,
```

```
    SEEDING_MODE = MANUAL
    ),
'Linux_AOAG' WITH
  (
  LISTENER_URL = 'tcp://LinuxListener:5022',
  AVAILABILITY_MODE = SYNCHRONOUS_COMMIT,
  FAILOVER_MODE = MANUAL,
  SEEDING_MODE = MANUAL
  );

--Wait until the Availability Groups are synchronized

WHILE (SELECT COUNT(DISTINCT synchronization_state_desc)
FROM (
      SELECT
            ag.name
      , drs.database_id
      , drs.group_id
      , drs.replica_id
      , drs.synchronization_state_desc
      , drs.end_of_log_lsn
      FROM sys.dm_hadr_database_replica_states drs
      INNER JOIN sys.availability_groups ag
            ON drs.group_id = ag.group_id
      WHERE ag.name = 'HR'
            AND synchronization_state_desc = 'synchronized'
      ) a
) > 1
BEGIN
      WAITFOR DELAY'00:00:05' ;
END

--Assign the primary Availability Group, the secondary role

ALTER AVAILABILITY GROUP DistributedAG SET (ROLE = SECONDARY) ;

--Force the failover

ALTER AVAILABILITY GROUP DistributedAG FORCE_FAILOVER_ALLOW_DATA_LOSS ;
```

Synchronizing Uncontained Objects

Regardless of the method you use to fail over, assuming that all of the databases within the availability group are not contained, then you need to ensure that instance-level objects are synchronized. The most straightforward way to keep your instance-level objects synchronized is by implementing an SSIS package, which is scheduled to run on a periodic basis.

Whether you choose to schedule a SSIS package to execute or you choose a different approach, such as a SQL Server Agent job that scripts and re-creates the objects on the secondary servers, these are the objects that you should consider synchronizing:

- Logins

- Credentials

- SQL Server Agent jobs

- Custom error messages

- Linked servers

- Server-level event notifications

- Stored procedures in Master

- Server-level triggers

- Encryption keys and certificates

Adding Multiple Listeners

Usually, each availability group has a single Availability Group Listener, but there are some rare instances in which you may need to create multiple listeners for the same availability group. One scenario in which this may be required is if you have legacy applications with hard-coded connection strings. Here, you can create an extra listener with a client access point that matches the name of the hard-coded connection string.

As mentioned earlier in this chapter, it is not possible to create a second Availability Group Listener through SQL Server Management Studio, T-SQL, or even PowerShell. Instead, we must use Failover Cluster Manager. Here, we create a new Client Access Point resource within our HR role. To do this, we select Add Resource from the context menu of the HR role and then select Client Access Point. This causes the New Resource

Wizard to be invoked. The Client Access Point page of the wizard is illustrated in Figure 8-6. You can see that we have entered the DNS name for the client access point and specified an IP address from each subnet.

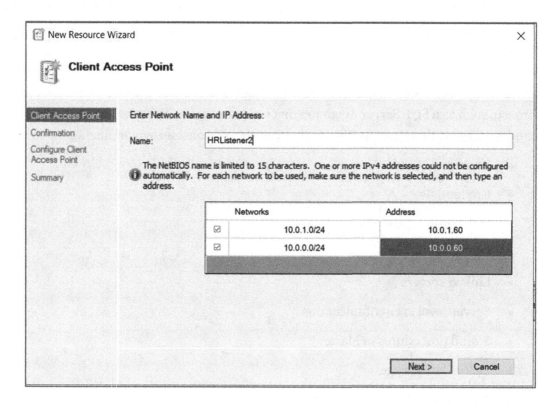

Figure 8-6. *The Client Access Point Page*

On the Confirmation page, we are shown a summary of the configuration that will be performed. On the Configure Client Access Point page, we see a progress indicator, before we are finally shown a completion summary on the Summary page, which is illustrated in Figure 8-7.

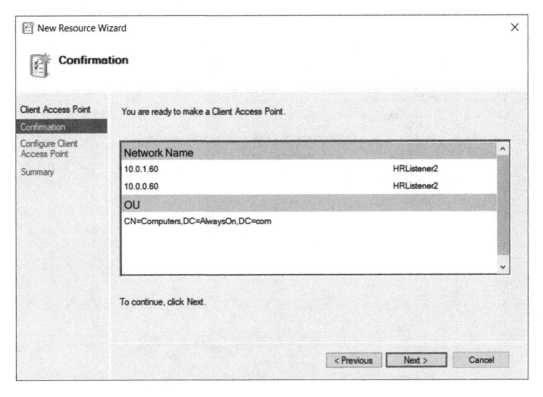

Figure 8-7. *The Confirmation Page*

Now, we need to configure the Availability Group resource to be dependent upon the new client access point. To do this, we select Properties from the context menu of the HR resource and then navigate to the Dependencies tab. Here, we add the new client access point as a dependency and configure an OR constraint between the two listeners, as illustrated in Figure 8-8. Once we apply this change, clients are able to connect using either of the two listener names.

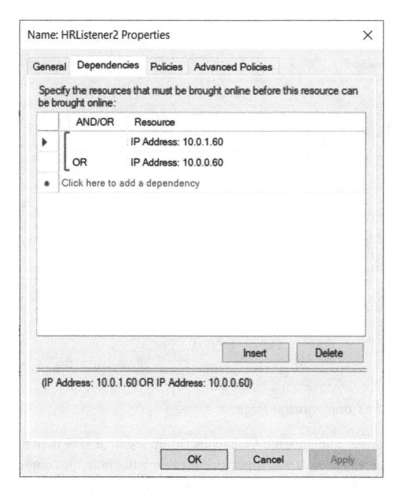

Figure 8-8. *The Dependencies Tab*

Other Administrative Considerations

When databases are made highly available with AlwaysOn Availability Groups, several
limitations are imposed. One of the most restrictive of these is that databases cannot be
placed in single_user mode or be made read only. This can have an impact when you
need to safe-state your application for maintenance. This is why in the "Failover" section
of this chapter, we disabled the logins that have users mapped to the databases. If you
must place your database in single-user mode, then you must first remove it from the
availability group.

A database can be removed from an availability group by running the command in Listing 8-8. This command removes the Customers database from the Sales availability group.

Listing 8-8. Removing a Database from an Availability Group

```
ALTER DATABASE Customers SET HADR OFF ;
```

There may also be occasions in which you want a database to remain in an availability group, but you wish to suspend data movement to other replicas. This is usually because the availability group is in Synchronous Commit mode and you have a period of high utilization, where you need a performance improvement. You can suspend the data movement to a database by using the command in Listing 8-9, which suspends data movement for the Sales database and then resumes it.

Caution   If you suspend data movement, the transaction log on the primary replica continues to grow, and you are not able to truncate it until data movement resumes and the databases are synchronized.

Listing 8-9. Suspending Data Movement

```
ALTER DATABASE Sales SET HADR SUSPEND ;
GO

ALTER DATABASE Sales SET HADR RESUME ;
GO
```

Another important consideration is the placement of database and log files. These files must be in the same location on each replica. This means that if you use named instances, it is a hard technical requirement that you change the default file locations for data and logs, because the default location includes the name of the instance. This is assuming, of course, that you do not use the same instance name on each node, which would defy many of the benefits of having a named instance.

Summary

Failover to a synchronous replica in the event of a failure of the primary replica is automatic. There are instances, however, in which you will also need to fail over manually. This could be because of a disaster that requires failover to the DR site, or it could be for proactive maintenance. Although it is possible to fail over to an asynchronous replica with the possibility of data loss, it is good practice to place the databases in a safe-state first. Because you cannot place a database in `read-only` or `single_user` mode, if it is participating in an availability group, safe-stating usually consists of disabling the logins and then switching to Synchronous Commit mode before failover.

To monitor availability groups throughout the enterprise, you need to use a monitoring tool, such as Systems Operation Center. If you need to monitor a small number of availability groups or troubleshoot a specific issue, however, use one of the tools included with SQL Server, such as a dashboard for monitoring the health of the topology, and an extended events session, called the AlwaysOn Health Trace.

One benefit of achieving high availability for SQL Server is that doing so allows you to minimize downtime during planned maintenance. On a two-node cluster, you can upgrade the passive node, fail over, and then upgrade the active node. For larger clusters, you can perform a rolling patch upgrade, which involves removing half of the nodes from the possible owners list and upgrading them. You then fail over the instance to one of the upgraded nodes and repeat the process for the remaining nodes. This mitigates the risk of mixed version, across the possible owners.

CHAPTER 9

Monitoring AlwaysOn Availability Groups

Once you have implemented Availability Groups, you need to monitor them and respond to any errors or warnings that could affect the availability of your data. If you have many availability groups implemented throughout the enterprise, then the only way to monitor them effectively and holistically is by using an enterprise monitoring tool, such as SOC (Systems Operations Center). If you only have a small number of availability groups, however, or if you are troubleshooting a specific issue, then SQL Server provides the AlwaysOn Dashboard and the AlwaysOn Health Trace. You can also create your own Extended Events sessions to monitor Availability Groups. This chapter will discuss each of these monitoring possibilities.

AlwaysOn Dashboard

The AlwaysOn Dashboard is an interactive report that allows you to view the health of your AlwaysOn environment and drill through, or roll up elements within the topology. You can invoke the report from the context menu of the Availability Groups folder in Object Explorer, or from the context menu of the availability group itself. Figure 9-1 shows the report that is generated from the context menu of the HR availability group. You can see that currently synchronization is in a healthy state. The Add/Remove columns button has been used to add the Estimated Recovery Time and Estimated Data Loss measures. Estimated Data Loss is helpful when you have asynchronous replicas, so that gauge impact in the event of an incident.

The three possible synchronization states that a database can be in are SYNCHRONIZED, SYNCHRONIZING, and NOT SYNCHRONIZING. A synchronous replica should be in the SYNCHRONIZED state, and any other state is unhealthy. An asynchronous

© Peter A. Carter 2020
P. A. Carter, *SQL Server 2019 AlwaysOn*, https://doi.org/10.1007/978-1-4842-6479-9_9

replica, however, will never be in the SYNCHRONIZED state, and a state of SYNCHRONIZING is considered healthy. Regardless of the mode, NOT SYNCHRONIZING indicates that the replica is not connected.

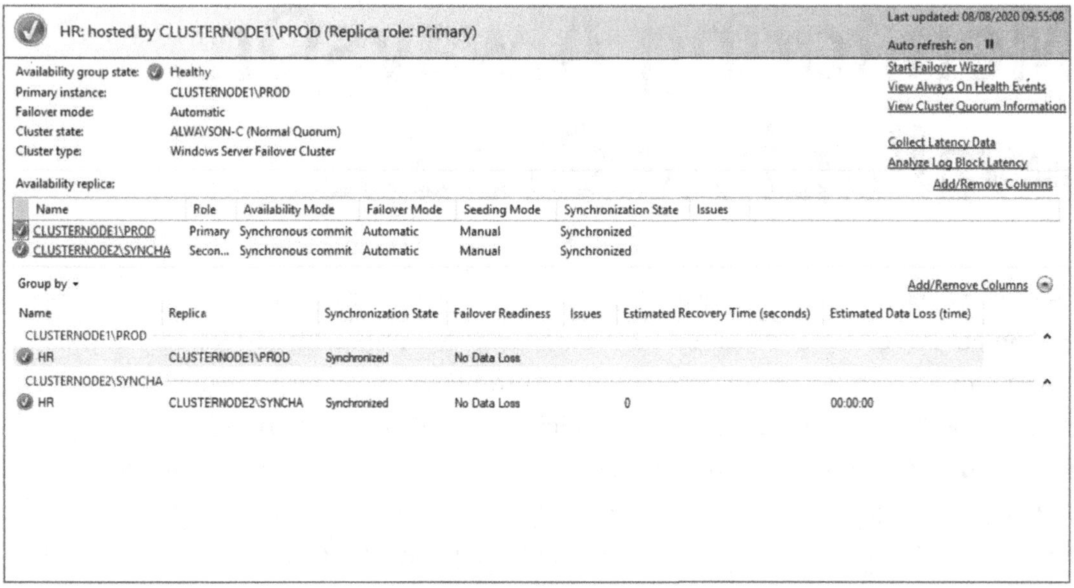

Figure 9-1. *The Availability Group Dashboard*

Note   In addition to the synchronization states, a replica also has one of the following operational states: PENDING_FAILOVER, PENDING, ONLINE, OFFLINE, FAILED, FAILED_NO_QUORUM, and NULL (when the replica is disconnected). The operational state of a replica can be viewed using the sys.dm_hadr_ availability_replica_states DMV.

At the top right of the report, there are links to the failover wizard, which we discussed earlier in this chapter; the AlwaysOn Health events, which we discussed in the next section; and also a link to view cluster quorum information. The Cluster Quorum Information screen, which is invoked by this link, is displayed in Figure 9-2.

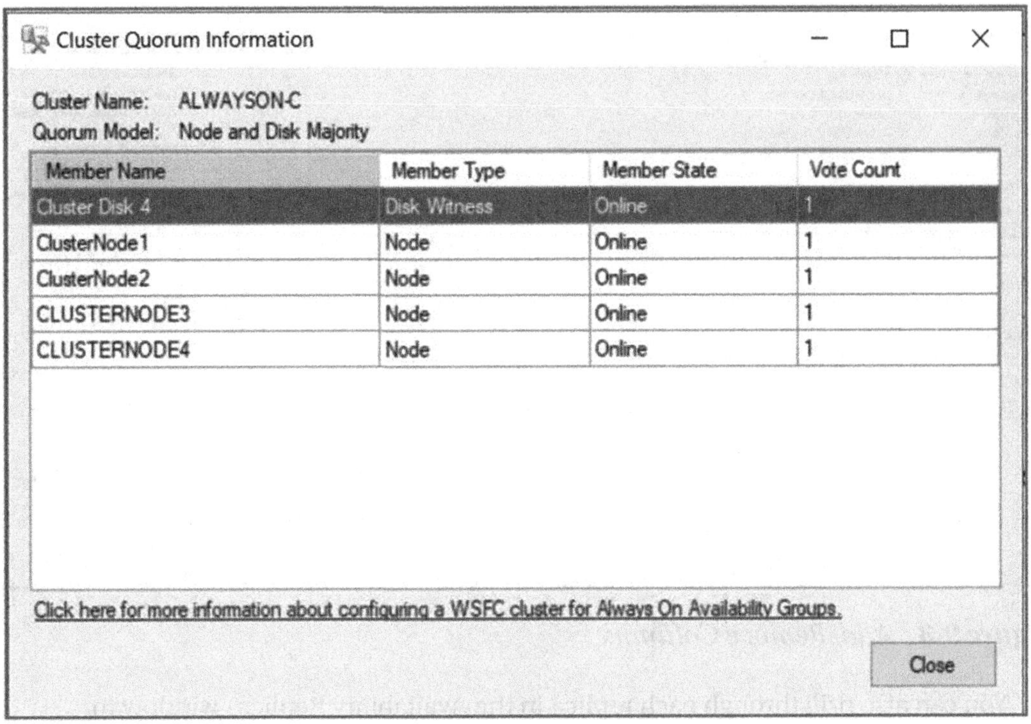

Figure 9-2. *The Cluster Quorum Information Screen*

The Add/Remove Columns link will display a context menu, where you can dynamically add or remove columns from the display. Figure 9-3 shows that Suspend and Suspend Reason have been added.

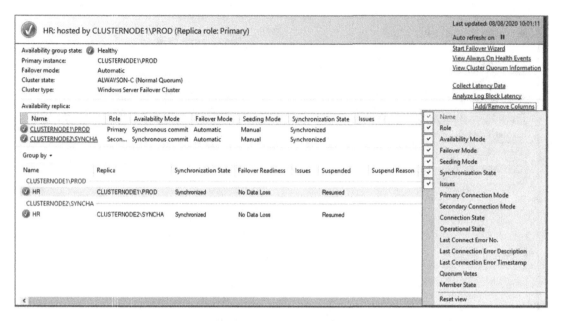

Figure 9-3. *Add/Remove Columns*

You can also drill through each replica in the Availability Replicas window to see replica-specific details. The Group by button will allow you to group Availability Databases by Replica, Database, Synchronization state, Failover Readiness, or Issue.

AlwaysOn Health Trace

The AlwaysOn Health Trace is an Extended Events session, which is created when you create you first availability group. It can be located in SQL Server Management Studio, under Extended Events ➤ Sessions, and via its context menu, you can view live data that is being captured, or you can enter the session's properties to change the configuration of the events that are captured. It can also be accessed by using the View AlwaysOn Health Events link in the AlwaysOn Dashboard.

Drilling through the session exposes the session's package, and from the context menu of the package, you can view previously captured events. Figure 9-4 shows that the latest event captured was Database 5 (which, in our case, is HR), which was waiting for the log to be hardened on the synchronous replica.

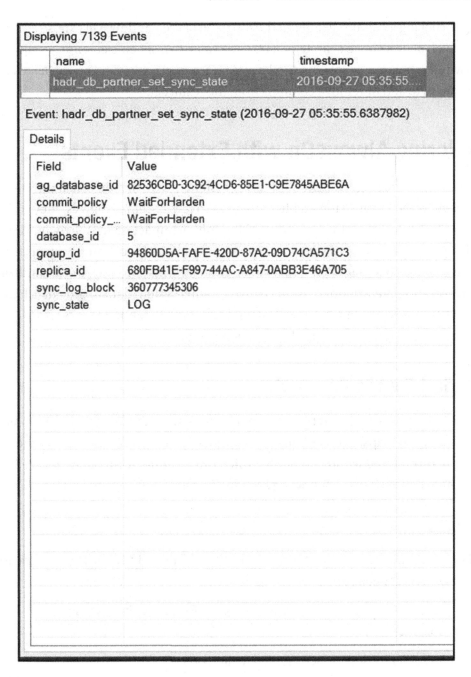

Figure 9-4. *The Target Data*

Right-clicking a column header in the top pane of the window will expose a context menu, which allows you to search for a text or a value in a specific column, group by the values within a column or sort the results sets by a specific column. You can also use the context menu to add or remove columns from the result set.

Monitoring AlwaysOn with Extended Events

Extended Events are a lightweight monitoring system in SQL Server, which capture events using WMI. Because the architecture uses so few system resources, they scale very well and allow you to monitor instances, with minimal impact on user activity. They are also highly configurable, giving you a wide range of options for capturing details from a very fine grain, such as page splits, to courser-grain information, such as CPU utilization. You can also correlate Extended Events with operating system data to provide a holistic picture when troubleshooting issues. The predecessor to Extended Events was SQL Trace and its GUI, called Profiler, which is deprecated.

Extended Events Concepts

Extended Events have a rich architecture, which consists of Events, Targets, Actions, Predicates, Types, Maps, and Sessions. These artifacts are stored within a Package, which is, in turn, stored within a module, which can be either a .dll or an executable. We discuss these concepts in the following sections.

Packages

A package is a container for the objects used within Extended Events. Here are the four types of SQL Server package:

- Package0 – The default package, used for Extended Events system objects.

- Sqlserver – Used for SQL Server–related objects.

- Sqlos – Used for SQLOS-related objects.

- SecAudit – Used by SQL Audit; however, its objects are not exposed.

Events

An event is an occurrence of interest that you can trace. It may be a SQL batch completing, a cache miss, or a page split, or virtually anything else that can happen within the Database Engine, depending on the nature of the trace that you are configuring. Each event is categorized by channel and keyword (also known as category). A channel is a high-level categorization, and all events in SQL Server 2016 fall into one of the channels described in Table 9-1.

Table 9-1. *Channels*

Channel	Description
Admin	Well-known events with well-known resolutions. For example, deadlocks, server starts, CPU thresholds being exceeded, and the use of deprecated features.
Operational	Used for troubleshooting issues. For example, bad memory being detected, an AlwaysOn Availability Group replica changing its state, and a long IO being detected are all events that fall within the Operational channel.
Analytic	High-volume events that you can use for troubleshooting issues such as performance. For example, a transaction beginning, a lock being acquired, and a file read completing are all events that fall within the Analytic channel.
Debug	Used by developers to diagnose issues by returning internal data. The events in the Debug channel are subject to change in future versions of SQL Server, so you should avoid them when possible.

Keywords (or categories) are much more fine grain. All events relating to AlwaysOn fall into the AlwaysOn and HADR categories. SQL Server exposes 122 events relating to AlwaysOn. These events are listed in Table 9-2.

Table 9-2. *AlwaysOn Events*

Event	Description
hadr_ddl_failover_execution_state	Raised when a DDL command alters the Availability Group failover state
hadr_transport_dump_message	Traces HADR transport messages throughout the system
hadr_transport_dump_config_message	Traces HADR configuration messages
hadr_transport_dump_failure_message	Traces HADR failure messages
hadr_transport_dump_preconfig_message	Traces HADR preconfig messages
hadr_transport_dump_dropped_message	Traces trace dropped HADR transport messages throughout the system
hadr_transport_session_state	Raised when a HADR transport session changes states
hadr_transport_configuration_state	Raised when session state changes
hadr_transport_ucs_registration	Raised when UCS registration state changes
hadr_transport_ucs_connection_info	Raised when the USC connection ID associated with the AlwaysOn transport replica is registered or changes
hadr_transport_flow_control_action	Raised when a flow control action has occurred for a particular replica
hadr_database_flow_control_action	Raised when a flow control action has occurred for a particular replica
hadr_db_manager_state	Raised when the state of db_manager changes
hadr_db_manager_lsn_sync_msg	Traces Log Sequence Number synchronization messages
hadr_db_manager_establish_db_msg	Raised when a DB message is established
hadr_db_manager_status_change	Traces DBReplicaStatusChange messages
hadr_db_manager_redo	Traces redo processing on secondary

(continued)

Table 9-2. (*continued*)

Event	Description
hadr_db_manager_undo	Traces undo processing on secondary
hadr_db_manager_db_queue_restart	Fires in response to the queue restart hadron database
hadr_db_manager_db_startdb	Fires in response to start hadron database
hadr_db_manager_db_shutdown	Fires in response to shutdown hadron database
hadr_db_manager_user_control	Fires in response to a change in user status for an AlwaysOn controlled database
hadr_db_manager_redo_control	Traces change log scan status for an AlwaysOn controlled database
hadr_db_manager_scan_control	Traces change log scan status for an AlwaysOn controlled database
hadr_db_manager_suspend_resume	Fires in response to a change in suspend/resume status for an AlwaysOn controlled database
hadr_db_manager_db_restart	Fires in response to a restart of an AlwaysOn controlled database
hadr_worker_pool_thread	Traces AlwaysOn worker pool thread actions
hadr_worker_pool_task	Traces AlwaysOn worker pool task actions
hadr_thread_pool_worker_start	Traces AlwaysOn thread pool worker thread, start actions
hadr_db_manager_page_request	Traces page Request/Response between servers
hadr_db_commit_mgr_update_harden	Fires in response to the update of the hardened Log Sequence Number for an AlwaysOn controlled database
hadr_db_commit_mgr_harden_still_waiting	Traces transaction Commit harden, still waiting for AlwaysOn Commit management
hadr_db_commit_mgr_harden	Traces transaction Commit harden result from AlwaysOn Commit management
hadr_db_commit_mgr_set_policy	Fires in response to a transaction Commit manager policy update

(*continued*)

Table 9-2. (*continued*)

Event	Description
hadr_db_partner_set_policy	Fires in response to an AlwaysOn partner commit policy update
hadr_db_partner_set_sync_state	Fires in response to a synchronization state change of an AlwaysOn partner
hadr_apr_added_corrupted_page	Fires when auto page repair added a corrupted page
hadr_apr_repaired_page	Fires when auto page repair repaired a corrupted page
hadr_apr_skipped_page_repair	Fires when auto page repair skipped a page repair
hadr_apr_failed_page_repair	Fires when auto page repair added a corrupted page
hadr_apr_sent_repair_request_for_page	Fires when auto page repair sent a page repair request
hadr_apr_received_page_repair_request	Fires when auto page repair received a page repair request
hadr_apr_deffering_page_repair_request	Fires when auto page repair is deferring the page repair request
hadr_apr_page_repair_failed	Fires when auto page repair failed to repair page
hadr_undo_of_redo_log_scan	Traces the amount of log scanned in Undo of Redo, and the total log needing to be scanned
hadr_db_manager_filemetadata_request	Fires in response to a File Metadata Request/Response between servers
hadr_capture_compressed_log_cache	Traces the hit/miss ratio for the compressed log block cache
hadr_db_manager_backup_sync_msg	Fires in response to a backup synchronization message
hadr_db_manager_backup_info_msg	Fires in response to a backup informational message
hadr_db_manager_primary_replica_file_list_msg	Fires in response to a Primary replica file list message
hadr_db_manager_seeding_request_msg	Fires in response to a seeding request message

(*continued*)

Table 9-2. (*continued*)

Event	Description
hadr_physical_seeding_backup_ state_change	Fires in response to a change in the state of a physical seeding, on the backup side
hadr_physical_seeding_restore_ state_change	Fires in response to a change in the state of a physical seeding, on the restore side
hadr_physical_seeding_ forwarder_state_change	Fires in response to a change in the state of a physical seeding, on the forwarder side
hadr_physical_seeding_ forwarder_target_state_change	Fires in response to a change in the state of a physical seeding, on the forwarder target side
hadr_physical_seeding_submit_ callback	Fires in response to a physical seeding submit callback
hadr_physical_seeding_failure	Fires in response to a physical seeding failure
hadr_physical_seeding_progress	Fires in response to a physical seeding progress
hadr_physical_seeding_ schedule_long_task_failure	Fires in response to a physical seeding schedule Long task failure
hadr_automatic_seeding_start	Fires when an automatic seeding operation is submitted
hadr_automatic_seeding_state_ transition	Fires when an automatic seeding operation changes state
hadr_automatic_seeding_success	Fires when an automatic seeding operation succeeds
hadr_automatic_seeding_failure	Fires when an automatic seeding operation fails
hadr_automatic_seeding_timeout	Fires when an automatic seeding operation times out
hadr_filestream_file_open	Fires when AlwaysOn FileStream transport opens a file
hadr_filestream_file_close	Fires when AlwaysOn FileStream transport closes a file
hadr_filestream_log_interpreter	Fires when AlwaysOn FileStream transport finds relevant log records when interpreting log
hadr_filestream_processed_ block	Fires when AlwaysOn FileStream transport has completed processing a log block

(*continued*)

Table 9-2. (*continued*)

Event	Description
hadr_filestream_directory_ create	Fires when AlwaysOn FileStream transport creates a directory
hadr_filestream_corrupt_message	Fires when AlwaysOn FileStream transport detects message corruption
hadr_filestream_message_ block_end	Fires when AlwaysOn FileStream transport traces a block end message
hadr_filestream_message_ dir_create	Fires when AlwaysOn FileStream transport traces a directory create message
hadr_filestream_message_ file_write	Fires when AlwaysOn FileStream transport traces a file write message
hadr_filestream_file_flush	Fires when AlwaysOn FileStream transport flushes a file
hadr_filestream_file_set_eof	Fires when AlwaysOn FileStream transport sets end of a file
hadr_filestream_undo_ inplace_update	Fires when AlwaysOn FileStream transport detects in-place update to undo
hadr_filestream_message_file_ request	Fires when HADR FileStream transport traces a file write message
hadr_wsfc_change_notifier_ status	Fires when Windows Server Failover Clustering change notifier status changes
hadr_wsfc_change_notifier_ start_ag_specific_notifications	Fires when Windows Server Failover Clustering change notifier starts receiving Availability Group–specific notifications
hadr_wsfc_change_notifier_ severe_error	Fires when Windows Server Failover Clustering change notifier encountered a severe error and will terminate
hadr_tds_synchronizer_ payload_skip	Fires when an AlwaysOn TDS Listener Synchronizer skipped a listener payload because there were no changes since the previous payload

(*continued*)

Table 9-2. (*continued*)

Event	Description
hadr_sql_instance_to_node_map_entry_deleted	Fires at the end of an API call that deletes a SQL Server instance to cluster node map entry
hadr_wsfc_change_notifier_node_not_online	Fires when Windows Server Failover Clustering change notifier detected that the local cluster node is not online
hadr_online_availability_group_first_attempt_failure	Fires if the first attempt to bring an AlwaysOn Availability Group resource online failed
hadr_online_availability_group_retry_end	Fires when SQL Server has either exhausted all retry attempts, or Windows Server Failover Cluster has accepted the command to bring an AlwaysOn Availability Group resource online
hadr_ar_api_call	Fires when an API call is made to an Availability replica
hadr_ar_manager_starting	Fires when the Availability Group replica manager is starting
hadr_ag_wsfc_resource_state	Fires in response to a state change of an Availability Group in the Windows Server Failover Cluster
hadr_ag_database_api_call	Fires in response to an API call to an Availability Group database replica
hadr_ag_lease_renewal	Fires in response to an Availability Group Lease Renewal
hadr_ar_manager_mutex_acquisition_state	Fires in response to an Availability Replica mutex acquisition state for synchronization of Availability Group manager startup and shutdown operations
hadr_ar_critical_section_entry_state	Fires in response to an Availability Replica critical section entry state
hadr_ag_config_data_mutex_acquisition_state	Fires in response to an Availability Group mutex acquisition state
hadr_database_replica_disjoin_completion	Fires when a Database Replica has been fully unjoined from the Availability Group

(*continued*)

Table 9-2. (*continued*)

Event	Description
hadr_ar_controller_debug	Fires when a replica controller outputs a debug message
hadr_apply_log_block	Fires when a secondary is going to append a log block to the log manager
hadr_capture_log_block	Fires when the primary has captured a log block
hadr_capture_vlfheader	Fires when the primary has captured a log block which starts new virtual file
hadr_apply_vlfheader	Fires when a secondary is going to apply a Virtual Log File header
hadr_scan_state	Fires when primary or secondary Database Replica is changing state
hadr_dump_log_block	Fires when a primary sends or secondary receives a log block message
hadr_log_block_send_complete	Fires after a log block message has been sent
hadr_dump_vlf_header	Fires when a primary sends or secondary receives a vlfheader message
hadr_dump_log_progress	Fires when a secondary sends a progress message
hadr_dump_primary_progress	Fires when a primary sends progress message
hadr_dump_sync_primary_progress	Fires when a synchronous secondary sends a progress message
hadr_send_harden_lsn_message	This event should not be used. It is for Microsoft internal testing
hadr_evaluate_readonly_ routing_info	Fires when evaluating read-only routing information on a local primary database replica
hadr_db_log_throttle	Fires when a database log generation throttle changes
hadr_db_log_throttle_input	Fires when the Fabric log management component updates the log throttle

(*continued*)

Table 9-2. (*continued*)

Event	Description
hadr_db_marked_for_reseed	Fires when a secondary database falls too far behind the primary and is marked for reseed
hadr_db_log_management_ configuration_parameters	Occurs when automatic log management configurations are read
hadr_db_long_running_xact_ aborted	Fires when a long-running transaction is forced to terminate by the system to avoid log becoming full
hadr_db_remote_harden_failure	Fires when a harden request, which was part of a commit or prepare, failed due to a remote failure
hadr_partner_log_send_ transition	Fires in response to a log send transition between the log writer and the log capture
hadr_partner_restart_scan	Fires when a replica scans for its partner, on restart
hadr_transport_sync_send_ failure	Fires when a synchronous send fails in transport
hadr_xrf_deleteAllXrf_ beforeEntry	Fires immediately before all extended recovery forks are deleted
hadr_xrf_deleteRecLsn_ beforeEntry	Fires immediately before the recovery Log Sequence Number is deleted from the metadata
hadr_xrf_updateXrf_ partialUpdate	Fires during an updating secondary's recovery forks stack. Specifically, it fires after deleting extra entries in the secondary stack, but before copying new entries from primary
hadr_xrf_updateXrf_before_ recoveryLsn_update	Fires during an updating secondary's recovery forks stack. Specifically, it fires after updating the stack but before saving the recovery Log Sequence Number in the metadata
hadr_xrf_copyXrf_partialCopy	Fires after deleting a secondary's stack entries, but before copying primary's entries

(*continued*)

Table 9-2. (*continued*)

Event	Description
alwayson_ddl_executed	Fires when AlwaysOn DDL statement is executed
availability_replica_state	Fires when an Availability Replica is starting or shutting down
availability_replica_state_change	Fires when the state of the Availability Replica has changed
availability_replica_manager_state_change	Fires when the state of the Availability Replica Manager has changed
availability_group_lease_expired	Fires when there is a connectivity issue between the cluster and the Availability Group, which has caused a failure to renew the lease
availability_replica_automatic_failover_validation	Fires when the failover validates the readiness of replica as a primary
availability_replica_database_fault_reporting	Fires when a database reports a fault to the availability replica manager
before_redo_lsn_update	Fires immediately before the update of the EOL Log Sequence Number
read_only_route_complete	Fires when a read-only routing operation successfully completed
read_only_route_fail	Fires when a read-only routing operation failed

Targets

A target is the consumer of the events; essentially, it is the device to which the trace data will be written. The targets available within SQL Server 2016 are detailed in Table 9-3.

Table 9-3. *Targets*

Target	Synchronous/Asynchronous	Description
Event counter	Synchronous	Counts the number of events that occur during a session
Event file	Asynchronous	Writes the event output to memory buffers and then flushes them to disk
Event pairing	Asynchronous	Determines if a paired event occurs without its matching event, for example, if a statement started but never completed
ETW (Event Tracking for Windows)	Synchronous	Used to correlate Extended Events with operating system data
Histogram	Asynchronous	Counts the number of events that occur during a session, based on an action or event column
Ring buffer	Asynchronous	Stores data in a memory buffer, using first-in, first-out (FIFO) methodology

Actions

Also known as Global Fields, Actions are commands that allow additional information to be captured when an event fires. An action is fired synchronously when an event occurs and the event is unaware of the action. There are 50 actions available that allow you to capture a rich array of information, including the statement that caused the event to fire, the security context under which the statement ran, the transaction ID, the CPU ID, and the call stack.

Predicates

Predicates are filter conditions that you can apply before the system sends events to the target. It is possible to create simple predicates, such as filtering statements completing based on a database ID, but you can also create more complex predicates, such as only capturing the role change of an AlwaysOn Availability Group replica if it happens more than twice.

Predicates also fully support short-circuiting. This means that if you use multiple conditions within a predicate, then the order of predicates is important, because if the evaluation of the first predicate fails, the second predicate will not be evaluated. Because predicates are evaluated synchronously, this can have an impact on performance. Therefore, it is sensible to design your predicates, so that predicates which are least likely to evaluate to true are placed before predicates that are very likely to evaluate to true.

For example, imagine that you are planning to filter on a specific database (with a database ID of 6), but this database accounts for a high percentage of the activity on the instance. You also plan to filter on a specific user ID (UserA), which is responsible for a low percentage of the activity. In this scenario, you would use the WHERE `((([sqlserver].[username]='UserA') AND ([sqlserver].[database_id]=(6)))` predicate to first filter out activity that does not relate to UserA, before then filtering out activity that does not relate to database ID 6.

Types

All objects within a package are assigned a type. This type is used to interpret the data stored within the byte collection of an object. Objects are assigned one of the following types:

- Action
- Event
- Pred_compare (retrieve data from events)
- Pred_source (compare data types)
- Target
- Type

Maps

A map is a dictionary that maps internal ID vales to strings that DBAs can understand. Map keys are only unique within their context and are repeated between contexts. For example, within the statement_recompile_cause context, a map_key of 1 relates to a map_value of Schema Changed. Within the context of a database_sql_statement type, however, a map_key of 1 relates to a map_value of CREATE DATABASE. You can find a complete list of mappings by using the sys.dm_xe_map_values DMV.

Sessions

A session is essentially a trace. It can contain events from multiple packages, actions, targets, and predicates. When you start or stop a session, you are turning the trace on or off. When a session starts, events are written to memory buffers and have predicates applied before they are sent to the target. Therefore, when creating a session, you need to configure properties, such as how much memory the session can use for buffering, what events can be dropped if the session experiences memory pressure, and the maximum latency before the events are sent to the target.

Creating an Event Session to Monitor Availability Group

You can create an event session using either the New Session Wizard, the New Session Dialog Box, or via T-SQL. To create a session using the New Session Wizard, drill through Management ➤ Extended Events in Object Explorer, and select New Session Wizard from the context menu of Sessions. This will cause the Introduction page of the New Session Wizard to be displayed.

After passing through the Introduction page, you will find the Set Session Properties page, as displayed in Figure 9-5. Here, you can configure a name for the Session and also specify if the Session should automatically be started on creation.

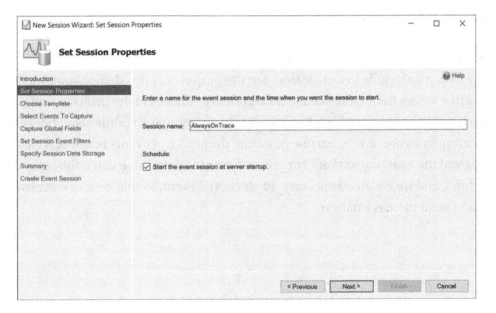

Figure 9-5. *Set Properties Page*

On the Choose Template page of the wizard, which is illustrated in Figure 9-6, you can either select a predefined template, which will give you a starting point for commonly required sessions, or you can start with a blank canvas and define the entire session manually. We will choose the latter option.

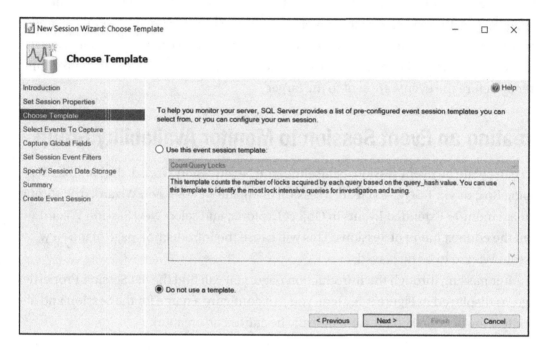

Figure 9-6. *Choose Template Page*

Figure 9-7 shows the Select Events To Capture page. Here, we can choose what events we want to include in our session. For the purposes of this demonstration, imagine that we are frequently seeing the secondary fall behind the primary, and we are trying to determine the cause. Specifically, do we have an IO bottleneck? Because we are trying to answer a very narrow question, the choice of events to select is clear. We will need the hadr_db_marked_for_reseed event to determine when the secondary falls behind, and we will need the long_io_detected event, so that we can correlate the times, and see if there is a pattern.

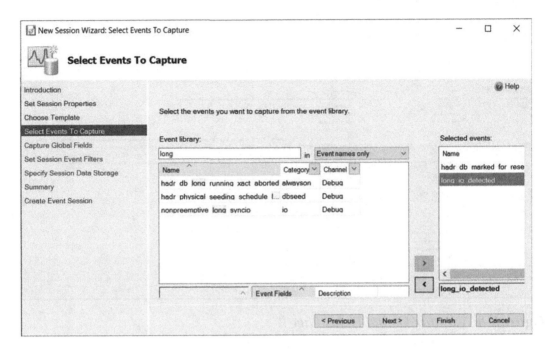

Figure 9-7. *Select Events To Capture Page*

The Capture Global Fields page will allow us to specify any Actions that we wish to capture. In our scenario, we will capture the NT Username and SQLText actions. This will allow us to trace any long IOs back through, to see if they are caused by an inefficient query. The Capture Global Fields page is illustrated in Figure 9-8.

Figure 9-8. *Capture Global Fields Page*

The Set Session Event Filters page, shown in Figure 9-9, allows you to configure Predicates on the Session. We will configure a Predicate which filters operations on system databases.

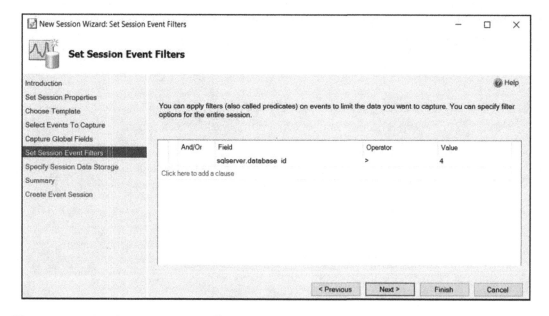

Figure 9-9. *Set Session Event Filters Page*

The Specify Session Data Storage page of the wizard is where we can configure the Target. The wizard provides the choice of a file or ring buffer target, along with the option to specify size and rollover options. We will configure a file target, as illustrated in Figure 9-10.

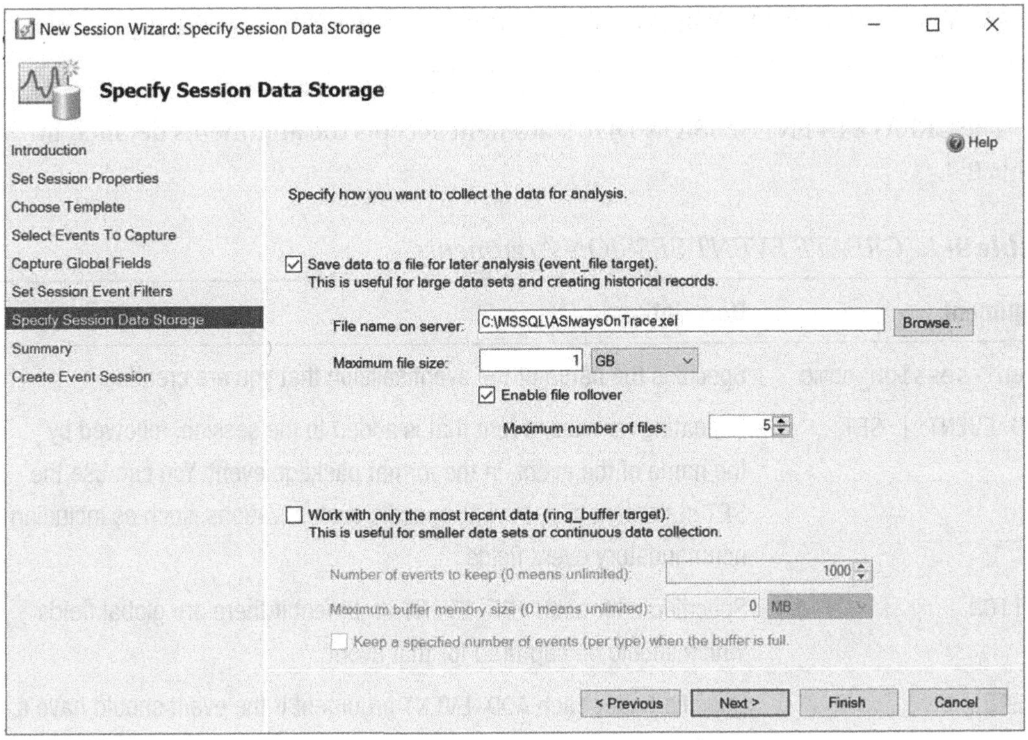

Figure 9-10. *Specify Session Data Storage*

The Summary page of the wizard will confirm the actions that the wizard will perform. After the Session has been created, the Completion page will provide the option of watching live data upon exit. To create the same Session using T-SQL, you could use the script in Listing 9-1.

Listing 9-1. Create an Event Session

```
CREATE EVENT SESSION AlwaysOnTrace ON SERVER
ADD EVENT sqlserver.hadr_db_marked_for_reseed(
    ACTION(sqlserver.nt_username,sqlserver.sql_text)
    WHERE (sqlserver.database_id>(4))),
```

```
ADD EVENT sqlserver.long_io_detected(
    ACTION(sqlserver.nt_username,sqlserver.sql_text)
    WHERE (sqlserver.database_id>(4)))
ADD TARGET package0.event_file(SET filename='C:\MSSQL\ASlwaysOnTrace.xel')
WITH (MAX_MEMORY=4096 KB,EVENT_RETENTION_MODE=ALLOW_SINGLE_EVENT_LOSS,MAX_
DISPATCH_LATENCY=30 SECONDS,MAX_EVENT_SIZE=0 KB,MEMORY_PARTITION_
MODE=NONE,TRACK_CAUSALITY=OFF,STARTUP_STATE=ON) ;
```

The CREATE EVENT SESSION DDL statement accepts the arguments detailed in Table 9-4.

Table 9-4. *CREATE EVENT SESSION Arguments*

Argument	Description
event_session_name	Specifies the name of the event session that you are creating
ADD EVENT | SET	Repeating for every event that is added to the session, followed by the name of the event, in the format package.event. You can use the SET statement to set event-specific customizations, such as including nonmandatory event fields
ACTION	Specified after each ADD EVENT argument if there are global fields which should be captured for that event
WHERE	Specified after each ADD EVENT argument if the event should have a predicate associated with it
ADD TARGET | SET	Specified for each target that will be added to the session. You can use the SET statement to populate target-specific parameters, such as the filename parameter for the event_file target

The CREATE EVENT SESSION statement also accepts a number of WITH options, which are detailed in Table 9-5.

Table 9-5. *CREATE EVENT SESSION WITH Options*

WITH Option	Description
MAX_MEMORY	Specifies the maximum amount of memory that the event session can use for buffering events before dispatching them to the target(s)
EVENT_RETENTION_MODE	Specifies the behavior if the buffers become full. Acceptable values are ALLOW_SINGLE_EVENT_LOSS, which indicates that a single event can be dropped if all buffers are full; ALLOW_MULTIPLE_EVENT_LOSS, which indicates that an entire buffer can be dropped if all buffers are full; and NO_EVENT_LOSS, which indicates that tasks that cause events to fire are to wait until there is space in the buffer
MAX_DISPATCH_LATENCY	Specifies the maximum amount of time that events can reside in the session's buffers before being flushed to the target(s), specified in seconds
MAX_EVENT_SIZE	Specifies the maximum possible size for event data from any single event. It can be specified in kilobytes or megabytes and should only be configured to allow events that are larger than the MAX_MEMORY setting
MEMORY_PARTITION_MODE	Specifies where event buffers are created. Acceptable values are • NONE – Which indicates that the buffers will be created within the instance • PER_NODE – Which indicates that the buffers will be created for each NUMA node • PER_CPU – Which means that buffers will be created for each CPU
TRACK_CAUSALITY	Specifies that an additional GUID and sequence number will be stored with each event so that events can be correlated
STARTUP_STATE	• Specifies if the session automatically starts when the instance starts. ON indicates it does • OFF indicates it does not

> **Tip** For a deeper discussion around Extended Events, I highly recommend the Apress book *Pro SQL Server 2019 Administration*, which can be purchased from `www.apress.com/gp/book/9781484250884`.

Summary

SQL Server provides rich tools for monitoring the health of AlwaysOn Availability Groups. The AlwaysOn Dashboard is an interactive report within SQL Server Management Studio, which will allow you to assess the health of your Availability Groups and Replicas. It also provides links to view quorum configuration information and live health data.

Live health data is captured by an extended events session, which is created when you create the first Availability Group on an instance, and runs in the background, capturing preconfigured events. It is possible to customize this trace; I would recommend leaving it with default configurations and creating a new Event Session, if you require a custom capture.

Creating an Event Session allows you to capture either very fine-grain points of interest, or just courser-grain information, depending on your requirements. Extended Events are implemented using WMI and are a very lightweight framework, meaning you can identify issues and trend, without compromising the performance of your instance.

CHAPTER 10

Troubleshooting AlwaysOn

SQL Server exposes a wealth of metadata, pertaining to high availability and disaster recovery objects, especially around the AlwaysOn feature set. This metadata can be used to quickly identify a configuration, find the root cause of an issue, or script automated responses to events that may occur. The following sections will discuss the metadata that is available and provide examples of how it can be used.

AlwaysOn Failover Clustered Instance Metadata

From inside the database engine, it is possible to view a large amount of metadata regarding a clustered instance, and the Windows Cluster that hosts it. This information can prove invaluable to a DBA. The following section will introduce some of the most useful and interesting metadata objects.

Discovering the Node That Hosts an Instance

Naturally, a DBA will need to know which node within a cluster is hosting a failover clustered instance, especially when attempting to diagnose connectivity or performance issues. If your organization has a policy that DBAs are not allowed operating system access, however, then Failover Manager can't be used. Luckily, there is a DMV (Dynamic Management View) within SQL Server that will expose this information. The `sys.dm_os_cluster_nodes` DMV will return the columns detailed in Table 10-1.

© Peter A. Carter 2020
P. A. Carter, *SQL Server 2019 AlwaysOn*, https://doi.org/10.1007/978-1-4842-6479-9_10

Table 10-1. *sys.dm_os_cluster_nodes Columns*

Column	Description
NodeName	The name of the cluster node
status	The current status of the node. Possible values are • 0 – Indicates the node is up • 1 – Indicates the node is down • 2 – Indicates the node is paused • 3 – Indicates the node is currently joining the cluster • 4 – Indicates that the status is unknown
status_description	A textual description of the status. Possible values are • Up • Down • Paused • Joining • Unknown
is_current_owner	Indicates if the instance is currently hosted by the node. Possible values are • 0 – Indicates the node does not own the instance • 1 – Indicates that the node does own the instance

The query in Listing 10-1 will return the name of the cluster node that currently hosts the instance.

Listing 10-1. Discover the Node That Hosts the Instance

```
SELECT NodeName
FROM sys.dm_os_cluster_nodes
WHERE is_current_owner = 1 ;
```

Viewing Health Check Configuration

If assisting the Windows administration team, with the repeated failover of a clustered instance, a DBA may wish to expose details of what conditions can cause a failover, to ensure that an appropriate level is configured. This can be achieved by using the sys.dm_os_cluster_properties DMV, which returns the columns detailed in Table 10-2.

Table 10-2. *sys.dm_os_cluster_properties Columns*

Column	Description
VerboseLogging	Indicates the logging level used by the cluster. Possible values are • 0 – Indicates that logging is turned off • 1 – Indicates that only errors are logged • 2 – Indicates that errors and warning are logged
SQLDumperDumpFlags	Specifies the type of dump file that SQLDumper will generate. Possible values are • 0x0120 – Indicates a Minidump • 0x0110 – Indicates a Full Dump • 0x8100 – Indicates a Filtered Dump
SQLDumperDumpPath	Specifies the file path where SQLDumper will output the dump files
SQLDumperDumpTimeOut	The timeout value for SQLDumper, when creating a dump file. Specified in milliseconds
FailureConditionLevel	The level of failure that will cause a failover to occur. A full description of failure condition levels can be found in Table 10-3
HealthCheckTimeout	The duration that the database engine will wait for health information to be returned before it will decide that the instance is unresponsive

The possible failure condition levels, returned by the FailureConditionLevel column, are detailed in Table 10-3.

Table 10-3. *Failure Condition Levels*

Condition Level	Description
0	Automatic failover does not occur
1	Automatic failover occurs when the SQL Server service is down
2	Automatic failover will occur when • Level 1 conditions are met • The HealthCheckTimeout value is exceeded
3	Automatic failover will occur when • Level 2 conditions are met • The health check returns System Error
4	Automatic failover will occur when • Level 3 conditions are met • The health check returns Resource Error
5	Automatic failover will occur when • Level 4 conditions are met • The health check returns Query_Processing_Error

The query in Listing 10-2 will return the current failover condition level and the current health check timeout value.

Listing 10-2. Return Health Check Configuration

```
SELECT
      FailureConditionLevel
      , HealthCheckTimeout
FROM sys.dm_os_cluster_properties ;
```

The current health of the instance can be determined manually by using the sp_server_diagnostics system stored procedure. The procedure accepts a single parameter: @repeat_interval, which specifies how often the procedure should return results, specified in seconds. If the parameter is omitted, then results will only be returned once. If a value is passed for the parameter, then it must be greater than 5. The procedure returns the result set detailed in Table 10-4.

Table 10-4. *Columns Returned by sp_server_diagnostics*

Column	Description
creation_time	Indicates the time that the row was created
component_type	Indicates the type of component. Possible values are • Instance • AlwaysOn: Availability Group
component_name	Indicates the name of the component. Possible values are • system • resource • query_processing • io_subsystem • events • [Availability Group name]
state	The health status of the component. Possible values are • 0 – Indicates that the state is unknown • 1 – Indicates that the state is clean (meaning healthy) • 2 – Indicates that there are warnings • 3 – Indicates that there are errors
state_desc	A textual description of the component's state. Possible values are • Unknown • Clean • Warnings • Errors
data	An XML representation of component-specific data. For example, the resource component includes element specifying the available physical and available virtual memory. It also includes attributes including a count of out of memory exceptions

The script in Listing 10-3 will return the complete result set of the sp_server_diagnostics system stored procedure, alongside values which have been shredded from the XML column, to provide a quick view of the overall server CPU utilization, the CPU utilization of the instance, and a count of any out of memory exceptions that may have occurred.

Tip   A discussion around shredding XML is beyond the scope of this book. However, I recommend the Apress title *Expert Scripting and Automation for SQL Server DBAs*, where a discussion around working with XML for administrative purposes can be found. The book can be purchased at www.apress. com/9781484219423.

Listing 10-3. Retrieving Diagnostic Information

```
CREATE TABLE #Server_Diagnostics
(
creation_time       DATETIME,
component_type      NVARCHAR(8),
component_name      NVARCHAR(128),
[state]             TINYINT,
state_desc          NVARCHAR(8),
[data]              XML
) ;

INSERT INTO #Server_Diagnostics
EXEC sp_server_diagnostics ;

SELECT *,
data.value('(/system/@systemCpuUtilization)[1]','int') AS
SystemCPUUtilization
,data.value('(/system/@sqlCpuUtilization)[1]','int') AS SQLServerCPU
,data.value('(/resource/@outOfMemoryExceptions)[1]','int') AS
OutOfMemoryExceptions
FROM ##Server_Diagnostics ;

DROP TABLE #Server_Diagnostics ;
```

AlwaysOn Availability Group Metadata

Metadata can also be used to troubleshoot issues with Availability Groups. The following sections will discuss some of the most useful and interesting metadata objects, relating the Availability Groups.

Determining the Last Failover Reason

If an Availability Group has failed over, one of the first questions you are likely to want to answer is "when and why?". This question can be answered using the sys.dm_hadr_ availability_replica_states DMV. This object returns the columns detailed in Table 10-5.

Table 10-5. *sys.dm_hadr_availability_replica_states*

Column	Description
replica_id	The GUID of the Replica
group_id	The GUID of the Availability Group
is_local	Indicates if the Replica is local or remote. Possible values are • 0 – Indicates a remote secondary • 1 – Indicates a local Replica
role	Indicates the role that is currently assigned to the Replica. Possible values are • 0 – Indicates that the role is currently being resolved • 1 – Indicates that the Replica has the Primary role • 2 – Indicates that the Replica currently has the Secondary role
role_desc	A textual description of the Replica's current role. Possible values are • RESOLVING • PRIMARY • SECONDARY

(continued)

Table 10-5. (*continued*)

Column	Description
operational_state	Indicates the current operational state of the replica. Possible values are • 0 – Indicates a failover is pending • 1 – Indicates the state is pending • 2 – Indicates online • 3 – Indicates offline • 4 – Indicates failed • 5 – Indicates failed, with no quorum • NULL – Indicates the Replica is not local
operational_state_desc	A textual description of the operational state. Possible values are • PENDING_FAILOVER • PENDING • ONLINE • OFFLINE • FAILED • FAILED_NO_QUORUM • NULL
connected_state	Indicates if a Secondary Replica is currently connected to the Primary Replica. Possible values are • 0 – Indicates the Replica is disconnected from the Primary • 1 – Indicates that the Replica is connected to the Primary
connected_state_desc	A textual description of the connected state. Possible values are • DISCONNECTED • CONNECTED
recovery_health	Indicates if databases within the Availability Group are online. Possible values are • 0 – Indicates that at least one of the databases is not online • 1 – Indicates that all of the databases are online • NULL – Indicates the Availability Group is not local

(*continued*)

Table 10-5. (*continued*)

Column	Description
recovery_health_desc	A textual description of the recovery_health. Possible values are • ONLINE_IN_PROGRESS • ONLINE • NULL
synchronization_health	Indicates the synchronization state of the Availability Group's databases. Possible values are • 0 – Indicates that at least one database is in the NOT SYNCHRONIZING state. This is known as Not Healthy • 1 – Indicates that at least one database is not in the ideal synchronization state. This is known as Partially Healthy The ideal state will be • SYNCHRONIZED – For synchronous-commit Replicas • SYNCHRONIZING – For asynchronous-commit Replicas • 2 – Indicates that all databases are in the ideal state. This is known as Healthy
synchronization_ health_desc	A textual description of the synchronization health state. Possible values are • NOT_HEALTHY • PARTIALLY_HEALTHY • HEALTHY
last_connect_error_ number	The error number of the last connection error
last_connect_error_ description	The description of the last connection error
last_connect_error_ timestamp	The date and time of the last connection error

The query in Listing 10-4 demonstrates how to return the time and reason of the last connection error. This will indicate when and why failover occurred. One row will be returned for each combination of Replica and Availability Group. You will notice that we join the sys.dm_hadr_availability_replica_states DMV to the sys.availability_replicas and sys.availability_groups DMVs, to retrieve the names of the nodes that host the Replicas and the names of the Availability Groups.

Listing 10-4. Determine Last Failover Time and Reason

```
SELECT
       ar.replica_server_name
     ,ag.name
     ,ars.last_connect_error_description
     ,ars.last_connect_error_timestamp
FROM sys.dm_hadr_availability_replica_states ars
INNER JOIN sys.availability_replicas ar
     ON ar.group_id = ars.group_id
          AND ars.replica_id = ar.replica_id
INNER JOIN sys.availability_groups ag
     ON ag.group_id = ar.group_id ;
```

Assessing the State of Availability Databases

You may have noticed that the sys.dm_hard_availability_replica_states DMV will provide details of Availability Groups that contain databases that are not in a healthy state. The results are not granular enough, however, for you to discover which databases are not healthy. This information can be retrieved from the sys.dm_hadr_database_replica_states DMV, which returns the columns detailed in Table 10-6.

Table 10-6. *sys.dm_hadr_database_replica_states Columns*

Column	Description
database_id	The ID of the database
group_id	The Availability Group GUID
replica_id	The Availability Replica GUID
group_database_id	The ID of the database, within the Availability Group
is_local	Indicates if the database is local of remote. Possible values are • 0 – Indicates that the database is not local to the instance • 1 – Indicates that the database is local to the instance
is_primary_replica	Indicates if the database replica currently has the role of primary or secondary. Possible values are • 0 – Indicates a Secondary Database Replica • 1 – Indicates a Primary Database Replica
synchronization_ state	Indicates the state of the database synchronization. Possible values are • 0 – Indicates not synchronizing • 1 – Indicates synchronizing • 2 – Indicates synchronized • 3 – Indicates that the state is reverting. This means that the secondary is at the part of the undo stage, where it is retrieving pages from the primary • 4 – Indicates that the state is initializing. This means that the secondary is at the part of the undo phase, where required log records are currently being shipped and hardened
synchronization_ state_desc	A textual description of the synchronization state. Possible values are • NOT SYNCHRONIZING • SYNCHRONIZING • SYNCHRONIZED • REVERTING • INITIALIZING

(continued)

Table 10-6. (*continued*)

Column	Description
is_commit_ participant	Indicates if transaction commits are synchronized. Databases on asynchronous replicas will always report 0 and the value is only accurate for databases on synchronous replicas, for the primary database. Possible values are • 0 – Indicates that transaction commit is not synchronized • 1 – Indicates that transaction commit is synchronized
synchronization_ health	Indicates the synchronization state of the database. Possible values are • 0 – Indicates Not Healthy. This means that the database is not synchronizing • 1 – Indicates Partially Healthy. This means that the database is synchronizing • 2 – Indicates Healthy. This means that the database is synchronized
synchronization_ health_desc	A textual description of the synchronization health. Possible values are • NOT_HEALTHY • PARTIALLY_HEALTHY • HEALTHY
database_state	Indicates the current state of the database. The value reflects the value in the sys.databases catalog view. Possible values are • 0 – Indicates that the database is Online • 1 – Indicates that the database is Restoring • 2 – Indicates that the database is Recovering • 3 – Indicates that the database has a state of Recovery pending • 4 – Indicates that the database is Suspect • 5 – Indicates that the database is in Emergency mode • 6 – Indicates that the database is Offline

(*continued*)

Table 10-6. (*continued*)

Column	Description
database_state_desc	A textual description of the database state. Possible values are • ONLINE • RESTORING • RECOVERING • RECOVERY_PENDING • SUSPECT • EMERGENCY • OFFLINE
is_suspended	Indicates if the database is suspended. Possible values are • 0 – Indicates resumed • 1 – Indicates suspended
suspend_reason	If the database is suspended, the suspend_reason column indicates the reason. Possible values are • 0 – Indicates a user manually suspended the data movement • 1 – Indicates a suspension following a forced failover • 2 – Indicates that an error occurred during the redo phase • 3 – Indicates that there was an error during the log capture • 4 – Indicates that there was an error when writing the log • 5 – Indicates the database was suspended prior to a restart • 6 – Indicates that there was an error during the undo phase • 7 – Indicates a log chain mismatch error • 8 – Indicates that there was an error in the calculation of the secondary replica's synchronization point

(*continued*)

Table 10-6. (*continued*)

Column	Description
suspend_reason_desc	A textual description of the suspend_reason column. Possible values are • SUSPEND_FROM_USER • SUSPEND_FROM_PARTNER • SUSPEND_FROM_REDO • SUSPEND_FROM_CAPTURE • SUSPEND_FROM_APPLY • SUSPEND_FROM_RESTART • SUSPEND_FROM_UNDO • SUSPEND_FROM_REVALIDATION • SUSPEND_FROM_XRF_UPDATE
recovery_lsn	On the primary replica, recovery_lsn indicates the end of the transaction log (the final point in the transaction log for point-in-time recovery). On a secondary replica, the column indicates the point to which the resynchronization would be required. If the value is equal or greater than last_hardened_lsn, however, then it indicates that resynchronization would not be required
truncation_lsn	For a primary replica, the column indicates the minimum log truncation LSN across all secondaries. For a secondary replica, the column indicates the log truncation point for that specific database replica
last_sent_lsn	Indicates the end of the last log block that has been sent
last_sent_time	The date and time that the last log block was sent
last_recieved_lsn	Indicates the end of the last log block to be received
last_hardened_lsn	Indicates the start of the last log block to be hardened. The value will be NULL for asynchronous commit replicas
last_hardened_time	The date and time of the hardened LSN
last_redone_lsn	The LSN of the last log record to be redone on the secondary

(*continued*)

Table 10-6. (*continued*)

Column	Description
last_redone_time	The timestamp of the last LSN to be redone on the secondary
log_send_queue_size	The size of the log records that have not yet been sent to the secondary, specified in kilobytes
log_send_rate	The speed at which log records are being sent to the secondary, specified in kilobytes/sec
filestream_send_rate	The speed at which FILESTREAM files are being sent to the secondary, specified in kilobytes/sec
end_of_log_lsn	The LSN of the final log record within the log cache
last_commit_lsn	The LSN of the last committed transaction in the transaction log
last_commit_time	The timestamp of the last committed LSN in the transaction log
low_water_mark_for_ ghosts	The ghost cleanup task (which physically deletes rows that have already been logically deleted) uses the minimum value of this column, across all replicas of the database, to determine where to start cleaning up records
secondary_log_ seconds	The number of seconds that the secondary replica is behind the primary replica

The script in Listing 10-5 demonstrates how to assess the health availability database, within the HR Availability Group. You will notice that we use the DB_NAME() function to return the name of the database and join the sys.dm_hadr_database_ replica_states DMV to the sys.availability_groups and sys.availability_ replicas catalog views to return the names of the Availability Groups and Replicas.

Listing 10-5. Assessing the State of an Availability Database

```
SELECT
      DB_NAME(database_id)
      ,ag.name
      ,ar.replica_server_name
      ,is_primary_replica
```

```
    ,synchronization_state_desc
    ,synchronization_health_desc
    ,database_state_desc
FROM sys.dm_hadr_database_replica_states drs
INNER JOIN sys.availability_groups ag
    ON drs.group_id = ag.group_id
INNER JOIN sys.availability_replicas ar
    ON drs.replica_id = ar.replica_id
WHERE ag.name = 'HR';
```

Summary

SQL Server exposes a large amount of metadata that can help you troubleshoot issues and audit your configuration. While this chapter discusses some of the most helpful metadata, I strongly encourage you to explore the hadr DMVs further.

For failover clustered instances, the sys.dm_os_cluster_nodes DMV exposes the health status of nodes within a cluster. Further troubleshooting detail can be found by calling the sp_server_diagnostics system stored procedure.

Tip   The sp_server_diagnostics system stored procedure can also be used for troubleshooting AlwaysOn Availability Groups and returns a row for each Availability Group hosted on the instance.

The sys.dm_hadr_availability_replica_states DMV exposes details of the health status of Replicas, which host AlwaysOn Availability Groups. To drill down to view the health status of databases that participate within an Availability Group, the sys.dm_hadr_database_replica_states DMV can be queried.

Both of the DMVs mentioned earlier can be joined to the sys.availability_groups and sys.availability_replicas DMVs to obtain the textual information regarding the configuration, as opposed to GUIDs. The sys.dm_hadr_database_replica_states DMV can also be joined to sys.databases to obtain further information regarding database configuration.

Index

A

© Peter A. Carter 2020
P. A. Carter, *SQL Server 2019 AlwaysOn*, https://doi.org/10.1007/978-1-4842-6479-9

Printed in the United States
By Bookmasters